First World War

and Army of Occupation

War Diary

France, Belgium and Germany

49 DIVISION
Headquarters, Branches and Services
Commander Royal Artillery
31 March 1915 - 30 June 1915

WO95/2772A

The Naval & Military Press Ltd
www.nmarchive.com
Published in association with The National Archives

Published by

The Naval & Military Press Ltd

Unit 10 Ridgewood Industrial Park,

Uckfield, East Sussex,

TN22 5QE England

Tel: +44 (0) 1825 749494

www.naval-military-press.com

www.nmarchive.com

This diary has been reprinted in facsimile from the original. Any imperfections are inevitably reproduced and the quality may fall short of modern type and cartographic standards.

Contents

Document type	Place/Title	Date From	Date To
Heading	49th Division C.R.A. Apr-Dec 1915		
Heading	War Diary of 1st West Riding Divisional Artillery from 31st March 1915 to 30th April (Volume 1)		
War Diary	Doncaster	31/03/1915	09/04/1915
War Diary	Folkestone	10/04/1915	10/04/1915
War Diary	Doncaster	11/04/1915	12/04/1915
War Diary	Haure	13/04/1915	13/04/1915
War Diary	York	13/04/1915	13/04/1915
War Diary	Doncaster	13/04/1915	13/04/1915
War Diary	Bawtry	13/04/1915	13/04/1915
War Diary	Boulogne	14/04/1915	14/04/1915
War Diary	Merville	15/04/1915	15/04/1915
War Diary	Berguette	15/04/1915	15/04/1915
War Diary	Doneauter	14/04/1915	15/04/1915
War Diary	Woolwich	15/04/1915	16/04/1915
War Diary	Hull	16/04/1915	16/04/1915
War Diary	5 Kilometers Word Of Merville	16/04/1915	16/04/1915
War Diary	5 Kilometers N.W. Cy W of Estaires	17/04/1915	18/04/1915
War Diary	Harte Vent	19/04/1915	19/04/1915
War Diary	Croix Marraisse	19/04/1915	19/04/1915
War Diary	Touquet	19/04/1915	27/04/1915
War Diary	Bac St Mary	27/04/1915	30/04/1915
Miscellaneous	Times Table of (Tasks).		
Miscellaneous	Time Table of (Tasks).		
Miscellaneous	Time Table of Tasks. Special Tasks	21/05/1915	21/05/1915
Miscellaneous	Defence of 49th (W.R.) Division Front.	24/05/1915	24/05/1915
Miscellaneous	Instructions For Movement 8th Division And Attached Brigade Of West Riding Artillery.	30/04/1915	30/04/1915
Miscellaneous	Instructions for Movement 2nd W.R. Fa Bde in Conjunction With 8th Divn	30/04/1915	30/04/1915
Operation(al) Order(s)	Operation Order No. 1 by Brig Gen C.T. Caulfield CRA 1st W.R. Divn	22/04/1915	22/04/1915
Miscellaneous	Instructions for Movement and Relief of Brigade, R.F.A. and 1st and 3rd West Riding Brigades, R.F.A.	23/04/1915	23/04/1915
Miscellaneous	HdQrs. R.A. 49th (WR) Division Vol II 1-31.5.15.		
Heading	War Diary of Headquarters West Riding Divisional Artillery from May 1st 1915 to May 31st 1915 Volume II		
War Diary	Bac St Maur	01/05/1915	08/05/1915
War Diary	H 20b. 6.8	09/05/1915	10/05/1915
War Diary	Bac St Maur	11/05/1915	19/05/1915
War Diary	Fort Rompu	20/05/1915	31/05/1915
Heading	Appendices War Diary 49th (W.R) Divnl. Arty 1st to 31st May 1915		
Miscellaneous	H Qrs 49th W Rest Bun	01/06/1915	01/06/1915
Miscellaneous	Tactical Progress Report Meerut Division.	02/05/1915	02/05/1915
Miscellaneous	Instruction for Movement 2nd W.R. 7a Bde in Conjunction with 8th Divn.	30/04/1915	30/04/1915
Miscellaneous	Instructions for movements 2nd W.R. 7a & 8th Divn	01/05/1915	01/05/1915

Miscellaneous	Instructions For Movement 8th. Divisional And Attached Brigade Of West Riding Artillery.	30/04/1915	30/04/1915
Miscellaneous	Instructions for movement of 2nd W.R. La Bde to VIII Divn	03/05/1915	03/05/1915
Miscellaneous	Instructions For Movement 5th H.A. Brigade 2nd. West Riding Brigade	03/05/1915	03/05/1915
Miscellaneous	A Form. Messages And Signals.		
Miscellaneous	Front. W. R.F.A. Bde	06/05/1915	06/05/1915
Miscellaneous	Third W. R.F.A. Bde.	06/05/1915	06/05/1915
Miscellaneous	Officer Comdg W.R. D.A.C.	06/05/1915	06/05/1915
Map	Field Ambulances. Advanced Dressing 5th. Divisional Collection		
Operation(al) Order(s)	West Riding Divisional Artillery Order No. 2	07/05/1915	07/05/1915
Miscellaneous	Time Table Of Tasks 3rd W. Rid F.A. Bde. 1st Phase O.O. O. 10.		
Miscellaneous	Headqrs R.A. West Riding Divn	12/05/1915	12/05/1915
Miscellaneous	Arrangements for Artillery Defence of 3,4,5 & 6 Sections.	11/05/1915	11/05/1915
Miscellaneous	5.9th Howitzer Battery firing 4 to 5 p.m. May 10th 1915 from West of Fromelles.	10/05/1915	10/05/1915
Miscellaneous	Arrangements For Artillery Defence Of	10/05/1915	10/05/1915
Miscellaneous	H.Q. West Riding Divn Arty	13/05/1915	13/05/1915
Miscellaneous	Headquarters, R.A. 49th (West Riding) Division.	13/05/1915	13/05/1915
Miscellaneous	A Form Messages And Signals		
Miscellaneous	C Form (Duplicate). Messages And Signals		
Miscellaneous	A Form Messages And Signals		
Miscellaneous	1/3rd Highland F.A. (H) Bde	15/05/1915	15/05/1915
Miscellaneous	A Form. Messages And Signals.		
Miscellaneous	C Form (Duplicate). Messages And Signals.		
Miscellaneous	Officer Commanding	14/05/1915	14/05/1915
Miscellaneous	A Form Messages And Signals.		
Miscellaneous	Messages And Signals.		
Miscellaneous	A Form Messages And Signals.		
Miscellaneous	West Riding R.G.A., Heavy Battery. Progress Report.	15/05/1915	15/05/1915
Miscellaneous	A Form Messages And Signals.		
Miscellaneous	March Table Night of 16th/17th May 1915	16/05/1915	16/05/1915
Miscellaneous	A Form Messages And Signals.		
Miscellaneous	West Riding R.G.A., Heavy Battery.	16/05/1915	16/05/1915
Miscellaneous	Instructions for Movements Evening 17th May 1915	17/05/1915	17/05/1915
Miscellaneous	C Form (Duplicate). Messages And Signals.		
Miscellaneous	For Information Instruction For Movements Evening of 17th May 1915	17/05/1915	17/05/1915
Operation(al) Order(s)	49th Division Operation Order No. 7	17/05/1915	17/05/1915
Miscellaneous	W.R.D.A. No S/7/G	17/05/1915	17/05/1915
Operation(al) Order(s)	49th (West Riding) Division Operation Order No. 8	21/05/1915	21/05/1915
Operation(al) Order(s)	49th (W.R.) Divisional Artillery Order No. 3	22/05/1915	22/05/1915
Miscellaneous	Time Table of Tasks. 1st Phase O.O-O. 15		
Miscellaneous	Time Table Of Tasks.	21/05/1915	21/05/1915
Miscellaneous	Headquarters R.A. 49th (W.R) Divn	23/05/1915	23/05/1915
Miscellaneous		22/05/1915	22/05/1915
Miscellaneous	C.R.A.	22/05/1915	22/05/1915
Operation(al) Order(s)	Operation Order No. 17 By Lieut General Sir H.S. Rawlinson, Bt., K.C.B., C.V.O. Commanding 4th Army Corps.	22/05/1915	22/05/1915
Miscellaneous	Time Table And Tasks.	24/05/1915	24/05/1915
Miscellaneous	General Staff 9th W.Q. Div Arty	24/05/1915	24/05/1915

Miscellaneous	General Staff 49th W.R. Div Arty	24/05/1915	24/05/1915
Miscellaneous	General Staff 49th W.R. Div Arty	25/05/1915	25/05/1915
Miscellaneous	49th W. Rid Division, T.F.	25/05/1915	25/05/1915
Miscellaneous	Defence of 49th W.R. Divn. Front.	25/05/1915	25/05/1915
Miscellaneous	Programme Of Return Move Of VIII Division Batteries		
Miscellaneous	C.R.A.	26/05/1915	26/05/1915
Miscellaneous	C Form (Duplicate). Messages And Signals.		
Miscellaneous	A Form Messages And Signals.		
Miscellaneous	Programme of Moves Night 26th-27th May, 1915	27/05/1915	27/05/1915
Miscellaneous	C Form (Duplicate). Messages And Signals.		
Miscellaneous	A Form Messages And Signals.		
Miscellaneous			
Miscellaneous	West Riding R.G.A. Heavy Battery	25/05/1915	25/05/1915
Miscellaneous	From Capt nicholls at 12:35 ever	27/05/1915	27/05/1915
Miscellaneous	C Form (Duplicate). Messages And Signals.		
Miscellaneous	Defence of 49th W.R. Division Front.	27/05/1915	27/05/1915
Miscellaneous	Situation Reports. From 12 midnight 26/5/15, to 12 midnight 27/5/15	26/05/1915	26/05/1915
Miscellaneous	First Army Intelligence Summary		
Miscellaneous	8th Division Artillery Report	24/05/1915	24/05/1915
Miscellaneous	49th (W.R.) Division.	25/05/1915	25/05/1915
Miscellaneous	Divisional Artillery Orders by Brigadier General C.T. Caulfeild R.A. Commanding R.A. 49th (W.R) Division.	26/05/1915	26/05/1915
Miscellaneous	Operation on the Bois Grenier-Bridoux Road 22-25 May.	22/05/1915	22/05/1915
Miscellaneous	49th (W.R.) Division	24/05/1915	24/05/1915
Miscellaneous	Officer Commanding, 4th W. Rid (How) Bde	28/05/1915	28/05/1915
Miscellaneous	The Officer Commanding, 1/3rd West Riding Brigade R.F.A. (T)	28/05/1915	28/05/1915
Miscellaneous	Action To Be Taken By The 3rd West Riding Brigade R.F.A. In The Event Of A Sudden Attack On Any Section Of The Present 49th (W.R.) Division Line.		
Miscellaneous	49th (West Riding) Divisional Artillery.	28/05/1915	28/05/1915
Miscellaneous	C Form (Duplicate). Messages And Signals.		
Miscellaneous			
Miscellaneous	C Form (Duplicate). Messages And Signals.		
Miscellaneous	1/3rd West Riding Brigade R.F.A. (T) Situation Report No. 29	28/05/1915	28/05/1915
Miscellaneous			
Miscellaneous	C Form (Duplicate). Messages And Signals.		
Miscellaneous	1/3rd West Riding Brigade R.F.A. (T) Situation Report No. 28	27/05/1915	27/05/1915
Miscellaneous			
Miscellaneous	A Form Messages And Signals.		
Miscellaneous	B Form Messages And Signals.		
Miscellaneous			
Miscellaneous	C Form (Original). Messages And Signals.		
Miscellaneous			
Miscellaneous	C Form (Duplicate). Messages And Signals.		
Miscellaneous			
Miscellaneous	Report on the Shelling of the 1st N.R. Battery by the Germans at 5.	28/05/1915	28/05/1915
Miscellaneous			
Miscellaneous	B Form Messages And Signals.		
Miscellaneous	A Form Messages And Signals.		
Miscellaneous			

Miscellaneous	C Form (Duplicate). Messages And Signals.		
Miscellaneous			
Miscellaneous	C Form (Duplicate). Messages And Signals.		
Miscellaneous			
Miscellaneous	49th (W.R.) Divisional Artillery.	29/05/1915	29/05/1915
Miscellaneous	Officer Commanding 4th W.R. (How) F.A. Bde.	29/05/1915	29/05/1915
Miscellaneous	49th (W.R) Divisional Artillery	29/05/1915	29/05/1915
Miscellaneous	49th (W.R) Division.	29/05/1915	29/05/1915
Miscellaneous	8th Division Artillery Report	30/05/1915	30/05/1915
Miscellaneous			
Miscellaneous	Appendix Casualties.		
Miscellaneous			
Miscellaneous	G.Q. C.R.A.	31/05/1915	31/05/1915
Miscellaneous	Officer Commanding	31/05/1915	31/05/1915
Miscellaneous	49th Division Headquarters R.A. 49th Division Vol III 1-30.6.15		
War Diary	Fort Rompu	01/06/1915	28/06/1915
War Diary	Proven	29/06/1915	30/06/1915
Miscellaneous	Appendix to War Diary for Month of June		
Miscellaneous			
Miscellaneous	A Form Messages And Signals.		
Miscellaneous	Ammunition Expended.		
Miscellaneous	49th (W.R) Divisional Artillery	01/06/1915	01/06/1915
Miscellaneous			
Miscellaneous	A Form Messages And Signals.		
Miscellaneous			
Miscellaneous	49th (W.R.) Divisional Artillery Tactical Progress Report 6 p.m. June 1st to 6 p.m. June 2nd 1915	02/06/1915	02/06/1915
Miscellaneous			
Miscellaneous	A Form Messages And Signals.		
Miscellaneous	C Form (Duplicate). Messages And Signals.		
Miscellaneous			
Miscellaneous	49th (W.R.) Divisional Artillery.	03/05/1915	03/05/1915
Miscellaneous			
Miscellaneous	C Form (Duplicate). Messages And Signals.		
Miscellaneous	A Form Messages And Signals.		
Miscellaneous			
Miscellaneous	A Form Messages And Signals.		
Miscellaneous			
Miscellaneous	49th (W.R.) Divisional Artillery.	14/06/1915	14/06/1915
Miscellaneous			
Miscellaneous	A Form Messages And Signals.		
Miscellaneous			
Miscellaneous	49th (W.R) Divisional Artillery.	05/06/1915	05/06/1915
Miscellaneous			
Miscellaneous	C Form (Duplicate). Messages And Signals.		
Miscellaneous	A Form Messages And Signals.		
Miscellaneous			
Miscellaneous	49th (W.R.) Divisional Artillery.	06/06/1915	06/06/1915
Miscellaneous			
Miscellaneous	A Form Messages And Signals.		
Miscellaneous			
Miscellaneous	49th (W.R) Divisional Artillery.	07/06/1915	07/06/1915
Miscellaneous			
Miscellaneous	49th (W.R.) Divisional Artillery.	07/06/1915	07/06/1915
Miscellaneous			

Miscellaneous	49th (W.R) Divisional Artillery.	08/06/1915	08/06/1915
Miscellaneous			
Miscellaneous	A Form Messages And Signals.		
Miscellaneous			
Miscellaneous	49th (W.R) Divisional Artillery.	09/06/1915	09/06/1915
Miscellaneous			
Miscellaneous	A Form Messages And Signals.		
Miscellaneous			
Miscellaneous	A Form Messages And Signals.		
Miscellaneous			
Miscellaneous	49th (W.R) Divisional Artillery.	10/06/1915	10/06/1915
Miscellaneous			
Miscellaneous	A Form Messages And Signals.		
Miscellaneous			
Miscellaneous	49th (W.R) Divisional Artillery.	11/06/1915	11/06/1915
Miscellaneous			
Miscellaneous	A Form Messages And Signals.		
Miscellaneous	XXIV		
Miscellaneous	A Form Messages And Signals.		
Miscellaneous			
Miscellaneous	49th (W.R.) Divisional Artillery.	12/06/1915	12/06/1915
Miscellaneous			
Miscellaneous	A Form Messages And Signals.		
Miscellaneous			
Miscellaneous	49th (W.R) Divisional Artillery.	13/06/1915	13/06/1915
Miscellaneous			
Miscellaneous	A Form Messages And Signals.		
Miscellaneous			
Miscellaneous	49th (W.R.) Divisional Artillery	14/06/1915	14/06/1915
Miscellaneous			
Miscellaneous	A Form Messages And Signals.		
Miscellaneous			
Miscellaneous	49th (W.R) Divisional Artillery.	15/06/1915	15/06/1915
Miscellaneous			
Miscellaneous	49th (W.R.) Divisional Artillery.	16/06/1915	16/06/1915
Miscellaneous	A Form Messages And Signals.		
Miscellaneous			
Miscellaneous	49th (W.R.) Divisional Artillery	16/06/1915	16/06/1915
Miscellaneous			
Miscellaneous	A Form Messages And Signals.		
Miscellaneous			
Miscellaneous	A Form Messages And Signals.		
Miscellaneous			
Miscellaneous	49th (W.R.) Divisional Artillery	17/06/1915	17/06/1915
Miscellaneous			
Miscellaneous	A Form Messages And Signals.		
Miscellaneous			
Miscellaneous	Officer Commanding.	18/06/1915	18/06/1915
Miscellaneous	Programme of Moves of Brigade Ammunition Columns on June 17th and 18th 1915	17/06/1915	17/06/1915
Miscellaneous			
Miscellaneous	49th (W.R.) Divisional Artillery.	18/06/1915	18/06/1915
Miscellaneous			
Miscellaneous	A Form Messages And Signals.		
Miscellaneous			
Miscellaneous	49th (W.R) Divisional Artillery	18/06/1915	18/06/1915

Miscellaneous			
Miscellaneous	49th (W.R) Divisional Artillery.	19/06/1915	19/06/1915
Miscellaneous	49th Divisional Artillery.	19/06/1915	19/06/1915
Miscellaneous			
Miscellaneous	49th (W.R.) Divisional Artillery.	20/06/1915	20/06/1915
Miscellaneous			
Miscellaneous	C Form (Duplicate) Messages And Signals.		
Miscellaneous	A Form Messages And Signals.		
Miscellaneous			
Miscellaneous	A Form Messages And Signals.		
Miscellaneous			
Miscellaneous	Officer Commanding 10th West Riding Howitzer Battery.	22/06/1915	22/06/1915
Miscellaneous	A Form Messages And Signals.		
Miscellaneous	49th (W.R) Divisional Artillery.	21/06/1915	21/06/1915
Miscellaneous			
Miscellaneous	49th (W.R) Divisional Artillery.	22/06/1915	22/06/1915
Miscellaneous			
Miscellaneous	A Form Messages And Signals.		
Miscellaneous			
Miscellaneous	49th (W.R) Divisional Artillery.	23/06/1915	23/06/1915
Miscellaneous	A Form Messages And Signals.		
Miscellaneous			
Miscellaneous	49th (W.R.) Divisional Artillery.	24/06/1915	24/06/1915
Miscellaneous			
Miscellaneous	A Form Messages And Signals.		
Miscellaneous			
Miscellaneous	49th (W.R.) Divisional Artillery.	27/06/1915	27/06/1915
Miscellaneous			
Miscellaneous	49th (W.R) Divisional Artillery Order No. 6	26/06/1915	26/06/1915
Miscellaneous	March Table 49th (W.R.) Division Artillery night 26th/27th June 1915	26/06/1915	26/06/1915
Miscellaneous			
Miscellaneous	A Form Messages And Signals.		
Miscellaneous			
Miscellaneous	C Form (Duplicate) Messages And Signals.		
Miscellaneous	49th (W.R.) Divisional Artillery Order No. 8	27/06/1915	27/06/1915
Operation(al) Order(s)	49th (W.R.) Divisional Artillery Order No. 7	27/06/1915	27/06/1915
Miscellaneous	March Table 49th (W.R) Division Artillery	27/06/1915	27/06/1915
Miscellaneous	49th (W.R) Divisional Artillery.	26/06/1915	26/06/1915
Miscellaneous			
Miscellaneous	49th (W.R.) Divisional Artillery.	26/06/1915	26/06/1915
Operation(al) Order(s)	49th (W.R.) Divisional Artillery Operation Order No. 8		
Miscellaneous	49th (W.R.) Divisional Artillery Units allotted to Groups vide 49th (W.R.) Division O.O. No. 16		
Miscellaneous			
Miscellaneous	March Table 49th (W.R) D.A.C.		
Miscellaneous	H.Q. RA. 49th Div Nov Vol VIII		

49TH DIVISION

C. R. A.

APR-DEC 1915

Confidential.

War Diary

of

1st West Riding Divisional Artillery.

from 31st March 1915 to 30th April

(Volume 1)

1st West Riding Divisional Artillery.

(1)

Army Form C. 2118.

Instructions regarding War Diaries and Intelligence Summaries are contained in F. S. Regs., Part II. and the Staff Manual respectively. Title pages will be prepared in manuscript.

WAR DIARY
or
~~INTELLIGENCE SUMMARY.~~

(Erase heading not required.)

Hour, Date, Place	Summary of Events and Information	Remarks and references to Appendices
10 am 31/3/15 DONCASTER	Orders received verbally to prepare for Embarkation for the Continent on or about 18th April.	[illegible]
5/4/15	Mark IV 15 Pr Guns commenced to arrive from 1st London Divisional Artillery.	[illegible]
8.15 am 6/4/15	Capt Kitchen 1/4th W.R. F.A. Bde & Lieut Willey 1/3rd W.R F.A. Bde proceeded with Capt Page G.S.O 3 1/1st W.R. Div for landing & entraining duties at ports of disembarkation.	[illegible]
7 am 7/4/15	Preparations for embarkation proceeding. Fitting of Shields to ammunition wagons commenced at DONCASTER	[illegible]
	Preparations continued.	
8/4/15	— ditto —	[illegible]
~~9/4/15~~	~~— ditto —~~	
6.20 pm 9/4/15	Capt Allen proceeds to continent for billeting duties. Preparations continued	[illegible]
1 pm. 10/4/15 ~~Folkestone~~ FOLKESTONE	Capt Allen embarked for ~~Boulogne~~. BOULOGNE Preparations continued.	[illegible]

(9 29 6) W4141—463 100,000 9/14 H W V Forms/C. 2118/10

Army Form C. 2118.

Instructions regarding War Diaries and Intelligence Summaries are contained in F. S. Regs., Part II. and the Staff Manual respectively. Title pages will be prepared in manuscript.

WAR DIARY
or
~~INTELLIGENCE SUMMARY.~~
(Erase heading not required.)

Hour, Date, Place	Summary of Events and Information	Remarks and references to Appendices
11/4/15 DONCASTER	Sunday. Preparations continued.	[illegible]
2.20 am 12/4/15 — " —	Lieut Calvert Jones A.D.C with horses, 14 men + 2nd line transport left by train for SOUTHAMPTON + HAVRE.	
	Preparations continued.	
7.30 pm 12/4/15	Lieut Calvert Jones + party embarked at Southampton on S.S. Maidan for HAVRE	
7.0 am 13/4/15 HAVRE ~~Havre~~	advance party arrived Havre + went to rest camp.	[illegible]
6 pm — " —	Entrained at HAVRE + left at 10.30 pm.	
[illegible] am — " — YORK ~~York~~	1/1st W.R. F.A. Bde commenced ~~entraining~~ departure by train; completed at 6.40 am.	
	1/2nd W.R. Battery R.F.A. from HAVRE 2.25 am + 4.15 am + arrived Southampton same day.	
11.25 am — " — DONCASTER ~~Doncaster~~	H.Q. 1/1st W.R. Divisional Artillery consisting of Brig Gen C.T. Caulfeild CRA + Major L.W. Lewer. RA Bde Major RA + 4 other ranks left for FOLKESTONE where they embarked at 7.50 pm. + landed ~~arrived~~ BOULOGNE 10. pm.	
9 am — " —	Shields on ammunition wagons completed at DONCASTER.	

(9 29 6) W4141—463 100,000 9/14 H W V Forms/C. 2118/10

(3)

Army Form C. 2118.

Instructions regarding War Diaries and Intelligence Summaries are contained in F. S. Regs., Part II. and the Staff Manual respectively. Title pages will be prepared in manuscript.

WAR DIARY

or

~~INTELLIGENCE SUMMARY.~~

(Erase heading not required.)

Hour, Date, Place	Summary of Events and Information	Remarks and references to Appendices
4.15 pm. 13/4/15 BAWTRY ~~Bawtry~~	1/2nd W.R. F.A. Bde commenced movement by train to SOUTHAMPTON, all units away by 6.5 am. 14/4/15.	WB
2 pm. 14/4/15 BOULOGNE ~~Boulogne~~	G.O.C. RA + Bde Major RA by motor to MERVILLE arriving 4.30 pm.	References 1/20,000 France Sheets 36 NW + SW
6.15 pm to 6.55 am 15th.	3rd W.R. F.A. Bde from DONCASTER + GRIMSBY to SOUTHAMPTON arriving at last place by 5.0 pm 15th, embarked for HAVRE.	WB
12 noon 15th. MERVILLE ~~Merville~~	Lieut Calvert Jones arrived with horses + 2nd line transport from BERGUETTE.	
Evening ... BERGUETTE ~~Berguette~~	1st W.R. F.A. Bde arrived + went into temporary billets.	
~~6.15 am~~ 11.15 pm 14th to 3.45 am 15th. DONCASTER	4th W.R. F.A. Bde (How) left for SOUTHAMPTON + HAVRE	WB
~~4 pm~~ 9.30 pm 15th to 7.55 am 16th WOOLWICH A.	W.R. Div. A.C. left for SOUTHAMPTON + HAVRE	
6.15 am – 9.35 am 16th HULL	W.R. R.G.A. for SOUTHAMPTON + HAVRE	

(9 29 6) W4141—463 100,000 9/14 H W V Forms/C. 2118/10

Army Form C. 2118.

WAR DIARY
or
~~INTELLIGENCE SUMMARY.~~
(*Erase heading not required.*)

Instructions regarding War Diaries and Intelligence Summaries are contained in F. S. Regs., Part II. and the Staff Manual respectively. Title pages will be prepared in manuscript.

Hour, Date, Place	Summary of Events and Information	Remarks and references to Appendices
1 pm. 16th 5 Kilometres West of MERVILLE	1st W.R. F.A. Bde arrived & went into billets.	CWL References $\frac{1}{20,000}$ France Sheets 36 NW & SW
3 pm 17th 3 Kilometres N.W by W of ESTAIRES	2nd W.R. F.A. Bde arrived & went into billets.	CWL — —
2 pm 18th 4 Kilometres N.N.W of ESTAIRES	3rd W.R. F.A. Bde arrived & went into billets	CWL — —
10.30 am 19th ~~Haute~~ HARTE VENT	4th W.R. F.A. Bde — " — " —	—
6. pm 19th ~~La~~ ~~Touquet~~ ~~Croix~~ CROIX ~~Marraisse~~ MARRAISSE	W.R. R.G.A. — " — " —	—
9 pm. 19th ~~La~~ LE ~~Touquet~~ TOUQUET	D.A.Col. — " — " —	CWL —

Army Form C. 2118.

WAR DIARY
or
~~INTELLIGENCE SUMMARY.~~
(Erase heading not required.)

Instructions regarding War Diaries and Intelligence Summaries are contained in F. S. Regs., Part II. and the Staff Manual respectively. Title pages will be prepared in manuscript.

Hour, Date, Place	Summary of Events and Information	Remarks and references to Appendices
20th	(1) All units completing equipment still outstanding & training remounts, practicing telephone carts & laying out lines of communication (2) Cols, Majors & 3 subalterns of 1st, 2nd & 3rd FA Bdes attached to VIIth & VIIIth Divns for instruction in trench warfare.	Lwt.
~~21st~~		
21st	(1) Continued (2) Adjutant, BSMs, Nos 1, Captains & Subalterns of same FA Bdes relieve those out for same instruction.	Lwt.
22nd	— ditto	Lwt.
23rd	(1) 2nd W. R. Bde RFA less 1 Section 6th Battery attached to VIIth Division & went into action near LAVENTIE night 23/24	Appendix (1) References 1/20,000 France Sheets 36 N.W. & S.W.
	(2) 3rd W. R. FA Bde less Amm Col to VIIIth Divisional Area & went into action near FLEURBAIX night 23/24	(2)
	(3) 1st W.R. FA Bde less Amm Col to VIIIth Divnl. Area to Wagon Lines E of BAC ST MAUR night 23/24.	(3)

Army Form C. 2118. (6)

Instructions regarding War Diaries and Intelligence Summaries are contained in F. S. Regs., Part II. and the Staff Manual respectively. Title pages will be prepared in manuscript.

WAR DIARY

or

~~INTELLIGENCE SUMMARY.~~

(Erase heading not required.)

Hour, Date, Place	Summary of Events and Information	Remarks and references to Appendices
23rd	(4) W. R. R. G. A to H. A. Reserve + into action square H 25 a (Sheet Series B) 36 N.W. night 23/24th	Append ix (4)
	(5) Bde A.C 1st W. R. Bde RFA from Artillery area to 2 Area 3pm.	—— (5) RWL
24th	(1) 1st W. R. F.A. Bde preparing gun pits in vicinity of Rue des LOMBARDES square H 27 d, H 28 c, H 33 a + H 33 d.	
	(2) 2nd W R F.A. Bde in action S. W. LAVENTIE	
	(3) 3rd W R. F.A. Bde in action H 28, H 28 b, H 29 b	
	(4) 4th W R F.A. Bde still in Artillery Area	
	(5) W. R. R. G. A as on night 23rd	
	(6) Divisional A.C from Artillery Area to No 1 Area.	Append ix (6) RWL

(9 29 6) W 4141—463 100,000 9/14 H W V Forms/C. 2118/10

(7)

Army Form C. 2118.

WAR DIARY
or
~~INTELLIGENCE SUMMARY.~~
(Erase heading not required.)

Instructions regarding War Diaries and Intelligence Summaries are contained in F. S. Regs., Part II. and the Staff Manual respectively. Title pages will be prepared in manuscript.

Hour, Date, Place	Summary of Events and Information	Remarks and references to Appendices
25th April	(1) 4th W.R. How: F.A. Bde marched 9 am to join First Corps; arrived LA TOMBE WILLOT 12.30 pm.	Appendix (7)
	(2) 4th Section D.A.C. marched 10 am to GONNEHEM for supply of ammunition to 4th W.R. How. Bde.	
	(3) 1st W.R. F.A. Bde preparing gun pits.	
	(4) 2nd W.R. F.A. Bde with VII th Division.	
	(5) 3rd W.R. F.A. Bde — VIII th Division registering.	[initials]
26th April	(1) Bde A.C.s 1st & 3rd Bde move to Square H 8 C 8.4 arrived by 2.30 pm.	Appendix (8)
	(2) 1st W.R. F.A. Bde with VIII th Division registering.	
	(3) 2nd W.R. F.A. Bde as before	
	(4) 3rd W.R. F.A. Bde as before.	[initials]

Army Form C. 2118. (8)

Instructions regarding War Diaries and Intelligence Summaries are contained in F. S. Regs., Part II. and the Staff Manual respectively. Title pages will be prepared in manuscript.

WAR DIARY
or
~~INTELLIGENCE~~ SUMMARY.
(Erase heading not required.)

Hour, Date, Place	Summary of Events and Information	Remarks and references to Appendices
27th. April 12.2 pm.	Instructions issued to Artillery re Hose pipes in Enemy Trenches.	Appendix (9).
	FA Bdes as before.	
BAC St Maur 4 pm.	Divisional Artillery H.Q. moved to BAC St Maur on move of H.Q. Division	[illegible]
28th. April	Report re unusual Activity in hostile trenches about N6d.	Appendix (10)
	Instructions issued to 1st & 3rd Bdes to keep sharp look out & register to spot.	
	Registration by Bdes as before.	
29th. April	Registration continued.	[illegible] Appendix (11).
30th. April	Wagon line 3rd RFA Bde changed to H 14 C 4,8.	
	One section 4th, 5th, 6th Batteries move to	

(9 29 6) W 4141—463 100,000 9/14 H W V Forms/C. 2118/10

Army Form C. 2118.

Instructions regarding War Diaries and Intelligence Summaries are contained in F. S. Regs., Part II. and the Staff Manual respectively. Title pages will be prepared in manuscript.

WAR DIARY
or
INTELLIGENCE SUMMARY.
(*Erase heading not required.*)

Hour, Date, Place	Summary of Events and Information	Remarks and references to Appendices
30th April	relief of O, Z & AQU batteries & taking up following positions 4th Battery to ~~H33 a 8.5~~ N33 c 4.8 5th — " — H33 a 8.5 6th — " — N34 a 9.5. Move completed by 12 midnight Remaining units continued Registration.	Appendix (12). hwz
24th – 30th.	Ammunition expended. 948 rounds 15 Pr BLC. Casualties. One driver (telephonist) wounded.	hwz

(9 29 6) W 4141—463 100,000 9/14 H W V Forms/C. 2118/10

SECRET. **TIME TABLE OF TASKS. (1).** Copy No. 34........

References 1/20,000 & 1/10,000 numbered Maps. 1st Phase 0.0 - 0.15

UNIT.	TIME	OBJECTIVE	REMARKS	ROUNDS PER GUN DEEMED SUFFICIENT.
5th Battery R.F.A.	0.0 - 0.15	Wire cutting 100x to 200x WEST of Pt 976		20 Shrapnel.
36th -------"-----	----"----	Wire cutting Pt 976 to 100x WEST.		20 Shrapnel.
72nd ------"-----	-----"-----	Wire cutting Pt 976 to 100x EAST.		20 Shrapnel.
112th ------"-----	-----"-----	Wire cutting 100x to 200x EAST of Pt 976.		20 Shrapnel.
	0.15 to 0.20		Pause.	

References 1/20,000 & 1/10,000 numbered Maps.

TIME TABLE OF TASKS. (2)

2nd Phase 0.20 -0.50

UNIT.	TIME.	OBJECTIVE	REMARKS	ROUNDS DEEMED SUFFICIENT.
5th Battery R.F.A.	0.20 - 0.30	100 to 200 WEST of Pt 976	Bombardment of enemy's front trenches,	50 Shrapnel per Battery.
36th ------"-----	----"-----	Pt 976 to 100 WEST	----------"---------	--------"------
72nd ------"-----	----"-----	Pt 976 to 100 EAST	----------"---------	--------"------
112th -----"-----	----"-----	100 to 200 EAST of Pt 976	----------"---------	--------"------
3rd W.R. Battery.	----"-----	100 EAST of Pt 966 to 175 EAST.	----------"--------	1 round per gun per minute.
3rd W.R. F.A. Bde.	----"----	175 EAST of Pt 966 to 400 EAST.	----------"--------	-------"--------
3rd Highland (H) Bde.	----"----	100 EAST of pt 966 to 350 EAST.	----------"-------	--------"------
4th W.R. (How) Bde.	----"----	250 EAST of Pt 976 to 500 EAST	----------"------	--------"------
	0.30 - 0.35		Pause.	
	0.35 - 0.45	All batteries repeat Bombardment.	18 prs fire 50 ~~H.E.~~ shrapnel per battery ~~instead of Shrapnel.~~ (not HE)	
	0.45 - 0.50		Pause.	
	0.50 - 0.60	All batteries repeat Bombardment,	18 prs fire 50 ~~percussion~~ HE ~~Shrapnel~~ per battery. (not Shrapnel)	

S E C R E T.

References 1/20,000 & 1/10,000 numbered Maps

TIME TABLE OF TASKS. (3)

SPECIAL TASKS.

UNIT.	TIME	OBJECTIVE	REMARKS	ROUNDS PER GUN DEEMED SUFFICIENT.
1st W.R. F.A. Bde less 3rd Battery	0.20 - 0.30	966 - 967 - 968.	To form a barrage	1 round per gun per minute.
	0.30 - 0.35		Pause.	
	0.35 - 0.45	Repeat		
	0.45 - 0.50		Pause.	
	0.50 - 0.60	Repeat		
55th Battery R.F.A.	0.20 - 0.60	(1) Pts 940, 941, 953, 954, 955 (Communication Trenches) (2) 974 - 975 (3) Communication Trenches from RUE DES BOIS BLANCS		1 round per gun per minute Shrapnel.
One 18 pr Gun 6th Divn.	0.20 - 0.60	Hostile Machine guns in salient 500 x EAST Pt 976		No limit.

21/5/15.

[signature]
Major R.A.,
Brigade Major R.A. 49th (W.R.) Division.

SECRET.

G.O.C. 148th Infy Bde

Defence of 49th (W.R.) Division Front.

Owing to 5th Brigade R.H.A. having been ordered to move from its present position, the entire defence of the front will be taken up as follows :-

A. 2nd W.R. F.A. Bde. covering sections 1 B & 2 for direct defence.
1st W.R. F.A. Bde, covering sections 3 & 4 for direct defence.
3rd W.R. F.A. Bde. covering sections 5 & 6 for direct defence.
4th W.R. F.A. Bde. 10th Battery covering sections 1 B, 2 & 3.
11th Battery covering sections 4, 5 & 6 for defence under orders of G.O.C.R.A.49th(W.R.)Divn.

B. O.C's Bdes will arrange that batteries overlap on both flanks and are able to fire on the approaches leading towards Sections on either flank.

C. (1) O.C. 2nd W.R. F.A. Bde. to arrange for 4th Battery to be able to fire on approaches in N 14 a and N 14 b on demand from H.Q. 33rd F.A. Bde.

(2) O.C. 3rd W.R. F.A. Bde to arrange for 8th Battery to be able to fire on approaches in I 31 d and I 32 a and c on demand from H.Q. 53rd F.A. Bde. (same H.Qrs as 12th F.A. Bds).

D. For the information of 4th W.R. (H) Bde. R.F.A. 1 B consists of 1 R, 1 S and 2 P.

E. INTER COMMUNICATION.

(1) 2nd W.R. F.A. Bde., with

(a) 146th Infantry Brigade.
(b) 33rd F.A. Bde.
(c) 1st W.R. F.A. Bde.

(2) 1st W.R. F.A. Bde., with

(a) 147th Infantry Brigade.
(b) 2nd W.R. F.A. Bde.
(c) 3rd W.R. F.A. Bde.

(3) 3rd W.R. F.A. Bde., with

(a) 148th Infantry Brigade.
(b) 1st W.R. F.A. Bde.
(c) 53rd F.A. Bde.

F. Night Lines.

F. <u>NIGHT LINES 4th W.R. (How:) F.A. Bde.</u>

10th Battery FROMELLES CHURCH.

11th Battery LEMAISNIL CHURCH.

G. <u>ZONE allotted 4th W.R.(How:) F.A. Bde.</u>

Both batteries the whole length of 49th (W.R.) Division front.

H. <u>TIME & DATE</u>.

These arrangements come into force from 8.30 p.m. 27th May, 1915.

I. O.C's Bdes will forward their arrangements for mutual support in case of S.O.S. call from Infantry.

R W Lewer

Major R.A.,

27/5/15. Brigade Major R.A. 49th (W.R.) Division.

SECRET.   Copy No. 2

(12)

INSTRUCTIONS FOR MOVEMENT
8th DIVISION AND ATTACHED BRIGADE OF WEST RIDING ARTILLERY.

Reference 1/20,000 sheets FRANCE 36 N.W. & 36 S.W.

30-4-15.

1. 4 Guns "O" battery to march at 8 p.m. tonight via LA CROIX LESCORNEX - Road junction H 31 b 3.0 - Road junction H 31 a 6.6 - LAVENTIE - road junction M 4 C 10.3 - four cross roads M 9 d 8.2 - four cross roads M 15 C 1.2 into position at M 21 a 5.2

4 Guns "Z" battery to march at 8.5 p.m. tonight following the same route as "O" battery as far as Road junction M 15 C 7.6 thence to position at M 21 b 7.7

1 Section 36th battery to march at 8.45 p.m. tonight via ROUGE DE BOUT - LAVENTIE - Road junction M 4 C 10.3 - four cross roads M 9 d 8.2 into position at M 15 b 5.5

1 Section "A,Q,U" battery to march at 8.30 p.m. tonight via CROIX BLANCHE - LA CROIX LESCORNEX into position at N 1 a 9.9

1 Section 5th WEST RIDING battery at M 21 b 7.7 to march at 8.45 p.m. via Road junction M 15 C 7.6 - four cross roads M 15 C 1.2 - fork road M 14 b 6.7 - LAVENTIE - ROUGE DE BOUT and thence as ordered by B.G.C.R.A. WEST RIDING DIVISION.

1 Section 6th WEST RIDING battery at M 21 a 5.3 to march at 8.55 p.m. via four cross roads M 15 C 1.2 and thence to follow 5th WEST RIDING battery.

1 Section 4th WEST RIDING battery at M 16 a 6.6 to march at 8.55 p.m. via four cross roads LAVENTIE - ROUGE DE BOUT and thence as ordered by B.G.C.R.A. WEST RIDING DIVISION.

2. On completion of movement Horses and 1st line wagons will move to -

"O" and "Z" batteries	-	M 1 d 5.3
"A & U" battery	-	G 34 b 4.2
36th battery	-	M 3 C 1.7

Accommodation must be found in present wagon lines for incoming units until relief is completed and wagon lines and gun positions can be completely handed over.

K.T. Johnson

Issued at...11 AM.   Major. R.A.

Brigade Major 8th Division Artillery.

Secret

Copy No 2

Instructions for movement
2nd W R F a Bde in conjunction with 8th Divn

Reference 1/20,000 Sheets France 36 N W & 36 S W

30. 4. 15

(1) These instructions are to be followed in conjunction with instructions issued by 8th Divnl Arty d/30/4/15.

(2) 1 Section 5th W R Battery to march at 8.45 pm via Road Junction M15 C 7.6 - 4 X ~~Roads~~ M15 C1.2 - Fork Road M14 b 6.7 - LAVENTIE - ROUGE DE BOUT - Road Junction N 31 a 6 6 - Road Junction N 31 b 3.0 - LA CROIX LESCORNEX - CROIX BLANCHE - H 33 a 8.5

1 Section 6th W R Battery to march at 8.5? pm via 4 X roads M15 C 1.2 + thence to follow 5th W R Battery to N 34 a 9 5 via RUELLE DU BOIS FIEREIZ

1 Section 4th W R Battery to march at 8.55 pm via 4 Cross roads LAVENTIE - ROUGE DE BOUT - Road Junction N 31 a 6.6 - Road Junction N 31 b 3.0 - LA CROIX LES-CORNEX - CROIX BLANCHE to N 33 C 4 8.

3\. Wagon line
1st line Wagons & horses to H 19 a 8 8 on completion of move.

3 Contd.

Accommodation to be found in present wagon lines for incoming ~~units~~ units until relief is completed and wagon lines and gun positions can be completely handed over.

4 Bde HQs will not move till tomorrow instructions will be issued when it is to go.

L.W. Lewer Major RA
Bde Major RA
W.R. Divn.

Issued at 3.15 pm.

Copy No 1.

Operation Order No 1
by
Brig Gen C.T. Caulfeild
CRA 1st W. R Divn

22nd April 1915

1 (a) West Riding Division will take over defence of Nos 3, 4, 5 & 6 Sections of trench line now held by 8th Divn.

(b) Troops of West Riding Division moving into 8th Division area will come under the command of G.O.C 8th Division.

(c) The transfer will be completed by 6 am 28th April at which hour G.O.C West Riding Division assumes command of the troops in Nos 3, 4, 5, & 6 Sections.

2. The 1st & 3rd F. A Bdes West Riding Division less ammn Cols will move so as to reach SAILLY Bridge at 7 pm, on 23rd April at which hour and place guides to be detailed by G.O.C RA 8th Division, will meet them.

3 Headquarters R.A. will move to BAC ST MAUR on 24th.

Issued at 6.55 pm
Copies to 1st & 3rd Fd. Bdes.

C W Lewer Major RA
Bde Major RA
1st West Riding Divn

COPY No...2....

INSTRUCTIONS FOR MOVEMENT AND RELIEF OF

33RD Brigade, R.F.A. and 1st and 3rd WEST RIDING Brigades, R.F.A.

23rd April, 1915.

3rd WEST RIDING Brigade (less Ammunition Column) arrives SAILLY BRIDGE at 7 p.m. 23-4-15. Guns and firing battery wagons will move via BAC ST MAUR road junction H 7 d 10.3 and FLEURBAIX into positions of 33rd F.A. Brigade. Brigade H.Q. will be established at H 28 a 8.3.

First line wagons will move via BAC ST MAUR - FORT ROMPU - and road junction H 8 c 9.9 - to wagon line position at H 8 a 7.4

1st WEST RIDING Brigade (less Ammunition Column) arrives SAILLY BRIDGE 7.30 p.m. 23-4-15. moves via BAC ST MAUR to H 8 c 6.8 Brigade Headquarters will be established at H 27 D 2.3

33rd F.A. Brigade will arrange to withdraw one section of each battery between 8 and 8.30 p.m. which will be moved into position on RUE PETILLON and at H 33 D 5.1

One section of each battery 33rd F.A. Brigade will be left in action in their present positions until the evening of 25th April.

R H Johnson Major. R.A.

Issued at 9 a.m. Brigade Major 8th Division Artillery.

23 4 15

Received 6-20 pm 23/4/15

On His Majesty's Servic[e]

H^d Qrs. R.A. 49th (W.R.) Division.

Vol II 1 – 31. 5. 15.

CONFIDENTIAL.

WAR DIARY

of

Headquarters West Riding Divisional Artillery.

from May 1st 1915 to May 31st 1915

Volume II.

H.Q. West Riding Divn. Artillery (1.)

Army Form C. 2118.

Instructions regarding War Diaries and Intelligence Summaries are contained in F. S. Regs., Part II. and the Staff Manual respectively. Title pages will be prepared in manuscript.

WAR DIARY
-May-
~~INTELLIGENCE SUMMARY~~.
(Erase heading not required.)

References 1/20,000 FRANCE Sheets 36 N.W & 36 S.W.

Place	Date	Hour	Summary of Events and Information	Remarks and references to Appendices
BAC St MAUR	May 1st	All day	(1) 1st W.R.F.A Bde continued registration.	
		12.15 am	(2) 2nd W.R.F.A Bde 1 Section per Battery arrived & went into position & billets as follows:— 4th Battery H 33 c 4.8. 5th —"— H 33 a 10.8. 6th —"— H 34 a 8.4. These sections commenced registering.	Appendix I. [initials]
		All day 12 noon	(3) 3rd W.R.F.A. Bde continued registration. Bde A.C. moved up from FORT ROMPU to H 14 a 4.0.	
	2nd	—"—	(1) 1st W.R.F.A Bde as on 1st.	
		12.5 am	(2) 2nd W.R.F.A. Bde remaining Section per battery arrived & went into position & billets along side respective Section which arrived as shown on May 1st. Batteries continued registration. Defensive front allotted to this Bde 2, 3, 5 & 6 sections of W.R. Divn defensive front as follows. 4th Battery Section 2 & ½ 3 & to assist in flanking fire VIIIth Div. 5th ——— 3. 6th ——— Sections 5 & 6.	Appendix II [initials]
		2 pm	(3) Bde A.C. arrived from LAVENTIE & took up billets at FORT ROMPU. Bde H.Q. established at BARLETTE FARM.	

Instructions regarding War Diaries and Intelligence Summaries are contained in F. S. Regs., Part II. and the Staff Manual respectively. Title pages will be prepared in manuscript.

WAR DIARY

or

~~INTELLIGENCE SUMMARY.~~

(Erase heading not required.)

Army Form C. 2118. (2)

Place	Date	Hour	Summary of Events and Information	Remarks and references to Appendices
BAC ST MAUR	May. 3rd.	all day	(1) 1st W.R. F.A. Bde continued registration.	
			~~Bde A.C. moved out~~ Wagon line moved up from FORT ROMPU to H 13 d central.	
			(2) 2nd — — —	
		9 pm.	2nd W.R. F.A. Bde less Bde A.C. moved out of area to join VIIIth Div temporarily until return of VIIth Div.	III
		all day	(3). 3rd W.R. F.A. Bde continued registration.	Lw
	4th.	all day	(1) 1st W.R. F.A. Bde continued registration light bad.	
		2 pm	(2) Bde A.C. 2nd W.R. Bde left FORT ROMPU for VIIIth + VIIth Div Area at 2 pm	Lw
		all day	(3) 3rd — — —	
	5th.	— " —	(1) 1st — — —	Lw
		— " —	(2) 3rd — — —	
	6th.	— " —	(1) 1st — — —	Lw
		— " —	(2) 3rd — — —	
	7th	4 am	(1) 1st W.R. F.A. Bde A.C. moved from FORT ROMPU to H 13 d 7.7 (piecemeal)	
			1st — — — Wagon line from H 13 d 7.7 to H 26 ~~b~~. (piecemeal)	
			Batteries continued Registration.	
		— " —	(2). 3rd W.R. F.A. Bde A.C. moved from FORT ROMPU to H 14 a. 4.0 (piecemeal)	
			3rd — — — Wagon line from H 14 a. 4.0 to H 16 d. (piecemeal	
			Batteries continued Registration.	
		8 am	(3). 1st Section W.R. D.A.C. from ~~L 9~~ L 10 d ~~to~~ to H 13 d 7.7 by subsections at 1 hour interval	

1577 Wt. W10791/1773 500,000 1/15 D. D. & L. A.D.S.S./Forms/C. 2118.

Army Form C. 2118. (3)

Instructions regarding War Diaries and Intelligence Summaries are contained in F. S. Regs., Part II. and the Staff Manual respectively. Title pages will be prepared in manuscript.

WAR DIARY

or

~~INTELLIGENCE SUMMARY.~~

(Erase heading not required.)

Place	Date	Hour	Summary of Events and Information	Remarks and references to Appendices
BAC ST MAUR	May 7th	10am	(3) Contd. 2nd Section W.R D.A.C. from L10d to G 32 d central by Subsections at 1 hr interval	
		12am	3rd Section W.R. D.A.C. from L10d to H 14 a 4.0 by Subsections at 1 hour interval.	IV
		3pm	H.Q. D.A.C. from L10d to H14 a 4.0.	[illegible] V
		12 noon	Divisional Artillery order issued for offensive operations.	
	8th	5am	Offensive operations postponed till 9th	
			(1) 1st W.R. 79 Bde handed over to VIIIth Div & registration completed	
			(2) 3rd W.R. 79 Bde registration completed.	
		12 midnight	Advanced Report centre opened at H 20 b. 6.8.	[illegible]
H20b 6.8	9th	5am	Bombardment of enemy's position commenced in accordance with Divisional Artillery Order No 2 d/7/5/15 & tasks allotted.	
		am 5 - 5.10	Wire cutting 966 - 969 1st Phase.	
		am 5.10 - 5.25	Destruction of as much of enemy's parapet as possible opposite Section 6. 2nd Phase	
		am 5.25 - 9.45.	Watch & search the road from point 788 inclusive – LEMAISNIL and all approaches leading towards our front in that Area, fire not to be directed WEST of Road running NORTH from point 788. Any enemy's guns opening fire in that Area is to be silenced.	

1577 Wt. W10791/1773 500,000 1/15 D. D. & L. A.D.S.S./Forms/C. 2118.

Army Form C. 2118.

Instructions regarding War Diaries and Intelligence Summaries are contained in F. S. Regs., Part II. and the Staff Manual respectively. Title pages will be prepared in manuscript.

WAR DIARY
or
~~INTELLIGENCE~~ SUMMARY.
(Erase heading not required.)

Place	Date	Hour	Summary of Events and Information	Remarks and references to Appendices
	May			
A 20 b. 6. 8	9th	6.51 am	Third W.R. F.A. Bde reports "wire and parapets greatly damaged. Farm at 8th battery + at H 29 c1-4 on fire". "No Casualties".	
		7.50 am	Third W.R.F.A. Bde reports "Nothing to report. Batteries searching roads in zone, slow rate of fire." "No Casualties".	
		8.26 am	First W.R. F.A. Bde reports "Left attack seems to be temporarily held up" "No Casualties".	
		8.51 am	Fire of two batteries 3rd W.R. F.A. Bde ordered to turn fire on to RUE DES TURCS for a period of ½ hour. H.Q. Divn. Informed 9. 5 am	
		9.48 am	Third brigade reports "only one battery able on this point. First gun fire 9. 30 am H.Q. Division informed verbally	
		10.7 am	Third W.R. F.A. Bde report ½ hour up + are ordered to return to original task.	
		12.26 pm	"Shelling of hostile observing station at LE MAISNIL." "No Casualties". H.Q. Divn. informed verbally	
		2.41 pm	Third W.R. F.A. Bde reports "Enemy shelling our trenches section 5 + 6." "Guns not located	

Instructions regarding War Diaries and Intelligence Summaries are contained in F. S. Regs., Part II. and the Staff Manual respectively. Title pages will be prepared in manuscript.

WAR DIARY
or
~~INTELLIGENCE SUMMARY.~~
(Erase heading not required.)

Army Form C. 2118. (5)

Place	Date May	Hour	Summary of Events and Information	Remarks and references to Appendices
H 20 b. 6. 8	9th	4.6 pm	Third Brigade ordered to keep steady fire of one battery on road from Pt 478 to LE MAISNIL	
		7.45 pm	Third Brigade ordered to cease fire, but to co-operate with infantry when called upon & to knock out located machine guns.	
		9.17 pm	VIth Divn reports flashes of guns firing at 6.50 pm were 6° Right of FOURNES Church. Too long range for 3rd W.R.F.A Bde.	
		10.10 pm	Third W.R.F.A Bde ordered to keep up intermittent rate of fire on road Pt 478 – LE MAISNIL of one battery. Two batteries on approaches from road to our own front & to cooperate with our infantry to prevent the enemy repairing his parapet & wire.	
	10th	12.20 am	Third W.R. FA Bde reports "location of enemy's guns flashes 7 degrees Right of RADINGHEM Church from E in LE CROMBALOT. HQ Divn informed.	
		4.45 am	Third W.R. FA Bde reports "Batteries firing on trenches 4, 5 & 6. No machine guns located.	

1577 Wt. W10791/1773 500,000 1/15 D. D. & L. A.D.S.S./Forms/C. 2118.

Army Form C. 2118. 6

WAR DIARY
or
~~INTELLIGENCE SUMMARY.~~
(Erase heading not required.)

Instructions regarding War Diaries and Intelligence Summaries are contained in F. S. Regs., Part II. and the Staff Manual respectively. Title pages will be prepared in manuscript.

Place	Date	Hour	Summary of Events and Information	Remarks and references to Appendices
H 20b. 6.6.	10th	11.30am	H.Q. Divn. presents 4th Corps order to cease firing unless infantry requires it. Third W.R.F.A. Bde informed	
		11.45am	Third W.R.F.A. Bde states batteries firing 20 rounds per hour, Hole in parapet opposite 6. R.	Files 1, 2 & 3 & Registration of messages.
		11.50am	Third W.R.F.A. Bde cease firing.	VI
BAC ST MAUR		1pm	H.Q. Div & Divl Artillery returned to Headquarters BAC ST MAUR.	[illegible]
	11th	3.45pm	Third W.R.F.A. Bde reports "5.9 inch Guns firing on FLEURBAIX this morning reported on a line from H.29c 9-9 through F of FROMELLES. H.Q. Divn & C.R.A. VIIIth informed & enemy guns located as Target No 31 on 1:20000 FRANCE 36 S.W. Square N 22 c 6-3, corroborated by VI Divn Arty. First W.R.F.A. Bde returned to control of C.R.A. W.R. Divn.	VII
		4.30pm.	Instructions issued for artillery defence of 3, 4, 5 & 6 sections.	VIII
		4.59pm	Instructions to 1st ~~&~~ W.R.F.A. Bde re suspected sap head opposite 3 R.	IX

1577 Wt. W10791/1773 500,000 1/15 D. D. & L. A.D.S.S./Forms/C. 2118.

Instructions regarding War Diaries and Intelligence Summaries are contained in F. S. Regs., Part II. and the Staff Manual respectively. Title pages will be prepared in manuscript.

WAR DIARY
or
~~INTELLIGENCE SUMMARY.~~
(Erase heading not required.)

Army Form C. 2118. (7)

Place	Date May	Hour	Summary of Events and Information	Remarks and references to Appendices
BAC ST MAUR	12th	10.5am	H.Q. Div. sends copy of wire sent to 8th + Highland Divisions that 49th W.R Heavy Battery to remain in present position. Highland Division Howitzer Bde to proceed through SAILLY to BAC ST MAUR.	X
		12.35pm	VIII th Div. Arty reports 49th W.R Heavy Battery has been ordered by 4th Corps to rejoin own division, report when transfer is completed to 4th Corps, + asking when control will be taken over by CRA 49th (W.R) Division.	XI
		6pm.	VIII th Div. Arty informed control of 49th W.R Heavy Battery will be taken over at 6. am 13th.	XII
			Nomenclature of W.R. Division changed to 49th (W.R) Division.	
		11.40pm	3rd Highland Howitzer Bde passed through BAC ST MAUR, on attachment to 49th (W.R) Divisional Artillery, en route for Bivouac as follows:— Bde Crs Bde A.C to H 21 a, Bde AC to H 14 a.	List
	13th	6am	Control of W. R. Heavy Battery assumed. ~~at~~	XIII
		10am	Visited 3rd Highland How: Bde gun emplacements + gave instructions as to making up of the same; also saw 2nd W.R Battery emplacements.	
		6.55pm	Issued instructions as ~~to~~ zones to be covered by Highland How. Bde.	XIV
		9-10pm	1st RENFREW (Howitzer) Battery occupied prepared position H 34 a 9.5.	

1577 Wt. W10791/1773 500,000 1/15 D. D. & L. A.D.S.S./Forms/C. 2118.

Instructions regarding War Diaries and Intelligence Summaries are contained in F. S. Regs., Part II. and the Staff Manual respectively. Title pages will be prepared in manuscript.

WAR DIARY

or

~~INTELLIGENCE SUMMARY.~~

(Erase heading not required.)

Army Form C.2118.

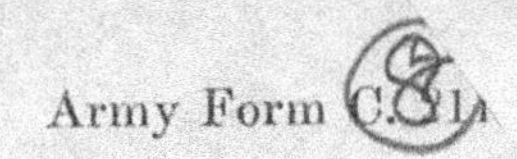

Place	Date	Hour	Summary of Events and Information	Remarks and references to Appendices
	May			
BAC ST MAUR	13th.	10.8pm	Orders issued to 1st + 3rd W.R. F.A. Bde & to 3rd Highland How Bde as to bombardment at 1am 14th & to take cover.	XIV
		10pm.	W.R. R.G.A ordered to open fire on LA PLOUICH exactly at 1am 14th, fire to last 5 minutes exactly	XV
BAC ST MAUR	14th.	2 ~~3.30~~ pm	W.R. R.G.A opened fire on LEMAISNIL, fire last 5 minutes.	XVI
		3.30pm	4th Section 51st Highland D.A.C. arrived H 19 a 10.9, 3rd Highland Bde A.C. not yet moved to H 19 a 8-6 according to orders, owing to congestion, moving on 15th.	XVII
		3.45pm	3rd Highland Howitzer Bde commenced registration with one gun in each battery	XVIII
		7pm.	Orders for bombardment at 9pm by W.R. R.G.A cancelled.	XIX
		9pm	2nd Highland Howitzer battery moved into emplacements at H 34 a 5.5.	
		9.30pm	Orders for bombardments by 1st, 3rd W.R. F.A. Bdes, W.R. R.G.A & 3rd Highland How Bde	XX
		12 midnight	W.R. R.G.A bombarded FOURNES, 1st + 3rd W.R. F.A. Bdes enemys trenches on night lines in accordance with instructions BM/24/G.	XX

Instructions regarding War Diaries and Intelligence Summaries are contained in F. S. Regs., Part II. and the Staff Manual respectively. Title pages will be prepared in manuscript.

WAR DIARY

or

~~INTELLIGENCE SUMMARY.~~

(Erase heading not required.)

Army Form C. 2118. (9)

Hour, Date, Place		Summary of Events and Information	Remarks and references to Appendices
BAC STMAUR May 15th	12.3am	1st + 3rd WR FA Bdes ceased firing	
	12.5am	——— recommenced firing	
	12.7am	——— + WR RGA ceased firing	
	4.45am to 4.55am	1st + 3rd WR FA Bdes wire cutting commenced as follows:— (a) 1st WR FA Bde pt 896 to 899 both inclusive (b) 3rd WR FA Bde pt 899 exclusive to pt 900 inclusive.	Fighting Map 1/10,000
	5am to 5.3am	1st + 3rd WR FA Bdes bombarded enemy trenches 3rd Highland Howitzer Bde N16 b 6.8 LECLOCHERS and N17 b 6.8 Fme DE LA MARLAQUE	
	5.5am to 5.7am	1st, 3rd WR FA Bdes + 3rd Highland Howitzer Bdes continued.	
	5.0am to 5.7am	WR RGA bombarded LEMAISNIL.	
	8.45am to 8.55am	1st + 3rd WR FA Bdes wire cutting as follows:— (a) 1st WR FA Bde pt 900 inclusive to 962 exclusive (b) 3rd WR FA Bde pt 963 to 964 both inclusive	Fighting Map 1/10,000

(9 29 6) W4141—463 100,000 9/14 H W V Forms/C. 2118/10

Army Form C. 2118. (10)

Instructions regarding War Diaries and Intelligence Summaries are contained in F. S. Regs., Part II. and the Staff Manual respectively. Title pages will be prepared in manuscript.

WAR DIARY
or
~~INTELLIGENCE SUMMARY.~~
(Erase heading not required.)

Hour, Date, Place	Summary of Events and Information	Remarks and references to Appendices
BAC ST MAUR May 15th 9am to 9.3am	1st & 3rd W.R. F.A. Bdes bombarded enemy trenches 3rd Highland Howitzer Bde bombarded N16d.4.6 & N17c6.7	Fighting Map 1/10,000.
9.5am to 9.7am	1st, 3rd W.R. F.A. Bdes & 3rd Highland How Bde continued.	
9am to 9.7am	W.R. R.G.A. bombarded FOURNES.	
afternoon	3rd Highland Howitzer Bde continued registration.	
6.40pm	Orders issued for bombardment as follows to commence at midnight & to last exactly 5 minutes. 1st W.R. F.A. Bde. 1st & 2nd Batteries on supporting trenches N11b10.8 to N12a5.10. 3rd Battery O1a3.3 to O1a5.4 3rd W.R. F.A. Bde. O1a5.4 exclusive to LE BRIDOUX. W.R. R.G.A. on RADINGHEM.	XXI
10.47pm	Orders issued to W. R. R.G.A. to stand ready at 3am to counter hostile batteries in neighbourhood of LA PLOUICH to assist Indian Corps advance if necessary	XXII

(9 29 6) W 4141—463 100,000 9/14 H W V Forms/C. 2118/10

Army Form C. 2118. (11)

Instructions regarding War Diaries and Intelligence Summaries are contained in F. S. Regs., Part II. and the Staff Manual respectively. Title pages will be prepared in manuscript.

WAR DIARY

or

~~INTELLIGENCE SUMMARY.~~

(Erase heading not required.)

Hour, Date, Place			Summary of Events and Information	Remarks and references to Appendices
BAC ST MAUR	May 16th	Midnight 15th–16th to 12.5 am 16th	1st WR FA Bde bombarded: 1st + 2nd Batteries N11 b 10.8 to N12 a 5.10; 3rd Battery O1 a 3.3 to O1 a 5.4	
			3rd WR FA Bde bombarded O1 a 5.4 exclusive to LE BRIDOUX	
			W.R. R.G.A. bombarded RADINGHEM.	
		3 am.	W.R. R.G.A. standing ready	XXII
		afternoon	3rd Highland How Bde Registration Continued.	
		5 pm.	Orders for move of 1 Section of each battery 2nd WR FA Bde from VIIIth Div to 49th WR Div issued	XXIII
		10.30 pm	2nd WR FA Bde, section from each battery arrived to new positions as shown in XXIII.	[initials]

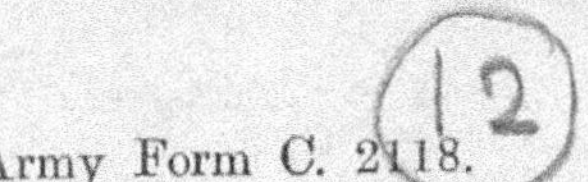

Army Form C. 2118.

Instructions regarding War Diaries and Intelligence Summaries are contained in F. S. Regs., Part II. and the Staff Manual respectively. Title pages will be prepared in manuscript.

WAR DIARY
or
~~INTELLIGENCE SUMMARY.~~
(Erase heading not required.)

Hour, Date, Place			Summary of Events and Information	Remarks and references to Appendices
BAC ST MAUR	May 17th	9.0 am	W. R. RGA ordered to open fire on LE PLOUICH batteries & search gradually south to LA CLIQUITERIE, telephoned & confirmed at 9.40 am	XXIV
		12.10 pm	W. R. RGA ordered to turn fire on Square T 16 a, 20 rounds to be fired & then to cease fire	XXIV
		10.30 am	2nd WR FA Bde ordered to move wagon lines during afternoon to new position H 25 d	XXV
			2nd WR FA Bde sections commenced registration	
		12.30 pm	2nd WR FA Bde, remaining sections & Bde AC ordered to move & join up with other sections in new position. Bde AC to move 18th.	XXVI
		2 pm	No 2 Section DAC ordered to move 18th to H 13 d 4.3	XXVII
		6 pm	Defence orders issued for Artillery defence of 49th (WR) Div Front.	XXVIII

(9 29 6) W 4141—463 100,000 9/14 H W V Forms/C. 2118/10

Army Form C. 2118. (13)

WAR DIARY
or
~~INTELLIGENCE SUMMARY.~~
(Erase heading not required.)

Instructions regarding War Diaries and Intelligence Summaries are contained in F. S. Regs., Part II. and the Staff Manual respectively. Title pages will be prepared in manuscript.

Hour, Date, Place	Summary of Events and Information	Remarks and references to Appendices
BAC ST MAUR May 17th 10.5pm	2nd W.R. F.A. Bde informed ~~that~~ VIII D.A. had instructed 33rd F.A. Bde to fire on hostile approaches in squares N15a + N15b on demand from 2nd F.A. Bde + that 2nd F.A. Bde is to search hostile approaches in N14a + N14b on demand from 33rd F.A. Bde.	XXIX
10.30pm	2nd W.R. F.A. Bde H.Q. + remaining sections of batteries arrived new position less 1 Section 5th Battery which went to wagon lines for the night	XXVI
11.55pm	Informed of continuance of operations of 1st Army on 18th + batteries within range of HAUT POMMEREAU + LORGIES (of 4th Corps) to be engaged	~~XXVII~~ XXX
18th 12.15am	W.R. R.G.A. ordered to engage batteries about HAUT POMMEREAU by searching fire to support 1st Army advance in the morning	~~XXVIII~~ XXX

(9 29 6) W4141—463 100,000 9/14 H W V Forms/C. 2118/10

Army Form C. 2118. (14)

Instructions regarding War Diaries and Intelligence Summaries are contained in F. S. Regs., Part II. and the Staff Manual respectively. Title pages will be prepared in manuscript.

WAR DIARY

or

~~INTELLIGENCE SUMMARY.~~

(*Erase heading not required.*)

Hour, Date, Place	Summary of Events and Information	Remarks and references to Appendices
BAC ST MAUR May 18th. 11am	2nd WR FA Bde AC arrived H19a 9-7 & went into billets	
Morning	WR RGA not required to open fire on HAUT POMMEREAU	
afternoon	3rd. Highland Howitzer Bde continued registration	
	2nd WR FA Bde continued registration	
6pm	No 2 Section 49th. WR DAC arrived H13d 4.3.	XXVII. [initials]
19th. 10am	Moved into new billets near FORT ROMPU.	
During day	2nd WR FA Bde & 3rd Highland How Bde continued registration	
10pm	Arrangements for S.O.S 1st & 2nd Sections of Trenches by 2nd. WR FA Bde	XXVIII [initials].

(9 29 6) W 4141—463 100,000 9/14 H W V Forms/C. 2118/10

Army Form C. 2118. (15)

Instructions regarding War Diaries and Intelligence Summaries are contained in F. S. Regs., Part II. and the Staff Manual respectively. Title pages will be prepared in manuscript.

WAR DIARY
or
~~INTELLIGENCE SUMMARY.~~
(Erase heading not required.)

Hour, Date, Place	Summary of Events and Information	Remarks and references to Appendices
FORT ROMPU May 20th	2nd W.R. F.A. Bde continued registration 3rd Highland How Bde — " —	
3.35pm	3rd Highland How Bde ordered to register hostile trench opposite I S in order to knock out trench mortar.	XXIX B
9.15pm	2nd W.R. F.A. Bde ordered to instruct 4th W.R. Battery to lay night lines on hostile trenches in N & d & to come under orders of O.C. 33rd F.A. Bde for purposes of defence. This was required on account of move of 5th & 36th F.A. Batteries from VIIIth Divn area to 49th Divn Area for temporary duty.	XXX B
11.30pm.	55th, 5th & 36th Batteries in new positions in 49th Divn Area as follows 55th H 28 d 5.4 5th H 29 c 4.9 36th H 29 b 2.6	XXXI [initials]

(9 29 6) W4141—463 100,000 9/14 H W V Forms/C. 2118/10

Army Form C. 2118. (16)

Instructions regarding War Diaries and Intelligence Summaries are contained in F. S. Regs., Part II. and the Staff Manual respectively. Title pages will be prepared in manuscript.

WAR DIARY
or
~~INTELLIGENCE SUMMARY.~~
(Erase heading not required.)

Hour, Date, Place	Summary of Events and Information	Remarks and references to Appendices
FORT ROMPU May 21st 9 am	49th W.R. D.A.C. moved back to old position near ESTAIRES by Subsections at ½ hour intervals	XXXII
During Day	5th, 36th + 55th Batteries dug themselves in, prepared gun pits + commenced registration.	
	2nd W.R. F.A. Bde + 3rd Highland How Bde continued registration.	
Afternoon	Selected positions for 4th W.R. How Bde, which was ordered back to 49th W.R. Divn from ALDERSONS force.	
9 pm	Received 49th (W.R.) Divn. operation order No 8 for offensive action by 148th Infantry Bde in neighbourhood of LA TOUQUET.	XXXIII
11.30 pm	Went down to show 4th W.R. F.A. Bde into positions near FLEURBAIX, unit did not arrive by midnight.	

RWB

(17)

Army Form C. 2118.

Instructions regarding War Diaries and Intelligence Summaries are contained in F. S. Regs., Part II. and the Staff Manual respectively. Title pages will be prepared in manuscript.

WAR DIARY

or

~~INTELLIGENCE SUMMARY.~~

(Erase heading not required.)

Hour, Date, Place	Summary of Events and Information	Remarks and references to Appendices
May		
FORT ROMPU 22nd. 9 am	4th W.R. How Bde arrived FLEURBAIX from ALDERSONS FORCE, reason of delay, unit still in action at 1.30 am near RICHEBOURG St VAAST & owing to communications having broken down did not receive orders to move in sufficient time	XXXIII B
12 noon	10th Battery went into position H 28 a 4 7 } single 11th ——— H 22 9 . 4 } gun at a time & commenced gun pits & cover.	
afternoon	5th, 36th & 55th batteries completed gun pits etc & continued registration 2nd F.A. Bde continued registration. Issued 49th W.R. Divl Artillery Order No 3 & time table of tasks in accordance with 49th W.R. Div Order No 8.	XXXIV
7.40 pm	No 4 Section W.R. D.A.C. reported.	XXXV
9 pm	Conference at H.Q. 49th W.R. Divn with reference to bombardment during night 23rd-24th. Zero to be 8 pm 23rd May.	XXXVI

[initials]

Army Form C. 2118. (18)

Instructions regarding War Diaries and Intelligence Summaries are contained in F. S. Regs., Part II. and the Staff Manual respectively. Title pages will be prepared in manuscript.

WAR DIARY

or

~~INTELLIGENCE SUMMARY.~~

(Erase heading not required.)

Hour, Date, Place	Summary of Events and Information	Remarks and references to Appendices
FORT ROMPU May 23rd: 1.35am	Detached Section Bde A.C. for 55th Battery arrived H 21 a 3.3	XXXVII
11.10am	Issued instructions to 4th W.R. F.A. Bde & 3rd Highland How Bde to register certain points.	XXXVIII
12 noon	Issued Time table of tasks for bombardment at 10pm 12 midnight & 2am	XXXIX
3.20pm	Operations for 23rd & night 23/24 postponed for 24 hours, units informed verbally & in writing at 6.10pm	~~XXX~~ XL
6pm	Informed by 49th W.R. Divn ~~that~~ working parties will be in front of No 6 Section of ~~trench~~. First, Third, Fourth W.R. F.A. Bdes & Third Highland F.A. Bde informed.	XLI
12 midnight	Germans occupying new trench ~~opposite section~~ 6. 3rd Bde ordered to be ready to open fire on house just N of pt 946 to assist infantry attack; order sent by telephone & confirmed by telegraph	Cancelled by request of Brig Gen Dawson [initials]

Army Form C. 2118.

(19)

Instructions regarding War Diaries and Intelligence Summaries are contained in F. S. Regs., Part II. and the Staff Manual respectively. Title pages will be prepared in manuscript.

WAR DIARY
or
~~INTELLIGENCE SUMMARY.~~
(Erase heading not required.)

Hour, Date, Place	Summary of Events and Information	Remarks and references to Appendices
FORT ROMPU May 24th 12.2am	Germans reported occupying new trench opposite Section 6. 3rd FA Bde ordered by telephone at 12.8am to be prepared to support infantry if called on. 1st FA Bde ordered to stand by. Verbal instructions to 3rd Bde confirmed by wire	XLII
12.32am	Trench Mortars in Pt 375 annoying 6th West Yorks. 3rd Highland How. Bde ordered to fire one gun of 2nd Battery on this point till mortars silenced. Order by telephone personally. 146th Inf. Bde report mortars silenced 1.45 am.	XLIII
2.30am	Information received that trench has been reoccupied, only slight opposition.	XLII
During Day	All units registered preparatory to the attack.	
3.50pm	Orders Recd ~~that~~ 49th Divn Report Centre will remain at FORT ROMPU	XLIII

Instructions regarding War Diaries and Intelligence Summaries are contained in F. S. Regs., Part II. and the Staff Manual respectively. Title pages will be prepared in manuscript.

Army Form C. 2118. (20)

WAR DIARY

or

~~INTELLIGENCE SUMMARY.~~

(Erase heading not required.)

Hour, Date, Place	Summary of Events and Information	Remarks and references to Appendices
FORT ROMPU May 24th 3pm	4th Howitzer Bde ordered to turn a battery onto House at I 31 d 1.2. & level it to the ground.	The fire was effective only row of sandbags left.
8pm	Offensive operations commenced according to programme whole of detail is shown on Registers of Communications & attached orders. up to 1.55pm 25th.	XLIV
25th 3pm	Situation & Progress reports for 25th.	XLV
3.10pm & 3.14pm	Recd. call for howitzer fire on Trench Mortars. Battery of 4th W.R. How. Bde ordered to open fire on Trench	
3.20pm	Recd Call for help against hostile artillery, not located by infantry	XLVI
4.5pm	Further call for help. Howitzer battery turned on to Trench & another battery to bring down house in vicinity	

Army Form C. 2118. (21)

Instructions regarding War Diaries and Intelligence Summaries are contained in F. S. Regs., Part II. and the Staff Manual respectively. Title pages will be prepared in manuscript.

WAR DIARY
or
~~INTELLIGENCE~~ SUMMARY.
(Erase heading not required.)

Hour, Date, Place	Summary of Events and Information	Remarks and references to Appendices
FORT ROMPU May 25th 5.30pm	Orders issued for return of 5th, 36th & 55th Batteries R.A. to 8th Divn.	XLVII
11pm	5th, 36th & 55th Batteries left 49th Divl Area.	
26th 10am	Request from H.Q. Divn to punch off houses opposite No 6 Section near new Trench. Complied with.	XLVIII
11.15am	148th Inf. Bde asked for Artillery help. Complied with.	XLIX
11am	Informed Armoured Train O.C. 9.2 gun & W.R.R.G.A. that they came under orders of G.O.C. R.A. 49th (W.R.) Divn.	L

(9 29 6) W4141—463 100,000 9/14 H W V Forms/C. 2118/10

22

Army Form C. 2118.

WAR DIARY

or

~~INTELLIGENCE SUMMARY.~~

(Erase heading not required.)

Instructions regarding War Diaries and Intelligence Summaries are contained in F. S. Regs., Part II. and the Staff Manual respectively. Title pages will be prepared in manuscript.

Hour, Date, Place	Summary of Events and Information	Remarks and references to Appendices
FORT ROMPU May 26th. 5 pm	Issued orders for return of 3rd Highland How: Bde to 51st (Highland) Divn.	L I
	Hostile gas bags up most of the day	L II
8.15 pm	Further help asked for from Infantry. + in conjunction with 8th Divl Arty fired on N 30 b 4.7 + N 23 d 7.7. Enemy's guns silenced 9.30 pm	L III
9.45 pm	10th W.R. Battery to new position H 34 a 5 5.	L I
11 pm	3rd Highland Howitzer Bde left 49th Divn Area.	
27th 12.35 am	Infantry ask for further help against trench mortars + rifle grenades. 11th How Battery ordered to sweep 200 yards each side of Pt 975. Effect good.	L IV
4.25 pm	Further help against enemy trench asked for, ...	L V
7.30 pm	Fresh orders issued for defence of 49th Divn front consequent on removal of 5th Brigade RHA	L VI
10 pm	5th Brigade RHA left 49th W.R. Divn Area.	

(9 29 6) W 4141—463 100,000 9/14 H W V Forms/C. 2118/10

Instructions regarding War Diaries and Intelligence Summaries are contained in F. S. Regs., Part II. and the Staff Manual respectively. Title pages will be prepared in manuscript.

WAR DIARY
or
~~INTELLIGENCE~~ SUMMARY.
(Erase heading not required.)

Army Form C. 2118.

(23)

Hour, Date, Place	Summary of Events and Information	Remarks and references to Appendices
Fort Rompu. All day.	a) Batteries. Continued registration. b) Situation normal.	LVII
28/5/15. (8-20pm)	Trench. Motor at 6th Sect silenced but not knocked out. reported moving about on trolley.	LVIII
25/5-15	a) Letter from 9 O.C. expressing satisfaction on work done on 24th. Also letter to Lancs from CRA. b) Operation report.	LVIX (in measure)
28/5/15.	a) Letter from "Brigade Major" to O.C. 4th W.R. Bde re move to new position of one section of 11th Battery. b) Also directions for accompanying section.	LX
" "	Letter from Adjutant 3rd W.R. Bde re Action to be taken in event of sudden attack on lines held by 49th (W.R.) Div. covering details of action	LXI
" "		

RWJ

Instructions regarding War Diaries and Intelligence Summaries are contained in F. S. Regs., Part II. and the Staff Manual respectively. Title pages will be prepared in manuscript.

WAR DIARY
or
~~INTELLIGENCE SUMMARY.~~
(Erase heading not required.)

Army Form C. 2118.

(24)

Hour, Date, Place MAY 29th	Summary of Events and Information	Remarks and references to Appendices
~~Fort Rompu~~ FORT ROMPU all day.	a/ Batteries continued registration } b/ Situation unchanged. }	LXII.
	c/ Progress Report.	
2·5. PM.	Enemy Field Gun fired at Infantry Hdqts. at 3C6·1. Information from OC 1st W R Bn →	LXIII. arranged with aeronautics at 6 pm a wireless plane & in conjunction with a. [illegible] to knock out Battery. }
3-30 pM.	Report of new German emplacement at N6C4·4½. →	Telephoned to Div at 3·45 PM
3-30 pM.	Enemy observation balloon up. →	LXIV Information received from OC 4th W R Battery.
4-18 pM.	an uncommon looking object reported immediately in rear of enemy's Trench about 75 yards W of point 883. Definition of object VIDE Appendix.	LXV
3-30. pM.	O.C. 5th West Riding Brigade reports having silenced hostile Trench mortar.	LXVI
6-5 pM	Orders from 4th Corps for move of 9·2 a verbal conversation later with General Hussey, deferred move for 24 hours.	LXVII from H.Q. 49th Div

Instructions regarding War Diaries and Intelligence Summaries are contained in F. S. Regs., Part II. and the Staff Manual respectively. Title pages will be prepared in manuscript.

WAR DIARY

or

~~INTELLIGENCE SUMMARY.~~

(Erase heading not required.)

Army Form C. 2118.

25

Hour, Date, Place	Summary of Events and Information	Remarks and references to Appendices
MAY 29th		
~~Fort Rompo~~ FORT RUMPO.		LXVIII
7-15 PM	German aeroplane reported as passing over in a South South Easterly direction.	Reports from OC 10th Battery
	OC 10th Battery reports firing 2 rounds on point near 883.	LXIX
8-45 p.m.	OC 1st W R Bde reports shelling of 1st Battery.	LXX
9. PM	Reports removal of suspicious cooking machine from Brigade Major 140th	Teleph to DIV
10-40 PM.	"A careful watch to be kept by units" received by wire from Div, originally coming from 140th Bde	

[signature]

(9 29 6) W4141—463 100,000 9/14 H W V Forms/C. 2118/10

Instructions regarding War Diaries and Intelligence Summaries are contained in F. S. Regs., Part II. and the Staff Manual respectively. Title pages will be prepared in manuscript.

WAR DIARY
or
~~INTELLIGENCE~~ SUMMARY.
(Erase heading not required.)

Army Form C. 2118.

(26)

Hour, Date, Place	Summary of Events and Information	Remarks and references to Appendices
MAY 30th FORT RAMPU		
4.45. p.m.	a. a german Balloon. observed to be again in Position at N 4. A 24.	LXXII
	b. 1st Battery again shelled by Field guns.	
9.2 P.M.	9.2 Howitzer left 49th Div on receiving Orders. —	
12.3 p.m.	Report of Conflagration observed behind wood in Enemy's lines opposite 3? and 3? Wire cutting appears to be at work. —	LXXI
	O.C. 2nd W. R. Brigade reports a) Balloon up. bearing 36 T 24d. b) Report from 5th W Yorks that enemy are [illegible] shelling their Headquarters. c) F.O.O. 4th W. R. Battery reports a curious [illegible] arrangement in Enemy's trenches.	LXXIII
	Situation remains unchanged.	LXXIII
9.30pm	OC 11th W.R Battery reports rejoining his other section in new position	

[signature]

Instructions regarding War Diaries and Intelligence Summaries are contained in F. S. Regs., Part II. and the Staff Manual respectively. Title pages will be prepared in manuscript.

WAR DIARY
or
~~INTELLIGENCE~~ SUMMARY.
(Erase heading not required.)

Army Form C. 2118.

(27).

Hour, Date, Place	Summary of Events and Information	Remarks and references to Appendices
MAY 31st		
FORT. ROMPU.		
11.AM.	Report re Handing over to 27th Division by 6th Division.	LXXXI
	Motor School Started at St Venant. Report of Officers detailed for course.	LXXVIII
1.PM.	Letter with reference to extreme activity in Enemy's lines also 49th Div artillery inclusive above.	
5.50pm.	Letter from O.C. armoured Train re temporary command.	LXXIV
7.5 pm.	Correspondence re obliteration of House at 6S.	LXXV
	Various correspondence. a) re report written b) re change to Indian Corps time from which change to take effect. '6 AM 31st May'	LXXVI
At intervals during day	F.O.O. 1st W.R. Battery reports smoke appearing from RUE de la LOMMERIE also shelling reported in area around RUE PETILLON + RUE DES BASSIERES	LXXIX
	also 11th W.R Battery reports a fire seen 12 degrees right of LE MAISNIL Church at 11.45am	

(27)

Army Form C. 2118.

WAR DIARY
or
INTELLIGENCE SUMMARY.
(*Erase heading not required.*)

Instructions regarding War Diaries and Intelligence Summaries are contained in F. S. Regs., Part II. and the Staff Manual respectively. Title pages will be prepared in manuscript.

Hour, Date, Place	Summary of Events and Information	Remarks and references to Appendices
MAY 31st FORT ROMPU.	Considerable activity observed on part of German Trenches reported opposite 2S Red & Green lights also observed.	LXXX
	Appendix for month of May containing (a) Casualty returns. (b) Ammunition returns (c) Cases of gallant conduct reported	LXXXII
		[initials]

- APPENDICES -

- WAR DIARY -

- 49th (W. R) Divnl. Arty -

1st to 31st May 1915.

G Bran

A Ors
49th W Rid: Div

The attached sample of progress report forwarded under your No G 820 d/31-5-16 is returned, as requested, with thanks.

Brigadier Gen. RA

1-6-16

TACTICAL PROGRESS REPORT, MEERUT DIVISION.

Up to 6.0 p.m., 2nd May 1915.

-:-:-:-:-:-:-:-:-:-:-:-:-

I. OPERATIONS. (a) The enemy's working parties in front of the Northern Section were fired on during the night by our Infantry and Machine guns. Our artillery shelled the enemy's working parties close to point 63, their trenches between points 51 and 63, and house 124.

(b) During the morning there was a little shelling by a Field Howitzer Battery, and about noon NEUVE CHAPELLE and "B" Sub-Section trenches were shelled by a Field Battery.
Snipers were more active than usual in front of the Northern Section.

II. INFORMATION. A number of Germans were seen in the redoubt at salient north of point 63, apparently dressed in nautical clothing.
Two pigeons were seen on the evening of the 30th, and two at 7.0 a.m. on the morning of the 2nd, flying over "D" Sub-Section, towards the BOIS DU BIEZ, on a bearing of about 130 degrees.
The enemy were heard working and hammering in rear of first line trenches in front of Southern Section during the night.
There appears to be a new parapet, about 50 yards behind the front trench between points V.6. and 59. Between this and the front trench for about 40 yards to the east of V.6., there appears to be some sort of low obstacle similar to that described in the Report attached to yesterday's Tactical Progress Report.
In the "covered way" about S.10.d. 3.6. there is the appearance of embrasures for half a dozen machine guns.
There is a new chevaux de frise in front of the fire trench just west of point 60. Length about 30 yards, consisting of planks 12 feet long, fastened together diagonally, with the ends sharpened; lying between the wire entanglement and the trench. High stakes have been driven in in front of left of "B" Sub-Section.
House 124 appears to be an observation post.
A fuze was picked up near the 14th Battery, which was the ordinary 10.5. c.m. D.A. type, marked HZ 14 SIMSON 15. Body of fuze of brass and nose of steel.

III. PROGRESS OF WORK. Work continued on new communication and assembly trenches. Machine gun emplacement at barricade across road in S.5.c. completed. Barricades put up across RUE DU BOIS at existing cut across road. Improvement and repair of fire and communication trenches continued.

J.S.M. Stewart

Captain,

3rd May 1915.

for General Staff, MEERUT Division.

R.W.D.

1423/3 1.32 pm

Secret

Copy No 3

(1)

Instructions for Deployment

2nd W.R. F.A. Bde. in conjunction with 8th Div[illegible]

Reference 1/20 000 Sheet Sheet 36 N.W. & 36 S.W.

30 & 35

(1) These instructions are to be followed in conjunction with instructions issued by 8th Divl Arty d/ [illegible]

(2) 1 Section 5th W.R. Battery to march at 8 [illegible] pm via Road Junction M 15 c 7.6 – 4 X Roads M 15 c 1.5 – Fork Road M 14 b 6.7 – LAVENTIE – ROUGE DE BOUT – Road Junction N 31 a [illegible] – Road Junction N 31 b 3.0 – LA CROIX LESCORNEX – CROIX BLANCHE – H [illegible]

1 Section 6th W.R. Battery to march at [illegible] via 4 X roads M 15 c 1.2 [illegible] to follow 5th W.R. Battery to N 34 a [illegible] via RUELLE DU BOIS FURREIZ

1 Section 4th W.R. Battery to march at [illegible] via 4 Cross roads LAVENTIE – ROUGE DE BOUT – Road Junction N 31 a 6.6 – Road Junction N 31 b 3.0 – LA CROIX LESCORNEX – CROIX BLANCHE – N 33 c [illegible]

3. (1) Wagon Lines

1st Line Wagons [illegible] to H 19 [illegible]

[illegible]

3 Contd

Accommodation to be found in present wagon lines for incoming ~~units~~ units until relief is completed and wagon lines and gun positions can be completely handed over.

4 Bde HQs will not move till tomorrow instructions will be issued when it is my go.

L W Lewis Major RA
Bde Major RA
W R Div

Issued at 3.15 pm.

Copy No 1

Secret

Instructions for movement
2nd W. R. F. A. & 8th Divn

Reference 1/20,000 Sheets France 36 N.W & 36 S.W.

1-5-15.

1. These instructions are to be followed in conjunction with those issued by VIII th Divisional Arty d/30-4-15.

2. Remaining section 5th West Riding Battery to march at 8.~~4~~5pm via Road Junction M15 c 7.6 - 4 X roads M15 c 1.2 - fork Road M14 b 6.7 - LAVENTIE - ROUGE DE BOUT - Junction Road H 31 a 6.6 - Junction Road H 31 b 3.0 - LA CROIX LESCORNEX - to H 33 b 0.8

Remaining section 6th W. R. Battery to march at 8.55pm via 4 X roads M15 c 1.2 & thence to follow ~~5th~~ 5th W. R. Battery to H 34 a 8.5 via RUELLE du BOIS FIERETZ - LA CROIX MARECHAL.

Remaining Section 4th W.R. Battery to march at 8.55pm via 4 X roads LAVENTIE - ROUGE DE BOUT and follow the same route as taken by 5th W R Battery to its own position at H 33 c 4.8.

3. Bde H.Q. 2nd W R F A Bde to be established by O.C. Bde either at BARLETTE Farm or LA CROIX LESCORNEX, O.C. Bde to inform this office at once which place he proposes to use, so ~~that~~ necessary arrangements for intercommunication can be established

Issued at 11.30 am.

R.W. Lewer Major RA
Bde Major W R Divl Arty

SECRET. COPY NO. 2

CONSTRUCTIONS FOR MOVEMENT
8th. DIVISIONAL AND ATTACHED BRIGADE OF WEST RIDING ARTILLERY.

Reference 1/20,000 sheets FRANCE 36 N.W. & 36 S.W.

30-4-15.

1. 1 Section "O" Battery to march at 8 p.m. tomorrow via LA CROIX LESCORNEX - Road Junction N 31b a 3.0 - Road Junction N 31 a 6.6 - LAVENTIE - road Junction M 4 c 10.3-four cross roads M 9 d 8.2 - four cross roads M 15 c 1.2 into position at M 21 a 5.2.

1 Section "Z" Battery to march at 8 p.m. tomorrow following the same route as "O" Battery as far as road junction M 15 c 7.6 thence to position at M 21 b 7.7

2 Sections 36th. Battery to march at 8-40 p.m. tomorrow via ROUGE DE BOUT - LAVENTIE - Road Junction M 4 c 10.3 - four cross roads M 9 d 8 . 2 into position at M 15 b 5.5

2 Sections " A.Q.U" Battery to march at 8-30p.m. tomorrow via CROIX BLANCHE - LA CROIX LESCORNEX into position at N i a 9.9.

1 Section 5th. West Riding Battery at M 21 b 7.7 to march at 8-45 p.m. via Road Junction M 15 c 7.6 - four Cross Roads M 15 c 1.2 - fork road M 14 b 6.7 - LAVENTIE - ROUGE DE BOUT and thence as ordered by B.G., C.R.A., WEST RIDING DIVISION.

1 Section 6th. West Riding Battery at M 21 a 5.3 to march at 8-55 p.m. via four cross roads M 15 c 1.2 and thence to follow 5th. WEST RIDING BATTERY.

1 Section 4th. WEST RIDING Battery at M 16 d 6.6 to march at 8-55 p.m. via four cross roads LAVENTIE - ROUGE DE BOUT and thence as ordered by B.G.,C.R.A., West Riding Division.

2. Brigade Headquarters 5th. Brigade R.H.A. to be establish ed at M 3 d 6.0 by 10 p.m. tomorrow night and telephonic communication established through 33rd. Brigade R.F.A. H.Q. to H.Q., R.A., 8th. Division.

3. O.C. 2nd. WEST RIDING BRIGADE R.F.A. will remain responsible for the Artillery Defence of C Section 8th. Division Lines until 10 p.m. 1.5.15 when the control will pass to O.C. 5th. Brigade R.H.A.

R H Johnson

Issued at 3pm MAJOR R.A.
BRIGADE MAJOR 8th. DIVISIONAL ARTY.

~~PLEASE ACKNOWLEDGE~~.

Copy No I.

Secret

Instructions for movement of 2nd W.R. Fd Bde to VIII th Divn.

(111)

Reference 1/20,000 Sheet FRANCE 36 SW + 36 NW.

---

(1) These instructions are to be followed in conjunction with those issued by CRA VIII th Divn.

2	Unit	Time	Starting Pt	Route	Destination
	4th Battery	9 pm	LACROIX LESCORNEX	CROIX BLANCHE	VIII D
	5th Battery	9.5 pm	— " —	— " —	— " —
	6th Battery	9.10 pm	— " —	LACROIX MARÉCHAL - H27 d 2.9 - CROIX BLANCHE	— " —

3 Bde Ammunition Column not to move tonight.

4 Report of departure ~~time reported~~ time from LACROIX LESCORNEX to be reported to this Office.

L.W. Lewer Major RA
Bde Major RA.
1st W.R. Divn

Issued at
5.35 pm.
3.5.15.

SECRET. COPY NO. 5

INSTRUCTIONS FOR MOVEMENT 5th, H.A.BRIGADE
and
2nd. WEST RIDING BRIGADE.

Reference 1/20,000 sheet FRANCE 36 S.W. & FRANCE & BELGIUM 36 N.W.

3 - 5 - 15.

1. (a). 5th. BRIGADE R.H.A. will march tonight as follows:-

UNIT.	TIME	STARTING Pt.	ROUTE	DESTINATION.
1 Sect. O.) 1 ,, Z)	8-15 p.m.	Road Junction M 15 c 6.6	LAVENTIE X RDS. ROUGE DE BOUTE Road Junction M 26 a 2.0- CROIX BLANCHE.	M 33 c 4.6 M 33 a10.9
2 Sects. O) 2 ,, Z)	10-45 p.m.	-do-	-do-	-do-

(b) 2nd. West Riding Brigade R.F.A. will march tonight as follows :-

UNIT.	TIME	STARTING Pt.	ROUTE	DESTINATION.
4th. Battery	9 p.m.	LA CROIX LESCORNEX	Road Junction M 6 d 2.0 - four cross roads LAVENTIE- Cross Roads M 16 b 7.7	M 16 d 5.8
5th & 6th) Batteries.)	9.5p.m.	-do-	Road Junction M 6 d 2.0 - Four X Roads LAVENTIE - Road Junction M 15 c 6.6	5th. Battery M 21 b 7.8 6th.Battery M 21 a 5.2

2. Brigade Ammunition Columns will not move tonight.

3. Horses and 1st Line wagons as follows :-
O & Z Batteries - M 19 a 9.9 (both sides of the road)

2nd.W.Riding Bde.R.F.A. -M 1 d 3.3(original wagon line)

4. Responsibility for defence of "C"Lines will remain with O.C.5th. Brigade R.H.A. until 10 p.m. tonight. At 10 p.m. tonight O.C. 2nd. W.Riding Brigade R.F.A. will become responsible for defence of "C" Lines and O.C.5th Brigade R.H.A. will assume responsibility held by O.C. 2nd.West Riding Brigade for assisting defence of Nos.2 and 3 Sections .

5. Completion of movement to be reported forthwith to H.Q. R.A. 8th. Division.

R H Johnson

Issued at 4 p.m. Major R.A.

Brigade Major 8th. Divisional Arty.

"A" Form. Army Form C. 2121.

MESSAGES AND SIGNALS.

No. of Message

Prefix Code m. | Words | Charge

Office of Origin and Service Instructions.

Sent
At m.
To
By

This message is on a/c of: O.H.M.S. *Service.*

Cecil Allen Capt
(Signature of "Franking Officer.")

Recd. at m.
Date
From
By

TO O.C. 2nd West Riding Bde Amm Col.

Sender's Number.	Day of Month	In reply to Number	AAA
* SCRA 6	4th		

Your	column	will	move	at
2pm	today	4th	AAA	Route
to	be	taken	BAC	St
MAUR	–	SAILLY	Road	junction
G32b2.8	to	old	billets	at
G32d	central			

From SCRA
Place West Rid: Div
Time

The above may be forwarded as now corrected.

Censor.

(Z) Cecil Allen Capt
Signature of Addressor or person authorised to telegraph in his name.

* This line should be erased if not required.

(632) —McC. & Co. Ltd., London.— W 11400/2045. 100,000 2/15. Forms C2121/10.

BM/11/9.

Secret

First W. R. F. A Bde. IV

(1) Move your wagon line up peacemeal to new wagon line H 20 d tomorrow morning 7th inst. as early as possible.

(2) Move your Bde A.C. up peacemeal to present position of wagon line H 13 d as early as possible & give instructions to O.C. Bde A.C. to leave room for 1st Section D.A.C to come in, this section will arrive peacemeal tomorrow.

(3) Although the number of rounds per gun has been estimated as will likely be required it does not mean that it is absolutely necessary to expend this amount unless it necessary according to the tactical situation. Ammunition is not to be wasted.

6. 5. 15.

R W Fewer Major RA
Bde Major RA
W. R. Div

Secret BM/111/G.

Third W. R. F. A. Bde. IV

(1) Move your wagon line up peacemeal to new wagon position H 16 a tomorrow morning 7th inst: as early as possible.

(2) Move your Bde A.C. up peacemeal to present position of wagon line H 14 b as early as possible & give instructions to O.C. Bde A.C. to leave room for 3rd Section A.C. to come in, this section will arrive peacemeal tomorrow.

(3) Although the number of rounds per gun will be estimated as will likely be required it does not mean that it is absolutely necessary to expend this amount it is necessary according to the tactical situation. Ammunition is not to be wasted.

6. 5. 15.

L. W. Lowe Major R.A.
Bde Major R.A. W R Div.

Ammunition Supply.

Secret

B.M./11/G.

IV

Officer Comdg.

W. R. D. A. C.

Owing to traffic arrangements the following is to be your procedure for the replenishment of ammunition during a general engagement.

1. Each section corresponding to the F.A Bdes will park in the same place as the Brigade Ammunition Columns.
2. Your refilling points will be ~~the~~ at your sections.
3. The positions of the Bde Ammunition Columns will be as follows

   1st W.R. F.A Bde H 13 d central

   2nd W.R. F.A Bde G 32 d central

   3rd W.R. F.A Bde H 14 a 4 0.

4. 1st & 3rd W.R. F.A Bde ACs move tomorrow to these positions from present positions.
5. You will move up your sections tomorrow to these positions by subsections at 1 hour intervals commencing at 9 am, & report to this office when the move has been completed.
6. Orders as to routes are being issued to the Park by Div H.Q. as follows, South of the River R LYS, ST VENANT – LA GORGUE, SAILLY SUR LA LYS, BAC ST MAUR – FORT ROMPU – H 14 a

Return route H 19 b.0.9 – BAC ST MAUR – CROIX DU BAC

(2)

and return to St VENANT NORTH of the River LYS.

7. You will replenish your section with the 30 rounds per gun 15 Pr Ammunition at your refilling points.

8. The attached is a copy of orders given to units, you will not indent for the 30 rounds per gun (on the Park) therein mentioned until the commencement of a general engagement i.e. although units will have drawn 30 rounds per gun from you tomorrow, these are not to be indented for on the Park.

9. Kindly acknowledge receipt stating that you are absolutely clear as to the course of action you are to take.

6. 5. 15

Issued at 8.22 pm

[illegible] Major RA.
Bde Major RA.
W. R. Div.

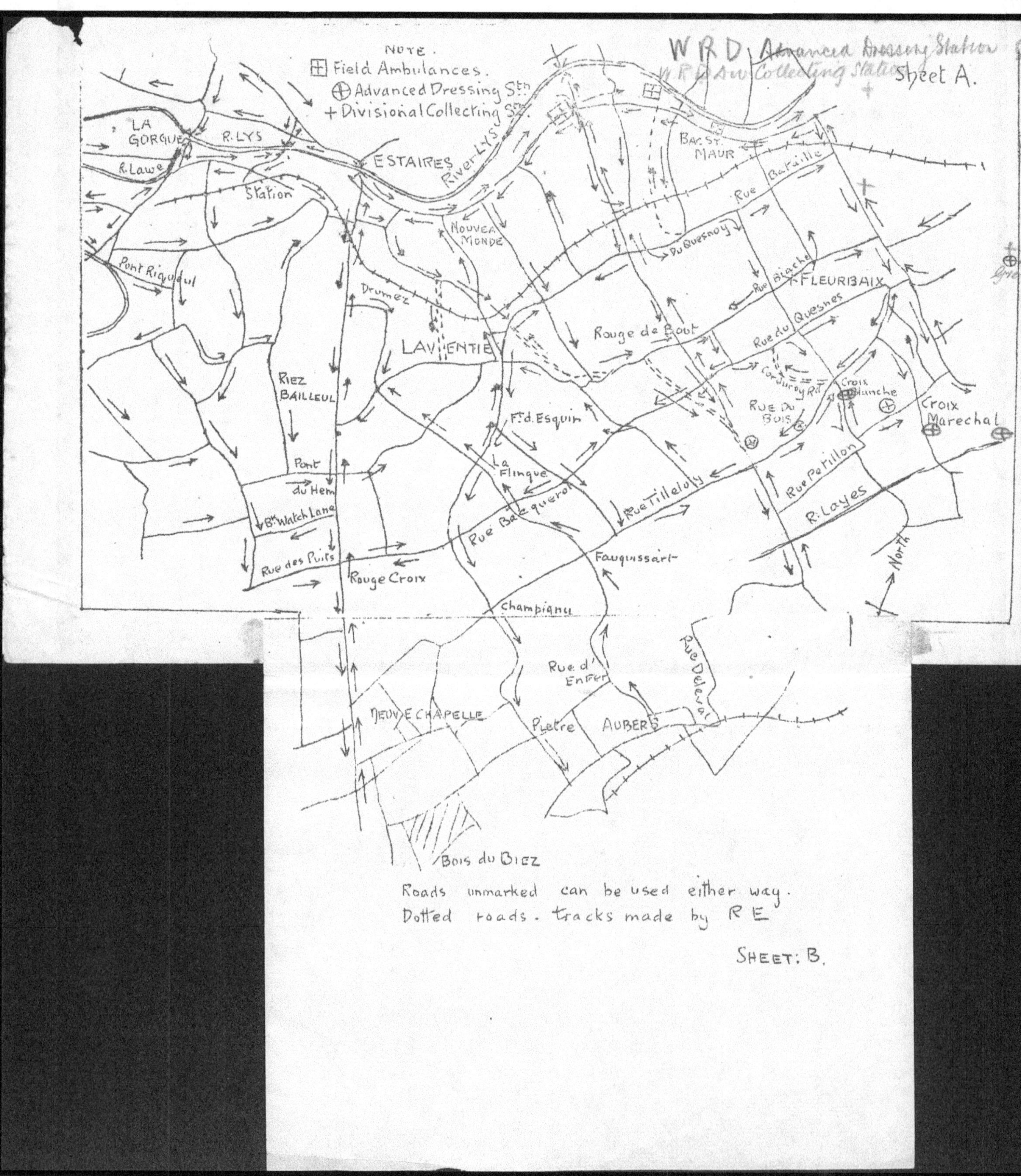
NOTE.
Field Ambulances.
Advanced Dressing Stn
+ Divisional Collecting Stn.
WRD Advanced Dressing Station
Sheet A.
LA GORGUE
R. LYS
R. Lawe
Station
ESTAIRES
River LYS
BAC ST. MAUR
Rue Bataille
NOUVEA MONDE
Du Quesnoy
Pont Riquedul
Drumez
LAVENTIE
Rue Biache
FLEURBAIX
Rouge de Bout
Rue du Quesnes
Corduroy Rd
Croix Blanche
RIEZ BAILLEUL
RUE DU BOIS
Croix Marechal
Ft d. Esquin
La Flinque
Pont du Hem
Rue Petillon
Rue Tilleloy
Bn Watch Lane
Rue Bacquerot
R. Layes
Rue des Puits
Rouge Croix
Fauquissart
North
Champigny
Rue d' Enfer
Rue Deleval
NEUVE CHAPELLE
Pietre
AUBERS
Bois du Biez
Roads unmarked can be used either way.
Dotted roads - tracks made by RE
SHEET: B.

Copy No:3

SECRET. West Riding Divisional Artillery Order ~~Order~~ No:2

7th May, 1915.

N.B. These orders are not to be taken into the Trenches.

Reference to 1/40,000 & 1/10,000 numbered Maps,

Information, 1. Offensive operations will be carried out at an early date. The front to be attacked by the 4th Corps is held by the 6th Bavarian Reserve Division. The 16th Bavarian Reserve Regiment of this Division holds, as far as is known, the Trenches to the West of the SAILLY - FROMELLES Road, and the 20th Bavarian Regiment Reserve Regiment holds the Trenches East of this Road. The German Reserves of this line are believed to be in HERLIES and FOURNES.

Behind the main line of German Trenches, there is a secondary line of Trenches running along the AUBERS - FROMELLES ridge,

Intention, 2. The G.O.C., R.A. intends to use the fire of the guns of the 3rd W.Rid:F.A.Bde. as follows:-

(a) To demonstrate ~~with 8th & 9th Batteries~~ against wire at certain points in front of trenches 5 & 6.

(b) The whole Brigade will then be employed to guard the left flank of the attacking Column, this will be effected by sweeping the approaches from the FROMELLES - LE MAISNIL Ridge E. of the road FLEURBAIX - FROMELLES.

Time table and allotted tasks will be issued later,

3rd W.RID:F.A.Bde, Wagon line will be at H.16a
1st - do - - do - at H.20d
1st - do - Ammunition Column & No:1 Section D.A.C. H.~~14a~~ 15d
(Supplies 2nd W.Rid:Infy.Bde.)
3rd - do - Ammunition Column & No: 3 Section D.A.C. H.14a
(Supplies 3rd W.Rid:Infy.Bde.)

Ammunition refilling points H.15d & H.14a.

H.QRS, W.Rid:Divn.Amn:Column, H.14a 4.0.

Medical Arrangements, 3. Advanced dressing stations will be established as under:-

H.33, c,d,
H.34 d 3.8.
H,35 d 2.9.
H.24 d 5.3.

Divisional collecting stations to which wounded, able to walk, should be directed:-

H.21 a 1.9.
H.22 a 5.2.

Supply, 4. Transfer point from supply wagons of train to cooks wagons BAC ST MAUR - FORT ROMPU Road.

Transport

Transport, 5, All transport not absolutely necessary will be kept clear of the road.

Traffic, 6, Maps showing traffic circuits are issued herewith.

Prisoners, 7. Prisoners of War will be handed over to A.P.M. at FLEURBAIX.

Flags, 8. Sketches of Flags used by 7th & 8th and Merrut Divisions are attached.

Reports, 9. Head Quarters, R.A. will be established at H.20 d 77.
2nd W.Rid: Infy.Bde, H.Qrs, at post 25)from midnight
3rd - do - - do - at post 29)proceeding the
)operation.

Issued at 12 noon

Major, R.A.,

Brigade Major, R.A., 1/1st W.Rid: Division.

Copy No: 1 to A.D.C. (for G.O.C., R.A.)

Copy No: 2 to Brigade Major, R.A.

Copy No: 3 to Office Copy.

Copy No: 4 to G.C.R.A.

Copy No: 5 to 1st W.Rid: F.A.Bde,

Copy No: 6 to 3rd - do -

Copy No: 7 to W.Rid: Division Amm: Column.

Copy No: 8 to W.Rid: Division,

SECRET. TIME TABLE OF TASKS 3rd W.Rid: F.A.Bde. Copy. No: 3

1st PHASE 0.0 - 0. 10.

Unit.	Time.	Objective.	Remarks.	Rounds per gun deemed sufficient.
3rd W.Rid:F.A.Bde.	0.0-0.10.	Wire cutting 988-989		25
		IInd PHASE 0-10 - 0.25.		15
3rd W.Rid: F.A.Bde.	0.10-0.25	To Destroy as much of enemy's parapet as possible opposite Section 6.		
		IIIrd PHASE 0.25	Fire to be very carefully controlled to avoid undue expenditure of ammunition,	
3rd W.Rid:F.A.Bde.	0.25-	To watch and search the road from point 798 inclusive - LEMAISNIL and all approaches leading towards our front in that Area, fire is not to be directed WEST OF Road running NORTH from point 798. Any enemys guns opening fire in that Area is to be silenced.		

Head Qrs
R.A. West Riding Divn

Reference attached.
If the guns mentioned have been located, will you kindly inform me where they are.

C H Hamilton
Major R.A.
for C.R.A. 6th Divn
12.5.15

Copy No 1.

W.R.D.A. No. 8/6/9.

VIII

S.E C R E T.

Arrangements for Artillery Defence of 3, 4, 5 & 6 Sections.

****

1. The control of the Artillery Defence of these Sections is assumed by B.G. C.R.A. West Rid: Division tasks are distributed to Brigades as follows :-

2. The O.C. 1st W.R. F.A. Bde. will be responsible for the direct defence of 3, 4 & 5 Sections, and will dispose his batteries as follows.

   1st Battery No 3 Section.
   2nd Battery No 4 Section.
   3rd Battery No 5 Section.

3. The O.C. Erd W.R. F.A. Bde will be responsible for direct defence of 5 & 6 Sections and will dispose his batteries as follows

   7th Battery No 5 Section.
   9th Battery No 6 Section.
   8th Battery No 6 Section.

4. The B.G. C.R.A. VIIIth Division has issued instructions to O.C. 5th H.A. Bde to have his batteries disposed as follows

   One battery to assist in covering No 3 Section.
   One battery to assist in covering No 4 Section.

   and to send Forward Observing Officers to Infantry holding No 3 & 4 Sections.

5. In case of alarm the guns in direct support will open fire on their night lines, switching as required; the guns not directly supporting the front attacked will fire on the flanks and approaches of the hostile attack.

4.30pm.
11.5.15.

L. W. Lewer. Major R.A.
Bde Major R.A
W R Divn.

5.9" Howitzer Battery firing 4 to 5 p.m. May 10th 1915. From West of FROMELLES.

****

Following indications were noticed.

1. From house N.30.b.1.5. I noted the sound as comming from between 1° and 5° right of FROMELLES Church, and at a greater range than the Church.

2. A pretty good groove at N.24.d.1½.4 gave magnetic bearing 125°

3. Major McGrath at convent N.24.d.2½.2. noted the time between sound of gun and arrival of shell as 6 seconds. If they were using No. 6 charge this indicates 5960 yards.

I believe it to be about N.22.b.South or S.W. It would be interesting to know if West Riding Division have located it.

They fired groups of 3 rounds. If there were not 3 howitzers the fire was very quick.

sd/ B.Butler, Major, R. F. A.

11/5/15. Commanding, 72nd Battery, R. F. A.

Copy No. 12

S E C R E T.

8th D.A. No. S/18/13

ARRANGEMENTS FOR ARTILLERY DEFENCE OF "C" "D" "E" and "F" lines and Nos.1 and 2 SECTIONS.

1. The control of the Artillery Defence of "C" "D" "E" and "F" lines, and Nos.1 and 2 Sections will be immediately assumed by the B.G.C.R.A. 8th Division.

2. Artillery Units responsible for the defence of these lines etc. as detailed below, will immediately open telephonic communication with H.Q.R.A. 8th Division.
The O.C. 3rd Brigade, R.H.A. will have tactical control of the 2nd WEST RIDING Brigade, R.F.A. for purposes of defence.

3. "C" lines - The 2nd WEST RIDING Brigade, R.F.A. will be responsible to Officer Commanding 3rd Brigade, R.H.A. for the direct Artillery defence of these lines and for maintaining communication with the infantry holding the lines and with Brigade Headquarters at M 3 D 5.0

4. "D" and "E" lines - 3rd Brigade R.H.A. will be responsible for the direct Artillery defence of these lines and for maintaining communication with the infantry holding the lines and with Brigade Headquarters at M 3 D 5.0

5. "F" Lines - 33rd Brigade R.F.A. will be responsible for the direct Artillery defence of these lines and for maintaining communication with the Infantry holding the lines and with Brigade Headquarters about N 9 a 3.6

6. Nos.1 and 2 Sections - 45th Brigade, R.F.A. will be responsible for the direct Artillery defence of these sections and for maintaining communication with the Infantry holding these sections, and with Brigade Headquarters, about N 9 a 3.6

7. Artillery units detailed for the direct Artillery defence of any portion of our lines, will have their guns laid at night on parallel lines to cover the most important portion of their area.

8. The 5th H.A. Brigade will establish communication with Headquarters of the WEST RIDING Infantry brigade holding Nos. 3 and 4 sections. They will have Forward Observing Officers with the Infantry holding No.2 Section and No.3 Section of WEST RIDING Division tonight and after tonight with No.3 Section and No.4 Section of WEST RIDING Division.
One battery will assist in covering No.2 section tonight and one in covering No.3 section.
From tomorrow night and after, one battery will assist in covering No.3 Section and one in covering No.4 section.

9. In case of alarm the guns in direct support will open fire on their night lines, switching as required; the guns not directly supporting the front attacked will fire on the flanks and approaches of the hostile attack.

10. H.Q.R.A. 8th Division will be re-established at G 17 C 7.9 at 10 a.m. tomorrow morning.

5 p.m.
10.5.15.

R.H.Johnson Major. R.A.
Brigade Major 8th Division Artillery.

SECRET 0/73.

~~O.C. Commanding.~~ 13-5-15.

H.Q. West Riding Div. Arty

The following Bombardment will be carried out at 1 a.m. until 1.5 a.m. precisely 14.5.15.

By 4.7" Batteries - Bombardment up to 10 rounds per gun, half of which is to be shrapnel where range admits.

OBJECTIVE		BATTERY
LE BAS WAILLY	by	118 Battery
LE PLOUICH	by	112 Battery
FOURNES	by	119 Battery
HERLIES	by	Highland Heavy Battery.

By 55th. HOWITZER BATTERY from 1 a.m. to 1.3 a.m. precisely 14.5.15 the hostile trenches registered by them immediately EAST of the SAILLY - FROMELLES road. Rounds allowed 3 per gun per minute shrapnel.

During this period the Infantry will open a hot rifle fire.

From 1.3 a.m. until 1.5 a.m. there will be dead silence save for the 4.7 batteries.

1.5 a.m. to 1.7 a.m. precisely 14-5-15 all 13pr. and 18pr. Batteries (except 5th. Brigade R.H.A. which will not fire) will fire on the German Trenches on their "Night L ines"-

Rounds allowed 3 per gun per minute shrapnel.

No firing by 15 p r. Batteries.

ACKNOWLEDGE by telephone.

R.T. Johnson Major R.A.

Brigade Major 8th. Divisional Arty.

10 p.m.
13.5.15

Headquarters, R. A.,

49th (West Riding) Division.

PROGRESS REPORT

from Midnight 13/14th to Midnight 14/15th May 1915.

Unit.	Time	Target Engaged.	Rounds Fired	Remarks
West Riding R.G.A. Heavy Battery.	~~12.15~~ 12.15 Am.	LE PLOUICH N27.d.10.4	23	
	2.25 P.m.	LE MAISNIL O.13.a.8.5	27	

Information obtained:-

Nil.

W. Graham Major,

Commanding West Riding R. G. A.

"A" Form. Army Form C. 2121.

MESSAGES AND SIGNALS. No. of Message

Prefix Code m.	Words	Charge	This message is on a/c of:	Recd. at m.
Office of Origin and Service Instructions.	Sent		OHMS Service.	Date XVII
	At m.			From
	To			
	By		(Signature of "Franking Officer.")	By

TO Third Highland How Bde

Sender's Number	Day of Month	In reply to Number	
BM/19	Thirteenth		AAA

Move	your	Bde	Amm	Column
to	H 19	a 8-6 to	a 10-9	tomorrow
morning	at	10 am.	AAA	Instruct
O	C	Column	to	leave
sufficient	room	for	No 4	Section
51st	Highland	D	A	C
which	will	arrive	tomorrow.	

From Bde Major 49th W

Place R Divn

Time 7 pm.

The above may be forwarded as now corrected. (Z) [illegible] Major RA

Censor. Signature of Addressor or person authorised to telegraph in his name

* This line should be erased if not required.

B. Ltd. Wt. W5673/619–50,000. 10/14. Forms C2121/10.

"C" Form (Duplicate). Army Form C. 2123.

42

MESSAGES AND SIGNALS. No. of Message

Service Instructions.	Charges to Pay. £ s. d.	Office Stamp. ARMY TELEGRAPHS 13.V.15

Handed in at Yhd Office 2 30 p m. Received 5 p m

TO 49th W R Div

Sender's Number	Day of Month	In reply to Number	AAA
Ga 291	13	G 323	

our howitzer section Dac will march to morrow by the same route as the brigade to H7D8.1 & should arrive about 3 30 pm

Copy sent to.
Q.
GOCRA } to see
ADM.

CH

Cocks Tower

CH

Received

G 20/M

FROM PLACE & TIME: 51 st High Divn 2 30 pm

(24932). M.R.Co.,Ltd. Wt.W9668/1672/50,000 Pads—1/15. Forms/C.2123.

"A" Form. Army Form C. 2121.

MESSAGES AND SIGNALS.

No. of Message

Prefix Code m.	Words	Charge	This message is on a/c of:	Recd. at m.
Office of Origin and Service Instructions.	Sent		Service.	Date
	At m.			From
	To			
	By		(Signature of "Franking Officer.")	By

TO 57th Highland Div

Sender's Number	Day of Month	In reply to Number	AAA
G 323		GA 286	

Howitzer Section DAC should be send tomorrow as we have no Howitzer Section Guns being away with another Corps

CRA
Q

HEADQUARTERS (GENERAL STAFF) 13/5/15 DIVISION T.F.

From HQ 51 H Div
Place
Time 12.30pm

The above may be forwarded as now corrected. (Z)

Censor. Signature of Addressor or person authorised to telegraph in his name

* This line should be erased if not required.

8350 S. B. Ltd. Wt. W4843/541—50,000. 9/14. Forms C2121/10.

XVIII

1/3rd Highland Fd (H) Bde
15. 5. 15

Situation Report

1/1st Renfrew (H) Bty

Registration partly completed and is being continued today.
Nothing special to report

1/2nd Renfrew (H) Bty

Registration partly completed and is being completed today
Nothing special to report

Peter C. Macfarlane, Lt Colonel
Commanding 1/3rd High Fd (H) Bde

Army Form C. 2121.

MESSAGES AND SIGNALS.

No. of Message

Prefix ______ Code ______ m.

Office of Origin and Service Instructions.

Words | Charge

Sent

At ______ m.

To

By

This message is on a/c of:

Service.

(Signature of "Franking Officer.")

Recd. at ______ m.

Date

From IX

By

TO ~~147th Bde~~ ~~148th Bde~~ ~~CRE~~ GOC RA

Sender's Number	Day of Month	In reply to Number	AAA
G 368	Fourteenth		

In view of certain reliefs in progress bombardment ordered for 9 pm tonight is cancelled AAA acknowledge.

From 49 Division

Place

Time 7 pm

The above may be forwarded as now corrected. (Z) H Nicholl Capt

Censor. Signature of Addressor or person authorised to telegraph in his name

*This line should be erased if not required.

3662 M. & Co. Ltd. Wt. W929/549—100,000. 6/14. Forms C2121/10.

"A" Form. Army Form C. 2121.

MESSAGES AND SIGNALS. No. of Message

Prefix Code m. | Words | Charge | This message is on a/c of: Highcastle Immediate Service. (Signature of "Franking Officer.") | Recd. at m.

Office of Origin and Service Instructions.

Sent At m. To By

Date From By

TO G.O.C RA 49 Division

* Sender's Number	Day of Month	In reply to Number	AAA
4359	fourteenth		

	The	bombardment	ordered	will
take	place	at	nine	pm
instead	of	ten	AAA	The
4·7	batteries	will	shell	following
to night	AAA	FOURNES	ILLES	HERLIES
LE BAS	WAILLY	AAA	Ten	rounds
per	gun	may	be	expended
AAA	duration	of	bombardment	five
minutes				

From 49 Division

Place

Time 4.52 pm

The above may be forwarded as now corrected. (Z) N. S. Nicholl Capt

Censor. Signature of Addressor or person authorised to telegraph in his name

* This line should be erased if not required.

8350 S. B. Ltd. Wt. W4843/541—50,000. 9/14. Forms C2121/10.

"A" Form. Army Form C. 2121.

MESSAGES AND SIGNALS.

No. of Message

Prefix Code m. Office of Origin and Service Instructions.	Words / Charge / Sent At m. To By	This message is on a/c of: Service. (Signature of "Franking Officer")	Recd. at m. Date From By

TO — 49th W. R. DIVISION ARTILLERY

Sender's Number	Day of Month	In reply to Number	AAA
*Bm. 55.	14.5.15		

Reference targets for 4.7 batteries tonights 9 pm bombardment AAA Propose to engage ILLIES HERLIES and LE BAS WAILLY with 4.7 batteries of this division will you please say if this is agreeable to you

From	6th	DIV	ARTY
Place			
Time	6.18 pm		

The above may be forwarded as now corrected. (Z) R H Johnson Maj RA.

Censor. Signature of Addressor or person authorised to telegraph in his name

* This line should be erased if not required.

C27642 P. G. Ltd. Wt. W14142/641—20,000 3/15. Forms C2121/10.

"C" Form (Duplicate). Army Form C. 2123.

MESSAGES AND SIGNALS. No. of Message 76

Charges to Pay. £ s. d.

Office Stamp. XDX 14. V. 15.

Service Instructions.

Handed in at Dro [illegible] Office 8 28 [illegible] m. Received 8 [illegible] m.

TO 49th WR Dvn

Sender's Number	Day of Month	In reply to Number	AAA
G 3543	14.5.15		

Bombardment of the enemys front will take place at midnight five am & 9 am aaa each bombardment will last for three minutes followed by a pause of two minutes followed by a further bombardment of two minutes aaa 18 pounders thirteen pounders & 15 pounders will fire at the rate of two rounds per gun per minute aaa 4.5 howitzers will not fire at all aaa 5 inch howitzers will only fire by day & not at enemys first line trenches make two rounds

FROM

PLACE & TIME

(24932). M.R.Co.,Ltd. Wt.W9668/1672. 50,000 Pads—1/15. Forms/C.2123.

"C" Form (Duplicate).

Army Form C. 2123.

MESSAGES AND SIGNALS.

No. of Message

Charges to Pay. £ s. d.

Office Stamp. YD1 14. V. 15. ARMY TELEGRAPHS

Service Instructions.

Handed in at Office m. Received m.

TO 2

Sender's Number	Day of Month	In reply to Number	AAA
G 8543			

per gun per minute aaa 4.7 will fire during the bombardment at selected localities aaa In addition to foregoing wire cutting by field artillery will be carried out before the bombardment at 5 am + 9 am at different places at expenditure of 10 rounds per gun

FROM PLACE & TIME 4 Corps 8 20 pm

(24932). M.R.Co.,Ltd. Wt.W9668/1672. 50,000 Pads—1/15. Forms/C.2123.

S E C R E T.

BM/24/9

Officer Commanding,

The following bombarment will be carried out - from 12 midnight to 12.7 a.m. precisely.

W.R. R.G.A. will bombard FOURNes

No. of rounds 10 per gun.

A. 1st and 3rd W.R. RA. Bdes 12 midnight to 12.3 a.m. precisely will bombard enemy's trenches on their night lines.

No. of rounds per gun per minute 2 viz 24 rounds per battery.

12.3 a.m. to 12.5 a.m. dead silence save for W.R. R.G.A.

1st and 3rd W.R. F.A. Bdes 12.5 a.m. to 12.7 a.m. precisely will bombard enemy's trenches on their night lines.

No. of rounds per gun per minute 2 viz 16 rounds per battery.

From 5 a.m. to 5.7 a.m. 15th precisely W.R. R.G.A. will bombard LEMAISNIL

No. of rounds ten per gun.

1st and 3rd W.R. F.A. Bdes 5 a.m. to 5.3 a.m. 15th precisely

B. will bombard enemy's trenches on different portions in their Sections than were done at mid-night.

5.3 a.m. to 5.5 a.m. dead silence except for W.R. R.G.A.

5.5 a.m. to 5.7 a.m. continue bombardment on enemys trenches.

No. of rounds allowed 2 per gun per minute.

From 5 a.m. to 5.3 a.m.

3rd Highland Howitzer Bde on N 16 b 6.8. LECLOCHERS and Fme DE LA MARLAQUE N 17 b 6.8.

5.3 a.m. to 5.5 a.m. dead silence.

5.5 a.m. to 5.7 a.m. repeat.

No. of rounds per gun per min one.

From 9 a.m. to 9.7 a.m.

W.R. R.G.A. will bombard FOURNES

10 rounds per gun per min allowed.

From 9 a.m. to 9.3 a.m.

C. 1st and 3rd W.R. F.A. Bdes repeat B but on different portions of enemy's trenches opposite their sections

2 rounds per gun per minute.

3rd Highland Howitzer Bde on N 16 d 4.6. and N 17 c 6.7.

1 round per gun per minute.

9.3 a.m. to 9.5 a.m. dead silence except for W.R. R.G.A.

9.5 a.m. to 9.7 a.m. repeat task allotted for 9 a.m. to 9.3 a.m.

In addition Wire Cutting commencing 4.45 a.m. to 4.55 a.m. precisely.

1st W.R. F.A. Bde from pt 896 to 899 both inclusive

D. 3rd -----------"--------- 899 exclusive to 900 inclusive

10 rounds per gun to be fired.

Commencing 8.45 a.m. to 8.55 a.m. precisely.

1st W.R. F.A. Bde from pt 900 inclusive to 963 exclusive

3rd ---------"---------- 963 to 964 both inclusive.

10 rounds per gun to be fired.

Acknowledge by telephone.

LW Lewis

Major R.A.,
Brigade Major R.A. 49th (W.R.) Division.

14th May 1915.
9.30pm.

MESSAGES AND SIGNALS. No. of Message

Prefix Code m. | Words | Charge

Office of Origin and Service Instructions.

Sent

At m.

To

By

This message is on a/c of: Service

(Signature of "Franking Officer.")

Recd. at m.

Date

From

By

TO

Sender's Number	Day of Month	In reply to Number	AAA
	fifteenth		

German	trenches	supporting	points	and
Communication	opposite	the	most	northerly
point	in	front	of	49th
Division	are	to	be	bombarded
at	12	midnight	to night	AAA
Bombardment		will	last	for five minutes
AAA	Ammunition	allowed	field	guns
and	howitzers	two	rounds	per
gun	per	minute	Shrapnel	only
AAA	4.7	guns	12	rounds
per	battery	Lyddite	AAA	

From 49 Division

Place

Time

The above may be forwarded as now corrected. (Z) H. J. Nicholl Capt

Censor. Signature of Addressor or person authorised to telegraph in his name

*This line should be erased if not required.

3662 M. & Co. Ltd. Wt. W929/549—100,000. 6/14. Forms C2121/10.

MESSAGES AND SIGNALS. No.

Prefix	Code	m.	Words	Charge	This message is on a/c of:	Recd. at
Office of Origin and Service Instructions.			Sent		Service.	Date
			At	m.		From
			To			
			By		(Signature of "Franking Officer.")	By

TO — CRA

* Sender's Number	Day of Month	In reply to Number	AAA
G390	15th		

Reference tonights bombardment the divisional Commander wishes the fire directed on enemys supporting points and communication and not against enemys trenches

From 49th WR Div

Place

Time 6.35 pm

The above may be forwarded as now corrected. (Z) C H Hampton Lt Col

Censor. Signature of Addressor or person authorised to telegraph in his name

* This line should be erased if not required.

8350 S. B. Ltd. Wt. W4843/541—50,000. 9/14. Forms C2121/10.

90

"A" Form. Army Form C. 2121.

MESSAGES AND SIGNALS. No. of Message

Prefix ___ Code ___ m.	Words	Charge	This message is on a/c of:	Recd. at ___ m.
Office of Origin and Service Instructions.	Sent		O H M Service.	Date
	At ___ m.			From
	To		(Signature of "Franking Officer.")	By
	By			

TO				
	FIRST	WEST	RIDING	ARTY
	THIRD	WEST	RIDING	ARTY
	WEST	RIDING	HEAVY	BATTERY

Sender's Number	Day of Month	In reply to Number	AAA
BM/25/G	Fifteenth		

Bombardment	to	take	place	precisely
at	midnight	tonight	and	to
last	for	five	minutes	AAA
FIRST	BDE	1 + 2	batteries	on
supporting	trenches	N 11 b 10-8	to	~~N12~~ N12
a 5-10.	3rd	Battery	supporting	Trench
O 1 a 3-8	to	O 1 a 5-6	AAA	THIRD
BDE	on	Supporting	Trench	O 1 a 5-4
inclusive	to	LE	BRIDOUX	AAA
Rate	of	fire	2	rounds
per	gun	per	min	AAA
HEAVY	BATTERY	R	RADINGHEM.	Twelve
rounds	in	all	Lyddite	

From	BDE	MAJOR	49th	W
Place	R	ARTY		
Time	6. 45 pm			

The above may be forwarded as now corrected. (Z) [signature] Major RA

Censor. Signature of Addressor or person authorised to telegraph in his name

* This line should be erased if not required.

8350 S. B. Ltd. Wt. W4843/541—50,000. 9/14. Forms C2121/10.

West Riding R. G. A., Heavy Battery.

PROGRESS REPORT.

From Midnight 15/16th to Midnight 16/17th May 1915.

Unit.	Time.	Target engaged.	Rounds fired	Remarks
West Riding RGA. Heavy Battery	mid-night to 12-5a.m.	RADINGHEM	12 Lyddite	

Information obtained:- N I L.

[signature] Graham Major,
Commanding West Riding R. G. A., H. B.,
49th (West Rid.) Division.

In the field
17-5-15.
9.am.

"A" Form. Army Form C. 2121.

MESSAGES AND SIGNALS. No. of Message

Prefix Code m. | Words | Charge | This message is on a/c of: Service. (Signature of "Franking Officer.") | Recd. at m. Date XXII From By

Office of Origin and Service Instructions. Secret

Sent At m. To By

TO WEST RIDING HEAVY BATTERY

Sender's Number: RM/26/G | Day of Month: Fifteenth | In reply to Number | AAA

As it is probable that the enemy will turn every available gun on to the Indian attack in the morning you will stand ready to act as a counter battery at 3 am AAA The batteries you will especially counter are those in the neighbourhood of LA PLOUICH AAA Should you be required to turn on to any other batteries you will be instructed accordingly

From: Bde Major 49th W R Artillery
Place
Time: 10.47 pm

The above may be forwarded as now corrected. (Z) [signature] Major RA

Censor. Signature of Addressor or person authorised to telegraph in his name

* This line should be erased if not required.

8350 S. B. Ltd. Wt. W4843/541—50,000. 9/14. Forms C2121/10.

MARCH TABLE NIGHT OF 16th/17th May 1915.

UNIT.	STARTING POINT	ROUTE	TIME of passing starting point	DESTINATION	REMARKS
2nd W.R. F.A. Brigade. 1 Section of each battery	~~Cross Roads~~ ~~H 31 c 8.8.~~ Four Cross Roads LAVENTIE.	~~Road Junction~~ ~~H 6 d 1.1.~~ ~~LAVENTIE.~~ ROUGE DE BOUT.	9 p.m.	4th H 31 a 5.5. 5th H 32 a 5.2. 6th H 32 b 1.10.	Wagon lines ~~take over from 45th F.A. Bde.~~ temporary. H 25 d 2.2

16/5/15.
5 pm

[signature]
Major R.A.,
Brigade Major R.A. 49th (W.R.) Division.

MARCH TABLE NIGHT OF 16th/17th May, 1915.

UNIT	STARTING Pt.	ROUTE	TIME (approximately)	DESTINATION	REMARKS
45th Brigade. 1 Section of each battery.	Cross roads M 31 c 8.2	Road Junction M 6 d 1.1 - LAVENTIE	9 p.m.	M 21 a 5.3 M 21 b 7.7 M 16 d 6.6	Wagon lines M 1 d Take over from 2nd West Riding Brigade.
2nd West Riding Brigade. 1 section of each battery.	Four cross roads LAVENTIE	ROUGE DE BOUT	9 p.m.	As directed by B.G.C.R.A. 49th W.R.Division.	As directed by B.G.C.R.A. 49th W.R. Divisio n.
55th Battery R.F.A.	Road junction M 31 a 6.6	Four cross roads LAVENTIE	10 p.m.	M 11 c 5.5	Wagon line M 5 c 3.2
5th Brigade, R.H.A.	Road junction M 26 a 1.1	ROUGE DE BOUT	10 p.m.	M 6 d 8.8 M 6 d 8.10	Wagon lines as at presen t.
Highland Heavy battery.	Road junction M 31 a 6.6	Road junction M 5 b 6.2	11 p.m.	M 5 a 8.8	Wagon line to remain as at present.

R.T. Johnson

3.15 pm

Major. R.A.

16-5-15. Brigade Major 8th Division Artillery.

"A" Form. Army Form C. 2121.

MESSAGES AND SIGNALS.

No. of Message

Prefix Code m.	Words	Charge	This message is on a/c of:	Recd. at m.
Office of Origin and Service Instructions.	Sent		XXIV	Date
	At m.		Service.	From
	To			
	By		(Signature of "Franking Officer.")	By

TO	W	R	R	G
	A			

Sender's Number	Day of Month	In reply to Number	AAA
*49th DA / 24 / G.	17th		

In confirmation of my 9am telephone message, open fire on battery near LE FAUVICH and search gradually South to LA CLIQUETERIE AAA These batteries are shelling our troops further South and require silencing

From	Bde	Major	RA	49th
Place	W	R	D'n	
Time	9.40 am			

The above may be forwarded as now corrected. (Z) [illegible] Major RA

Censor. Signature of Addressor or person authorised to telegraph in his name

* This line should be erased if not required.

8350 S. B. Ltd. Wt. W4843/541—50,000. 9/14. Forms C2121/10.

"A" Form. Army Form C. 2121.

MESSAGES AND SIGNALS.

No. of Message

Code m. Office of Origin and Service Instructions.	Words / Charge / Sent At m. To By	This message is on a/c of: Service. (Signature of "Franking Officer.")	Recd. at m. Date From By

TO: 49th West Riding Division Artillery

Sender's Number	Day of Month	In reply to Number	AAA
* BM91	17.5.15		

No 1 Group Heavy Artillery reserve report Heavy Howitzers enfilading RUE DU BOIS from direction HT POMMEREAU or WARNETON and ask for assistance AAA we are turning fire on to WARNETON F^me Square T16a and also on Squares T2C T2D and N32 ~~AAA~~

W.R. Heavy Battery ordered to turn on to Square T16a, 20 rounds to be fired

Time 1210 am

From: 8th DIV ARTY
Place
Time: 11.55 am

The above may be forwarded as now corrected. (Z) R.H. Johnson Major RA.

Censor. Signature of Addresser or person authorised to telegraph in his name

*This line should be erased if not required.

B562 M. & Co. Ltd. Wt. W929/549–100,000. 6/14. Forms C2121/10.

"A" Form. Army Form C. 2121.

MESSAGES AND SIGNALS. No. of Message

Prefix Code m. | Words | Charge | This message is on a/c of: | Recd. at m.

Office of Origin and Service Instructions. | Sent At m. To By | Service. (Signature of "Franking Officer.") | Date From By

TO WEST RIDING ARTILLERY

Sender's Number	Day of Month	In reply to Number	AAA
* BM 92	17.5.15		

Have just heard that the hostile shelling of the RUE DU BOIS has abated

From 8th DIV ARTY

Place

Time 12·25pm

The above may be forwarded as now corrected. (Z) R H Johnson Major RA.

Censor. Signature of Addressor or person authorised to telegraph in his name

*This line should be erased if not required.

8362 M. & Co. Ltd. Wt. W929/549—100,000. 6/14. Forms C2121/10.

West Riding R. G. A., Heavy Battery.

To:- Headquarters, R. A.,
49th (West Riding) Division.

PROGRESS REPORT.

From midnight 16/17th to midnight 17/18th May 1915.

Unit.	Time	Target engaged.	Rounds Fired	Remarks
West Riding R. G. A. Heavy Battery	9a.m to 11/30 am.	Opened fire on batteries in the vicinity of LE PLUICH and LA CLIQUETERTE Farm. Map places:- N.28 C 3.3 N.34 A.7.4 N.33 C.10.4 T. 3 C.6.4 T. 2 D.8.7 T. 2 B.2.6 T. 2 C. 7.3 T. 2 C. 7.8 T. 2 A.5.3	107 lyddite	12 rounds at each target with the exception of the last at which 11 rounds were fired
	12-15 pm.	WARNETON Fme and Chateau	20 lyddite	

Information obtained:- NIL

W. Graham Major,
Commanding West Riding R. G. A., H. B.,
49th (West Riding) Division.

In the field
18-5-15.
9.am.

Secret.

Instructions for Movements Evening 17th May/1915

XXVI

Reference $\frac{1}{20,000}$

1. 2nd W. R. T. A. Bde. The remaining Section will move to new positions.

4th Battery to H 31 a 5-5
5th " to Wagon Line
6th " to H 32 b 1-10

Starting point Town Cross roads LAVENTIE
Time 9pm
Route ROUGE DE BOUT
Wagon line H 25 d 4-4

2. Brigade A. Column. to H 19 a 9-7
Starting point Junction Roads M 4 b 4-9
Time 9am 18th inst.
Route RUE DU QUESNOY
To move by Sections at 1 hour interval

17/5/15
12.30 pm

[signature]
Major RA
Brigade Major RA 49th (WR) Divn

"C" Form (Duplicate). Army Form C. 2123.

MESSAGES AND SIGNALS. No. of Message

	Charges to Pay. £ s. d.	Office Stamp.
[illegible]		WR 17-5-15
Service Instructions.		

Handed in at ... Office ... m. Received ... m.

TO Hdqrs R A 49th (W R) Div.

Sender's Number	Day of Month	In reply to Number	AAA
TC 2132	17th		

Fourth sixth and one section 5th W R Batteries in positions as ordered at 10.30 p[illegible]

FROM 2nd W R Bde R F A

PLACE & TIME [illegible]

(24932). M.R.Co.,Ltd. Wt.W9668/1672. 50,000 Pads—1/15. Forms/C.2123.

For information.

S E C R E T.

INSTRUCTIONS FOR MOVEMENTS EVENING OF 17th MAY, 1915.

Reference to 1/40,000 map BELGIUM and part of FRANCE Sheet 36.

17-5-15.

1. 45th Brigade, R.F.A. (less 1 section of each battery)

Starting Point - Four cross roads H 31 C 8.2

Time. - 9 p.m.

Route - Road junction M 6 d 1.1

Destinations - Headquarters M 3 d 5.1
One battery to M 21 a 5.5
do. M 21 b 7.7
do. M 16 d 6.6

2. 2nd WEST RIDING Brigade, R.F.A. (less 1 section of each battery).

Starting Point - Four cross roads LAVENTIE.

Time - 9 p.m.

Route - ROUGE DE BOUT

Destination - as ordered by B.G.C.R.A. 49th WEST RIDING Division.

Major. R.A.

10 a.m. Brigade Major 8th Division Artillery.

Copy No......1

49th DIVISION OPERATION ORDER NO. 7.

XXVIII

Reference - Map, 1:20,000.   17th May, 1915.

1. The 146th Infantry Brigade and 2nd West Riding Brigade R.F.A. rejoin the Division today.

2. 146th Infantry Brigade will take over No. 2 Section, and No. 1 Section from its eastern end to the road (inclusive) which crosses 1 R trench line at N.9.a.0.0. (running south west from the SAILLY - FROMELLES road) on the night 18/19th May.

Arrangements for relief will be made direct with 23rd Infantry Brigade.

3. There will be no changes in the lines now held by 147th and 148th Brigades.

4. The two battalions at LAVENTIE will move today to billets on RUE DU QUESNE vacated by 24th Infantry Brigade. Arrangements to be made direct between Brigades.

H.Q. 146th Infantry Brigade will move to H.31.d.0.4 on 18th.

5. Two battalions 146th Brigade will take over the trench line mentioned in paragraph 2 on the 18th.

Two battalions will be in Brigade Reserve in the area between RUE BIACHE and RUE DU QUESNE.

6. 2nd Brigade R.F.A. will take up positions selected by 10 p.m. tonight, atvwhich hour the responsibility for the artillery defence of the front east of the house about N.9.c.0.8. will devolve upon G.O.C.R.A., 49th (W.R.) Divn.

5th Brigade R.H.A. will retain its present positions and will come under the orders of 49th (W.R.) Divn. for tactical purposes only.

7. The dividing line between 8th and 49th Divisions will be from G.17.d.7.9. through G.24.a.3.0.- G.30.a.9.7. - H.31.a.1.0. - H.31.c.7.0 - N.8.a.7.9 to N.9.a.0.0.

8. 146th Brigade will be responsible for the following defended posts, to which suitable permanent garrisons will be allotted :-

1X, 1B, 1C, 2D, 2E, 20, 21.

C H Harington Lieut.-Colonel.
General Staff, 49th (W.R.) Division, T.F.

Issued at 7 a.m.

Copy No. 1 to G.O.C.R.A. , 49th (W.R.) Divn.
,, 2 C.R.E.
,, 3 Signal Coy.
,, 4 146th Bde.
,, 5 147th ,,
,, 6 148th ,,
,, 7 8th Divn.
,, 8 5th Bde. R.H.A.
,, 9 A.D.M.S.
,, 10 A.&.Q.
,, 11 A.P.M.
,, 12 A.D.C.(for G.O.C.).
,, 13 G.S.O.2 (Office copy).

SECRET.

Copy No 1

W.R.D.A. No S/7/6

17th May 1915.

Arrangements for Artillery defence of 49th W.R. Divn Front.
(H 9 c 0.8. Sec 1 to H 31 d 2.8. Sec 6)

Reference Map 1/20,000.

(1) The control of the Artillery defence of the new 49th W.R. Divn Front is assumed by B.G. C.R.A. 49th W.R.Divn from 8·30 p.m. tonight 17th instant.

(2). Positions and Zones of responsibility of Brigades will be as follows

(a) 5th Brigade R.H.A. (H.Q. BARLETTE FARM)
Z Battery (H 33 b 0.8.) to assist in covering No 4 Section.
O Battery (H 33 c 4.8.) to assist in covering No 3 Section,
and to send forward observing officers to Infantry holding No 3 & 4 Sections (147th Infy.Bde.) (H.Q.H 20 d 6.6.)

(b) 2nd W.R. F.A. Bde. (H.Q. H 31 a 8.9.) for support of 146th Infy.Bde. (H.Q. H 31 d 0.4.)
in direct defence of No.1 Section H 9 c 0.8. to H 9 c 9.5. & No.2 Section and will dispose his batteries as follows
4th Battery (H.31 a 5.5.) H 9 c 0.8. to H 9 c 9.5. No.1 Section
5th Battery (H 33 c 3.4.) }
6th Battery (H 32 b 1.10.) } No 2 Section.

In addition to be able to cover that portion of No.1 Section held by VIIIth Divn.
The H.Q. of 33rd Bde R.F.A. is at M 6 a 6.6. with whom communication must be established.

(c) Direct defence of Sections 3, 4, 5 & 6 by 1st & 3rd W.R. F.A. Bdes will be as laid down in W.R.D.A.No S/6/G dated 11/5/15.

(d) 3rd Highland How: Bde. (H.Q. H 28 a 8.4.) to cover the whole front with each battery in order to assist in defence when ordered by B.G. C.R.A. 49th W.R. Division.

(e) W.R. R.G.A. will be under orders of B.G. C.R.A. 49th W.R. Divn as counter battery.

(3) In cases of alarm the guns in direct support will open fire on their night lines switching as required; the guns not ~~in~~ directly supporting the front attacked will fire on the flanks and approaches of the hostile attack.

(4) The new portion of No.1 & 2 Sections is divided as follows from N 9 c 0.8.

R 1, S 1, and P 2 Section No.1 B
Q 2, R 2, S 2, Section 2.

(5) <u>Rocket signals between Infantry and Artillery.</u>

a Section No.1 B & 2 RED.
Sections 3 & 4 BLUE.
Sections 5 & 6 RED.

b The signal for immediate Artillery support will be two rockets close together. The signal will be repeated at intervals of about a minute until telephone acknowledgement is received from supporting battery, or the guns opens fire.

c The exact position from which rockets will be fired will be arranged direct between Infy.Bdes., and supporting Artillery.

d No batteries will open fire when any particular rockets are sent up, except those previously detailed to do so.

e The S.O.S. signal from Infantry to supporting Artillery

is only to be made in case of real necessity.
Tests will only be carried out when these have been arranged between Divisional R.A. and Infantry Brigades concerned and when carried out the word "TEST" will always precede "S.O.S." in the message sent by the Infantry.

(6). Positions of following Units

2nd W.R. F.A. Bde. A.C. H 19 a 9.6.

49th W.R. D.A.C. 2nd Section H 13d4.3.

Issued at 6pm

Major R.A.,
Brigade Major ~~R.A.~~ (49th W.R.Division.

SECRET.

Copy No.....4

49th (WEST RIDING) DIVISION OPERATION ORDER NO.8.

XXXIII

Reference - Map, Sheet 1/20,000.

21st May, 1915.

1. In conjunction with the main operations of the 1st Army about QUINQUE RUE, the 49th (West Riding) Division will carry out active offensive operations in the neighbourhood of TOUQUET, with the object of holding the enemy to his ground in our front and preventing his reserves from moving south.

2. 148th Infantry Brigade will capture the ruined houses on the west of the BOIS GRENIER - BRIDOUX road and will establish itself on that line, the flanks being thrown back to join up with the present line.

3. The date and hour of the operations will be notified later.

4. The trench line will be held by the troops as at present, supported by the following artillery :-

"O" and "Z" Batteries R.H.A.
2nd West Riding Brigade R.F.A.

5. (a) The artillery detailed for the above operations is as under :-

1st West Riding Brigade R.F.A.
3rd West Riding Brigade R.F.A.
4th West Riding (Howr.) Brigade R.F.A.
West Highland (Howr.) Brigade R.F.A.
55th Howitzer Battery.
2 Batteries R.F.A. (18-pr.) from 8th Div.
3 Batteries R.F.A. (18-pr.) from 6th Div.
1 18-pr. gun for special purpose.

} Wire cutting and bombardment as per time table attached (you no doubt have one)

Under Br. Genl. Hussey for counter battery guns :-

West Riding Heavy Battery.
119th Battery R.G.A.
1 9.2.
1 Armoured Train.

(b) Arrangements have been made with the IIIrd Corps for the batteries of the 6th Division, which are within effective range, to support the operation with fire against selected points in rear of the enemy's trench line.

(c) The batteries of the 8th Division which are within effective range will bring fire to bear on FROMELLES and VER TOUQUET.

6. <u>Medical arrangements.-</u>

Advanced Dressing Station : H.24.d.5.3. North of BOIS GRENIER.

Divisional Collecting Station, to which wounded able to walk should be directed : H.24.d.5.3. North of BOIS GRENIER.

7. The following stores will be sent to 148th Brigade tonight:-

40,000 sandbags.
100 ladders.
12 coils of wire.
1,500 stakes.
400 wire-cutters.
300 Hales Grenades.
150 Service Grenades.
33 Smoke Bombs and 3 Mortars,
Dietz Discs.

8. The West Riding Field Company is placed under the orders of G.O.C. 148th Brigade for the purpose of these operations.

2 Machine guns from 8th Division are also placed under the orders of G.O.C. 148th Brigade, and will be used in selected positions in the present parapet.

9. Divisional H.Q. and H.Q.R.A. will be established at H.29.b.3.2 from 10 p.m. previous to the operations commencing.

C H Harington Lieut.-Colonel.
General Staff, 49th (West Riding) Division.

Issued at 8 p.m.

Copy No. 1 to A.D.C. for G.O.C.
,, 2 G.S.O. 1.
,, 3 ,, 2. (Office copy).
,, 4 G.O.C.R.A.
,, 5 C.R.E.
~~,, 6 Divl. Signal Coy.~~ Cancelled
,, 7 148th Inf. Bde.
,, 8 A.&.Q.
,, 9 6th Div. (For information)
,, 10 8th ,, do.
,, 11 A.D.M.S.
,, 12 147th Inf. Bde. (For information).
,, 13 146 ——

XXXIV

SECRET.

Copy No. 2

49th (W.R.) Divisional Artillery Order No.3. 22nd May, 1915.

Reference Map Sheet 1/20,000.

1. The 49th W.R. Division will carry out active offensive operations in the neighbourhood of TOUQUET.

2. 148th Infantry Brigade has been detailed to capture the ruined houses on the West of the BOISGRENIER - BRIDOUX road.

3. Date and hour of operations will be notified later.

4. The present trench line will be held by the troops as at present, supported by

O and Z Batteries R.H.A.
2nd W.R. F.A. Bde.

5. (a) The following Artillery will take part in the offensive operations

1st W.R. F.A. Bde. 3rd W.R. F.A. Bde 4th W.R. (How) F.A. Bde. 3rd Highland (How) F.A. Bde. 5th Battery R.F.A. 36th Battery R.F.A. 55th (How) Battery R.F.A. 2 Batteries R.F.A. (18 pr:) from 6th Divn.	Time Table and ~~Take~~ Tasks attached.

1 18 pr: Gun for special purpose.

(b) W.R. R.G.A. Heavy Battery is placed under orders of Brig: General Hussey as counter battery.

6. Medical arrangements.

Advanced Dressing Station H 24 d 5.3. (North of BOIS GRENIER). Divisional Collecting Station to which wounded able to walk should be directed H 24 d 5.3. (N of BOIS GRENIER)

7. H.Q. R.A., will be established at H 29 b 3.2. from 10 p.m. previous to the operations commencing.

Issued at 10 a.m.

R W Lewer
Major R.A.,
Brigade Major R.A.49th (W.R.)Division.

Copy No.1 to A.D.C. for G.O.C.R.A.
----"-- 2 Brigade Major R.A.
----"-- 3 S.C.R.A.(Office Copy).
----"-- 4 49th (W.R.) Division.
----"-- 5 5th Bde. R.H.A.
----"-- 6 1st W.R. F.A. Bde.
----"-- 7 2nd W.R. F.A. Bde.
----"-- 8 3rd W.R. F.A. Bde.
----"-- 9 4th W.R. F.A. Bde.(Howitzer).
----"-- 10 3rd Highland F.A. Bde.(Howitzer).
----"-- 11 5th Battery R.F.A.
----"-- 12 36th Battery R.F.A.
----"-- 13 55th (How:)Battery R.F.A.
----"-- 14 W.R. R.G.A.

SECRET.

TIME TABLE OF (TASKS). (1). Copy No. 2........

References 1/20,000 & 1/10,000 numbered Maps.

1st Phase 0.0 - 0.15

UNIT.	TIME	OBJECTIVE	REMARKS	ROUNDS PER GUN DEEMED SUFFICIENT.
5th Battery R.F.A.	0.0 - 0.15	Wire cutting 100* to 200* WEST of Pt 976		20 Shrapnel.
36th ------"-----	----"----	Wire cutting Pt 976 to 100* WEST.		20 Shrapnel.
72nd ------"-----	-----"-----	Wire cutting Pt 976 to 100* EAST.		20 Shrapnel.
112th ------"-----	-----"-----	Wire cutting 100* to 200* EAST of Pt 976.		20 Shrapnel.
	0.15 to 0.20		Pause.	

References 1/20,000 & 1/10,000 numbered Maps.

TIME TABLE OF TASKS. (2)

2nd Phase 0.20 -0.60

UNIT.	TIME.	OBJECTIVE	REMARKS	ROUNDS DEEMED SUFFICIENT.
5th Battery R.F.A.	0.20 - 0.30	100x to 200x WEST of Pt 976	Bombardment of enemy's front trenches,	50 Shrapnel per Battery.
36th ------"-----	----"-----	Pt 976 to 100x WEST	----------"---------	--------"------
72nd ------"-----	----"-----	Pt 976 to 100x EAST	----------"---------	--------"------
112th -----"-----	----"-----	100x to 200x EAST of Pt 976	----------"---------	--------"------
3rd W.R. Battery.	----"-----	100x EAST of Pt 966 to 175x EAST.	----------"--------	1 round per gun per minute.
3rd W.R. F.A. Bde.	----"----	175x EAST of Pt 966 to 400x EAST.	----------"--------	-------"--------
3rd Highland (H) Bde.	----"----	100x EAST of pt 966 to 350x EAST.	----------"-------	--------"------
4th W.R. (How) Bde.	----"----	250x EAST of Pt 976 to 500x EAST	----------"------	--------"------
	0.30 - 0.35		Pause.	
	0.35 - 0.45	All batteries repeat Bombardment.	18 prs fire 50 H.E. per battery instead of Shrapnel.	
	0.45 - 0.50		Pause.	
	0.50 - 0.60	All batteries repeat Bombardment.	18 prs fire 50 percussion Shrapnel per battery.	

SECRET.

TIME TABLE OF TASKS.

SPECIAL TASKS.

References 1/20,000 & 1/10,000 numbered Maps

UNIT.	TIME	OBJECTIVE	REMARKS	ROUNDS PER GUN DEEMED SUFFICIENT.
1st W.R. F.A./Bde less 3rd Battery	0.20 - 0.30	966 - 967 968	To form a barrage	1 round per gun per minute.
	0.30 - 0.35		Pause.	
	0.35 - 0.45	Repeat		
	0.45 - 0.50		Pause.	
	0.50 - 0.60	Repeat		
55th Battery R.F.A.	0.20 - 0.60	(1) Pts 940, 941, 953, 954, 955 (Communication Trenches) (2) 974 - 975 (3) Communication Trenches from RUE DES BOIS BLANCS		1 round per gun per minute Shrapnel.
One 18 pr Gun 6th Divn.	0.20 - 0.60	Hostile Machine guns in saliont 500 EAST Pt 976		No limit.

21/5/15.

[signature]
Major R.A.,
Brigade Major R.A. 49th (W.R.) Division.

73

XXXV

Headquarters R.A.
49th (W.R.) Div.

I beg to report that Lieut. Walker & 4th (H) Section 49th (W.R.) D.A.C. reported here at 7.40 last night. As reported to you last night he is now billeted ~~at~~ N of letter C in Ct DE LA MALADERIE (Sheet HAZEBROOK 205A).

H. E. Aykroyd Lt-Col.
Comd. 49th (W.R.) D.A.C.

23/5/15.

Secret. G 572

XXXVI

CRA.

Zero has been ordered for 8 pm tomorrow 23rd May.

The Infantry advance will take place at 8.50 pm.

Reference your Artillery Time Table, the Divisional Commander wishes you to have your 0.35 – 0.45 bombardment with shrapnel and not HE but he wishes the 0.50 – 0.60 bombardment to be the one with H.E so that the Infantry go forward at the commencement of the HE. bombardment at 8.50 pm.

Will you please notify all concerned.

Div^l HQ will move forward to H.29 b.3.2 at 7 pm tomorrow evening.

C H Harington Lt Col
Gs.
49th W.R. Div

May 22nd/15.

<u>Secret</u>

C.R.A.

Reference Corps Commanders instructions today, after the bombardment is finished tomorrow night, the G.O.C 148th Bde has been informed that he can call on you during the night for assistance should the Enemy prove troublesome, otherwise your guns will not continue. Counter batteries will continue to fire at certain periods during the night.

C H Harington Lt Col
GS
49th W.R. Divn

May 22/15.

SECRET. Copy No. 2.

OPERATION ORDER NO. 17
BY
LIEUT. GENERAL SIR H.S. RAWLINSON, Bt., K.C.B., C.V.O.
Commanding 4th Army Corps.

Headquarters, 4th Corps.
22nd May, 1915.

1. With reference to Operation Order No. 16, dated 20th inst., the attack of the 49th (W.R.) Division will be delivered in accordance with the approved time-table of which zero will be at 8 p.m. on Sunday, May 23rd.

2. In order to divert the enemy's attention from the main operations of the 1st Army about QUINQUE RUE which will take place on the morning of the 24th instant, and to attract to the neighbourhood of BRIDOUX as large a number of the enemy as possible, the bombardment of selected points in the area north of FROMELLES (inclusive) will be carried out during the night of the 23rd/24th May by the artillery of the 49th and 8th Divisions, as well as by the group of guns under Br. General Hussey. These bombardments will take place at 10 p.m., 12 midnight, and 2 a.m., for a period of five minutes at each hour. The selection of the points for bombardment is left to Divisional Commanders, but they should include cross roads which the enemy is likely to use as well as the communication trenches behind the enemy's lines.

3. At 3.20 a.m. on the 24th, there will be a further bombardment of the enemy's front line trench opposite BRIDOUX by the 18-pounders and 5" Howitzers of the 49th Division for ten minutes. At this hour, also, the group of artillery under Br. General Hussey and the guns of the 8th Division will bombard the enemy's approaches for ten minutes at a moderate rate of fire.

4. The infantry of the 49th Division, which will have occupied the house on the BRIDOUX - BOIS GRENIER road after the bombardment on the evening of the 23rd, will dig in during

the night and join up the flanks with their present line of trenches, constructing likewise a communication trench on the south of the road.

5. All reports to be sent to 4th Corps Headquarters, MERVILLE.

(Signed) A.G. DALLAS, Br. General.
General Staff, 4th Corps.

Issued at 7.45 p.m.

Copy No. 1 to 8th Divn.
2 to 49th Divn.
3 to 6th Divn.
4 to 3rd Corps.
5 to B.G.R.A. 4th Corps.
6 File.

S E C R E T. TIME TABLE AND TASKS. (BOMBARDMENT) Night 23rd - 24th May

References 1/20,000 & 1/10,000 numbered Maps.

UNIT	TIME	OBJECTIVE	REMARKS	ROUNDS PER GUN DEEMED SUFFICIENT.
4th W.R. (How) Bde. 10th Battery.	10 p.m. to 10.5 p.m.	Road Junction N 12 a 1.5. to BAS MAISNIL N 12 a 8.3.	Special attention to Road Junctions	1 round per Gun per minute
11th Battery	----------"--------	LEBRIDOUX O 1b 3.7 and road thence to BOIS BLANCS I 32 d 8.9.	---------"-------	-------"------
3rd Highland How:Bde.				
1st Battery	10 p.m. to 10.5 p.m.	Road Junction O 7 a 9.6 to Road Junction O 2 c 3.4.	--------"------	-------"------
2nd Battery	------------"-------	Road Junction N 12 b 6.2. -------"------- O 7 a 5.0. & BACQUART O 7 b 1.3.	--------"-----	-------"-------

4th W.R. (How:) Bde. and 3rd Highland How: Bde., will repeat the above Tasks from 12 Midnight to 12.5 a.m. and from 2 a.m. to 2.5 a.m.

S E C R E T.

TIME TABLE AND TASKS (BOMBARDMENT 24th May).

Reference 1/20,000 & 1/10,000 numbered Maps. 3.20 a.m. to 3.30 a.m.

UNIT.	TIME	OBJECTIVE	REMARKS	ROUNDS PER GUN PER MINUTE.
1st W.R. F.A. Bde., less 3rd Battery.	3.20 a.m. to 3.30 a.m.	966 - 967 - 969	To form a Barrage	1 round per gun per minute.
3rd W.R. Battery.	---------"---------	100 x EAST of Pt 966 to 175 x EAST.	Front Trench	------"------
3rd W.R. F.A. Bde.	---------"---------	175 x EAST of Pt 966 to 400 x EAST.	-----"-----	------"------
5th Battery R.F.A.	---------"---------	Point 976 to 200 x W.	-----"----- Percussion Shrapnel.	----"------
36th Battery R.F.A.	---------"---------	Point 976 to 200 x E.	-----"----------	----"------
72nd or 112th Battery R.F.A. (as detailed by 6th Divn.)	---------"---------	200 x EAST of Pt 976 to 250 x EAST.	Front Trench, Slow rate of fire to make ammunition last. Time Shrapnel.	Remainder of 600 rounds allotted by IVth Corps.
3rd Highland How:Bde.	---------"---------	100 x EAST of Pt 966 to 550 x EAST.	Front Trench.	1 round per gun per minute.

4th W.R. (How) Bde.	3.20 a.m. to 3.30 a.m.	250x EAST of Pt 976 to 500x EAST	Front Trench	1 round per gun per minute.
55th How: Battery R.F.A.	------"----------	Communication Trenches (940 to 955 (974 to 975 (from RUE (DES BOIS BLANCS.	Time Shrapnel	------"------

23/5/15

Major R.A.,
Brigade Major R.A. 49th (W.R.) Division.

Issued at 12.15 p.m.

Offensive Operations 24th May commencing 8pm.

Register of communications received or despatched.

XLIV (1)

Date 24th May 1915 Branch General Staff 49th W.R. Div ARTY Station FORT ROMPU

Message Branch Index No.	Sender's No.	Time of receipt or despatch.	From.	To.	Subject &c.	Action &c.	File No.
1	150	8.38pm	1st WRFA Bde	49th W.R. ARTY	Hostile mortar shelling Sect 5 from direction of clump of trees about point N6 & 9.4 near point 967	Filed. Barrage formed by 1st FA Bde covers this point	2
2	153	9.14pm	— " —	— " —	2nd W.R. Battery reported under fire	Filed	2
3	133/W	9.20pm	3rd WRFA Bde	— " —	Telephone wires 8th & 9th batteries broken, being repaired	Filed	2
4	G 2	10.25pm	49th W.R. Div	— " —	4th Bn K.O.Y.L.I. went over parapet successfully at 8.50pm and are now established in new line	Filed	2

(2)

Register of communications received or despatched.

Date 24th May 1915 Branch General Staff: 49th W.R. Divn ARTY Station FORT ROMPU

Message Branch Index No.	Sender's No.	Time of receipt or despatch.	From.	To.	Subject &c.	Action &c.	File No.
1	BM/41/G	10.30pm	49th W R ARTY	5th & 6th Batteries RFA	Additional bombardments at 9 am & 12 noon 25th inst. (Ordered verbally by 4th Corps Commander at 10pm)	By telephone, confirmed by motor cyclist	1
2	BM/42/G	10.45pm	— " —	4th West Riding How Bde & 3rd Highland How Bde	— " —	— " —	1
3	BM/43/G	10.35pm	— " —	VIth Divn ARTY & VIIIth Divn ARTY	— " —	— " —	1
5	G 4	11.19pm	49th W R Divn	49th W R ARTY	Further report on success of operation.	Units informed over telephone of the success.	2

3

Register of communications received or despatched.

Date 24th May 1915 Branch General Staff 49th W.R. Divn. ARTY Station FORT ROMPU

Message Branch Index No.	Sender's No.	Time of receipt or despatch.	From.	To.	Subject &c.	Action &c.	File No.
6	G 6	11.40pm	49th W.R. Divn	49th W.R. Divn Arty	Confirmation of additional bombardments for 5 minutes at 8 am & 12 noon 25th instant.	Already acted on in my 1, 2 & 3	2
7	G 7	11.50pm	— " —	— " —	148th Inf. Bde report "Infantry digging in, telephone communication with advanced companies established & visual signalling being provided for. Ammunition stores sandbags etc being sent up. Wiring party out in advance of working parties laying wire between enemy's lines & ruined buildings" etc. Enemy unusually quiet.	Filed	2

(4)

Register of communications received or despatched.

Date 25th May 1915 Branch General Staff 49th W.R. Divn Arty Station FORT ROMPU

Message Branch Index No.	Sender's No.	Time of receipt or despatch.	From.	To.	Subject &c.	Action &c.	File No.
8	G10	4 am	49th W.R. Divn	49th W.R. Divn Arty	148th Infantry Bde report Shell falling very short just over our parapet at 5Q	All units informed by Telephone 4.2 am	2
4	BM/44/G	8.20am	49th W.R. Divn Arty	Third Highland How Bde	Fire 6 rounds on farm at point 841. Transport reported parked there. (Information received from wireless Aeroplane thro' Brig Gen Hussey)	Copy filed	1
9	Nil	8.25am	5th Battery RFA	49th W.R. Divn Arty	Reports four field gun shells falling short. Not 5th Battery	36th Battery warned	2
10	G652	8.36am	49th W.R Divn	— — —	Warning of Royal Artillery that party of 4th K.O.Y.L.I. are occupying ruined houses in new trench	Filed, R.A. units informed	2

5

Register of communications received or despatched.

Date 25th May 1915 Branch General Staff 49th W.R. Divn Arty Station FORT ROMPU

Message Branch Index No.	Sender's No.	Time of receipt or despatch.	From.	To.	Subject &c.	Action &c.	File No.
11	Nil	8.35am	36th Battery RFA	49th W.R. Divnl Arty	Reports F.O.O. observed no shells short & asks for further information of position of shells falling short	Informed on telephone	2
5	1341/65/9	8.36am	49th W.R. Divnl Arty	All R A units	Party of 4th KOYLI occupying ruined houses in new trench	By telephone to all units	1
12	Nil	8.56am	5th Battery RFA	49th W.R. Divnl Arty	Gasbag up true bearing 166° from 5th Battery at H 29 c 5.9 range about 9700	Filed. Gen Hussey shown telegram, but gas bag too far away to justify expenditure of ammunition	2
13	9666	1.55pm	49th W.R. Divn	— —	Orders for returns of 5th, 36th & 55th Batteries RFA to VIIIth Divn.	Units informed that they will move tonight & that detailed orders would be issued in due course.	2

XLV

From,

G.O.C.,R.A.,

49th W.Rid:Division,T.F.

To

Head Quarters,

49th W.Rid: Division,T.F.

Sir,

I have the honour to report that the situation remains unchanged.

Registrations have been carried out by 10th and 11th Batteries and also by the 3rd Highland Brigade R.F.A. and R.G.A.

The Headquarters 1st W.R. F.A. Bde., was shelled on the afternoon of the 24th inst., at 5.40 p.m., Casualties 1 Officer killed,(Capt. & Adjutant T.A. Abbott), 2 other ranks wounded, one since died of wounds.

O.C. 2nd W.R. F.A. Bde., reports one man slightly wounded at 9.20 a.m. About 24 H.E. Shell fell near CROIX LESCORNEX. Fuzes when dug up proved to broken to render any useful information.

At 4 p.m., 5 light shrapnel fell near 5th W.R. Battery, no damage done.

At 9.7 p.m. Twp H.E. Shells apparently 4.2 Howitzer fell near CROIX BLANCHE.

Enemy's air-craft observed over 11th Battery obviously ranging a hostile battery.

The house at 131 d 1.2. in possession of enemy was taken on and four direct hits were recorded.

Programme as laid out was adhered to as per 49th Div:Artillery Order No.3, and Bombardments were carried out at times specified viz 8 p.m., 10 p.m., 12 midnight, 2 a.m., 3.20 a.m., 8 a.m., & 12 noon.

I have the honour to be
Sir,
Your obedient Servant,

25th May, 1915.

Brigadier General R.A.,
G.O.C.R.A.49th (W.R.) Division.

Copy War diary

XLVII

SECRET.

Defence of 49th W.R. Divn. Front.

Officer Commanding,

2nd W.R. F.A. Bde.

From 6 a.m. 26th inst., the 4th W.R. Battery will resume its former night lines and will cease to be in direct communication with O.C. 33rd F.A. Bde., for direct defence of the right hand portion of No.1 Section of the trench line.

L.W.B.

Major R.A.,

25/5/15. Brigade Major R.A. 49th (W.R.) Division.

S E C R E T.

PROGRAMME OF RETURN MOVE OF VIII DIVISION BATTERIES.

Name of Unit.	Starting Point.	Time at Starting Point.	Route	Position	Wagon Line
5th Battery R.F.A.	Junction Roads M 28 a 9.3.	9.15 p.m.	CROIX DE ROME - RUE BIACHE - ROUGE DE BOUT - LAVENTIE - 4 Cross Roads M 16 b 7.7. thence to position.	M 16 d 6.6.	Former position.
55th How: Battery R.F.A.	--ditto--	9.25 p.m.	Follow 5th Battery route to 4 Cross Roads LAVENTIE thence to position.	M 10 d 8.2.	--ditto--
36th Battery R.F.A.	Cross Roads H 22 b 9.1.	9.30 p.m.	FLEURBAIX - RUE DE QUESNE to position.	N 1 a 9.10.	-ditto-

25/5/15.

R W Lewer.
Major R.A.,
Brigade Major R.A.49th (W.R.) Division.

Recd 10 am 26/5/15

HEADQUARTERS
(GENERAL STAFF)
Date G68y
WEST RIDING DIVISION, T.F.

C.R.A.

Please finish off the house in question if possible.

CHH.

26/5/15 Arranged for with 11th Howitzer Bde on 26th.

WR

"C" Form (Duplicate). Army Form C. 2123. 86

MESSAGES AND SIGNALS. No. of Message

	Charges to Pay. £ s. d.	Office Stamp.
Service Instructions.	X	ARMY XDV 25 NO TELEGRAPHS

Handed in at 148th Bde Office 10.30p m. Received 10.47p m.

TO D 49 WR Divn

Sender's Number	Day of Month	In reply to Number	AAA
BM 960	twentyfifth		

Situation	quiet	aaa	Enemy	shelled
all	supporting	points	heavily	this
afternoon	resulting	in	casualties	amounting
to	about	8	killed	including
one	officer	and	20	odd
wounded	aaa	Enemy	trench	~~mortars~~ mortars
was	troublesome	and	several	have
been	brought	into	this	area
or	else	one	or	two
are	moved	about	along	to
front	aaa	Our	howitzers	probably
caused	considerable	damage	there	searching
but	the	house	opposite	our
post	in	the	mined	building
has	not	been	touched	so
far	as	can	be	ascertained
aaa	The	two	coys	holding

FROM

PLACE & TIME

(24932). M.R.Co.,Ltd. Wt.W9668/1672. 50,000 Pads—1/15. Forms/C.2123.

"C" Form (Duplicate). Army Form C. 2123.

MESSAGES AND SIGNALS. No. of Message

Charges to Pay. £ s. d.

Office Stamp. ARMY YD1 – 25. V. 15. TELEGRAPHS

Service Instructions.

Handed in at 148th Bde Office 10 35p m. Received 10 47p m.

TO (2) 49 WR Divn

Sender's Number	Day of Month	In reply to Number	AAA

new	trench	line	have	been
relieved	without	incident	aaa	Addressed
49	Divn	Repeated	19th	Bde
147	Bde			

FROM PLACE & TIME 148 Inf Bde 10/30 pm

(24932). M.R.Co.,Ltd. Wt.W9668/1672. 50,000 Pads—1/15. Forms/C.2123.

"C" Form (Duplicate). Army Form C. 2123.

MESSAGES AND SIGNALS. No. of Message

Charges to Pay. £ s. d. Office Stamp. YD 1 26. V. 15. TELEGRAPHS

Service Instructions.

Handed in at 148th Bde Office 12-30 p m. Received 12-35 p m.

TO GOC RA

Sender's Number	Day of Month	In reply to Number	AAA
BM 776	26th		

Our howitzers are dealing successfully with the house just in enemy lines crossing Bois Grenier Bridoux road addressed 49 Div repeated GOC RA 19 and 147 Inf Bdes

FROM PLACE & TIME: 148 Inf Bde 12-20 pm

(24932). M.R.Co.,Ltd. Wt. W9668/1672. 50,000 Pads—1/15. Forms/C.2123.

"C" Form (Duplicate). Army Form C. 2123.

MESSAGES AND SIGNALS. No. of Message

11.15 am 26.5.15

Charges to Pay. £ s. d.	Office Stamp.
X	26.V.15.

Service Instructions. priority

Handed in at 148th Inf Brigade Office 11.0 am. Received 11.6 am.

TO C.R.A. 49 Div

Sender's Number	Day of Month	In reply to Number	AAA
Bm 770	twentysixth		

Enemy	artillery	shelling	new	trench
line	also	6 R	and	6 S
AAA	unable	to	locate	enemy
batteries	addressed	49	Div	repeated
C.R.A.				

FROM
PLACE & TIME 148 Inf Bde 10.55 am

(24932). M.R.Co.,Ltd. Wt.W9668/1672. 50,000 Pads—1/15. Forms/C.2123.

"A" Form. Army Form C. 2121.

MESSAGES AND SIGNALS.

No. of Message

Prefix Code m.	Words / Charge	This message is on a/c of:	Recd. at m.
Office of Origin and Service Instructions.	Sent	Service.	Date
	At m.		From
	To		
	By	(Signature of "Franking Officer.")	By

TO: Armoured Train / O C 9.2 12th Siege / W R Heavy Battery

Sender's Number	Day of Month	In reply to Number	AAA
* BM/47/7	Twentysixth		

Priority message received begins General Heavy artillery Command ceases to exist forthwith and following transfers of command take place on receipt of this telegram AAA 119th Heavy Battery RGA to 8th Div aaa West riding heavy battery RGA to 49th Div aaa The 9.2 gun twelfth Siege battery and armoured train to 49th Div temporarily aaa ends aaa Adjutant RA 49th Div is at H 13 b 3-4 AAA The present telephone communication will remain

From HQ W R ARTY

Place

Time 11 am

The above may be forwarded as now corrected. (Z) [signature] Major RA

Censor. Signature of Addressor or person authorised to telegraph in his name

* This line should be erased if not required.

158 S. B. Ltd. Wt. W5673/619–50,000. 10/14. Forms C2121/10.

XLI

S E C R E T.

PROGRAMME of MOVES NIGHT 26th - 27th May, 1915.

Name of Unit.	Starting Point	Time at Starting Point.	Route	Position	Wagon line.
Headquarters and 1st Battery 3rd Highland Brigade R.F.A.	Junction Roads H 28 a 9.2.	9.15 p.m.	CROIX de ROME - Junction Roads H 14 a 8.3 - RUE QUESNOY - Fork Roads M 4 b 4.9 - LAGORGUE - LESTREM -ZELOBES thence to Road Junction R 32 c	To join Highland Division.	
2nd Battery.	--ditto--	9.25 p.m.	----ditto---	"	
3rd Highland Bde.A.C.	Junction Roads ½ H 19 c 5.9.	10.30 p.m.	----ditto---		
10th W.R. Battery.	Present Position.	9.40 p.m.	H 28 d 6.8 - CROIX MARECHAL	H 34 a 5.5.	Same as present.

26/5/15.

[signature]
Major R.A.,
Brigade Major R.A. 49th (W.R.) Division.

"C" Form (Duplicate). Army Form C. 2123.

MESSAGES AND SIGNALS. No. of Message

Service Instructions.	Charges to Pay. £ s. d.	Office Stamp.
" 47 Parker	L	JWK 26th

Handed in at AW Office —m. Received 7 pm.

TO Bde Major R. A

Sender's Number	Day of Month	In reply to Number	AAA
—	26th	—	

Angular elevation to both gas bags reported this morning has just been read from same point and found to be 2 degs 20 mins

FROM PLACE & TIME O C W. R. RGA.

(24932). M.R.Co.,Ltd. Wt.W9668/1672. 50,000 Pads—1/15. Forms/C.2123.

"C" Form (Duplicate). Army Form C. 2123.

MESSAGES AND SIGNALS. No. of Message

Sm

ae
7c

Charges to Pay. £ s. d.

Office Stamp. HWR

Service Instructions.

Handed in at Office m. Received m.

TO C R A

Sender's Number	Day of Month	In reply to Number	AAA

Observed from point H19d 1-1 (a)
Gas bag, true bearing 151 pulled down
before elevations could be obtained
(b) Gas bag. true bearing 213½, elevation
3°.

repeated to 8th Div
3.15 pm

FROM Capt Edwards

PLACE & TIME W R - R G-Ava 3/10pm

(24932). M.R.Co.,Ltd. Wt.W9668/1672. 50,000 Pads—1/15. Forms/C.2123.

"C" Form (Duplicate).

Army Form C. 2123.

MESSAGES AND SIGNALS.

No. of Message ....

LAA on 27 FCW

Charges to Pay. £ s. d.

Office Stamp. FWK 25.5

Service Instructions.

Handed in at FCW. Office......m. Received......m.

TO HQ RA

Sender's Number	Day of Month	In reply to Number	AAA
139/W	26th		

Magnetic Bearing H29.c.8.8

179 deg 196deg respectively

FROM 3rd FA Bde

PLACE & TIME 11-6A m

(6900) W.9668-1672. 50,000 Pads—12/14. F. T. & Co., Ltd.—Forms/C.2123.

"C" Form (Duplicate). Army Form C. 2123.

MESSAGES AND SIGNALS. No. of Message

8m 1117 FCW Parkin

Charges to Pay. £ s. d.

Office Stamp. FWR 26 5 15

Service Instructions.

Handed in at FCW Office 10.50 m. Received 10.50 m.

TO Hdqtrs RA

Sender's Number	Day of Month	In reply to Number	AAA
136/W	26th		

2 Captive Balloons up 3am to 7.30am one has been moved from 8 deg right of LE MAISNIL to 17 deg right is close in & still up other distant and 1 deg right of FROMELLI

2. Reference my 136/W. magnetic bearings of balloons are 179 degrees and 196 degrees respectively

FROM
PLACE & TIME 3rd WR FA Bde 10

(6900) W.9668—1672. 50,000 Pads—12/14. F. T. & Co., Ltd.—Forms/C.2123.

"C" Form (Duplicate). Army Form C. 2123.

MESSAGES AND SIGNALS. No. of Message

Service Instructions.

Charges to Pay. £ s. d.

Office Stamp. 7WR 26th

Handed in at Office m. Received 9.55 a m.

TO 49th (WR) Divnl Arty

Sender's Number	Day of Month	In reply to Number	AAA
C 109	26th		

Observation balloon bearing 172 true from H14a 5.4

FROM O C Armoured Train

PLACE & TIME 9.45 am

(6900) W.9668—1672. 50,000 Pads—12/14. F. T. & Co., Ltd.—Forms/C.2123.

"C" Form (Duplicate). Army Form C. 2123.

MESSAGES AND SIGNALS. No. of Message

Parkin

Charges to Pay. £ s. d.

Office Stamp. FWR 26th 9.35

Service Instructions.

Handed in at Office m. Received 9.35 m.

TO C.R.A.

Sender's Number	Day of Month	In reply to Number	AAA
	26th		

Magnetic bearings.

Cross roads – Croix Blanche 169 degrees 30 min

Crossroads Betillon 162 d. 10 min

4th Batty Hqrs H 21A 33 161 d. 30 min

FROM PLACE & TIME 2nd. (W.R.) Bde. R.F.A. 9.30 a.m.

(24932). M.R.Co.,Ltd. Wt.W9668/1672. 50,000 Pads—1/15. Forms/C.2123.

"C" Form (Duplicate). Army Form C. 2123.

MESSAGES AND SIGNALS. No. of Message

	Charges to Pay. £ s. d.	Office Stamp.
Parker	8th 1K	7WR 26th
Service Instructions.		

Handed in at ... Office ... m. Received 8.60 m.

TO 49th (WR) Divisional Arty.

Sender's Number	Day of Month	In reply to Number	AAA
	26th		

O.	C.	4th	W.	R.
reports	as	follows	enemys	baloon
observing	on	our	front	behind
AUBERS	RIDGE	AAA	They	are
shelling	our	battery	and	have
just	smashed	our	mess	room

FROM PLACE & TIME: 2nd WR Bde R.F.A.

(24932). M.R.Co.,Ltd. Wt.W9668/1672. 50,000 Pads—1/15. Forms/C.2123.

"A" Form. Army Form C. 2121

MESSAGES AND SIGNALS.

No. of Message 37

Prefix Code 4C m. Words Charge

Office of Origin and Service Instructions.

Sent At m. To By

This message is on a/c of Service.

(Signature of "Franking Officer.")

Recd. at m. Date From By

TELEGRAPHS 20.V.15.

TO 4G Div

Sender's Number	Day of Month	In reply to Number	AAA
Bm 800	26		

Enemy shelling new trench and also 6 M trench aaa right section of left portion of new trench temporarily vacated during bombardment aaa Enemy guns on trench are thought to be firing from a wood half right looking from centre of BRIDOUX road aaa our artillery might shell enemy parapets during temporary vacation of portions of new trench if they cannot locate enemy battery

G.O.C.R.A. Forwarded

Priority 8.5 pm 26/5/15

From 145 Bde

Place

Time 7.40 pm

Over

The above may be forwarded as now corrected. (Z)

Censor. Signature of Addressor or person authorised to telegraph in his name

* This line should be erased if not required.

3350 S. B. Ltd Wt. W4843/541—50,000. 9/14. Forms C2121/10.

Action taken

In conjunction with 8th Div

W.R. Rly. are ordered to open line in

N 30 b 4.7 & N 23 d 7.7.

[illegible signature]

West Riding R. G. A., Heavy Battery.

49th (West Riding) Division.

PROGRESS REPORT.

Midnight 25/26th to Midnight 26/27th May 1915:-

Unit.	Time.	Target Engaged	Rounds Fired	Remarks.
West Riding R.G.A., Heavy Battery	Noon	~~N. 30b 4.7~~ O. 8d 6.7 O.14c 2.2	6 Shrap. 6 Shrap.	
	9.p.m.	N. 30b 4.7 N. 23d 7.7	7 Shrap. 8 Shrap.	

Information obtained : - NIL.

W Graham Major,
Commanding West Riding R. G. A., Heavy Battery.
49th (West Riding) Division.

In the Field.
27-5-1915.
9 a.m.

27. 5. 15.

From Capt Nicholls at [illegible] am

XLIV

Gen Dawson has just telephoned up to say that Germans are using rifle fire & rifle grenades & trench mortars against them and giving them rather a bad time in the new trench opposite 6 S. Can we turn some guns on to help.

11th. How Battery. 4th W.R. How Bde ordered to open fire 6 rounds per gun & sweep from 200 yards EAST of Point 975 to 200 yards WEST of same point. 12.45 am

27th. May

RWS.

"C" Form (Duplicate). Army Form C. 2123.

MESSAGES AND SIGNALS. No. of Message 68

Charges to Pay. £ s. d. Office Stamp. YD1 27.V.15. TELEGRAPHS

Service Instructions. Priority

Handed in at 5 KOYLI Office 6-51p m. Received 7.12p m.

TO C.R.A 1st W Rid Div

Sender's Number	Day of Month	In reply to Number	AAA
E 1	27th		

Eleven th battery line broken Col Moxon 5th KOYLI wishes eleven battery to fire twelve rounds on enemy's front trenches 100 yds each side of house I 31 d 1.3 at once

O.C. 11th Battery ordered to open fire 7.25pm

[illegible]

FROM PLACE & TIME O.H. Eddison Lt 5th KOYLI 6.51p.m.

(24932). M.R.Co.,Ltd. Wt.W9668/1672. 50,000 Pads—1/15. Forms/C.2123.

XCXVI

S E C R E T.

Defence of 49th W.R. Division Front.

Owing to the 5th Brigade R.H.A. having been ordered to move from its present position, the entire defence of the front will be taken up as follows :-

A. 2nd W.R. F.A. Bde. covering sections 1 B and 2 for direct defence.
1st W.R. F.A. Bde. covering sections 3 and 4 for direct defence.
3rd W.R. F.A. Bde. covering sections 5 and 6 for direct defence.
4th W.R. F.A. Bde. 10th Battery covering sections 1 B, 2 and 3.
11th Battery covering sections 4, 5 and 6 for defence under orders of G.O.C.R.A. 49th(W.R.)Divn.

B. O.C's Bdes will arrange that batteries overlap on both flanks and are able to fire on the approaches leading towards Sections on either flank.

C.(1). O.C. 2nd W.R. F.A. Bde. to arrange for 4th Battery to be able to fire on approaches in N 14 a and N 14 b on demand from H.Q. 33rd F.A. Bde.

(2). O.C. 3rd W.R. F.A. Bde. to arrange for 8th Battery to be able to fire on approaches in I 31 d and I 32 a and c on demand from H.Q. 53rd F.A. Bde.(same H.Qrs as 12th F.A. Bde).

D. For the information of 4th W.R. (H) Bde. R.F.A. 1 B consists of 1 R, 1 S and 2 P.

E. INTER COMMUNICATIONS.

(1). 2nd W.R. F.A. Bde., with
(a) 146th Infantry Brigade.
(b) 33rd F.A. Bde.
(c) 1st W.R. F.A. Bde.

(2) 1st W.R. F.A. Bde., with
(a) 147th Infantry Brigade.
(b) 2nd W.R. F.A. Bde.
(c) 3rd W.R. F.A. Bde.

(3) 3rd W.R. F.A. Bde., with
(a) 148th Infantry Brigade.
(b) 1st W.R. F.A. Bde.
(c) 53rd F.A. Bde.

F. Night Lines.

F. <u>NIGHT LINES 4th W.R. (How:) F.A. Bde.</u>

10th Battery FROMELLES CHURCH.

11th Battery LEMAISNIL CHURCH.

G. <u>ZONE allotted 4th W.R. (How:) F.A. Bde.</u>

Both batteries the whole length of 49th (W.R.) Division front.

H. <u>TIME & DATE.</u>

These arrangements come into force from 8.30 p.m. 27th May, 1915.

I. O.C's Bdes will forward their arrangements for mutual support in case of S.O.S. call from Infantry.

R.W. Lewis

Major R.A.,

27/5/15. Brigade Major R.A. 49th (W.R.) Division.

LVII.

SITUATION REPORTS.

From 12 midnight 26/5/15, to 12 midnight 27/5/15.

To Head Quarters,

49th (W.R.) Division.

Sir,

I have the honour to report that the situation remains normal.

Further Registration was carried out by the W.R. R.G.A.

The O.C. 11th Battery reports having opened fire between 1 and 2 a.m. the night of the 26th - 27th, on to the Right and Left of the redoubt I 31 d 1.3. This was repeated at about 7 p.m.

The 10th Battery occupied the position formarly held by the 2nd Renfrew Battery.

The 3rd Highland Brigade acting on orders received left this Division.

Section 5, Subsection P of the trench line reports having seen flashes from a gun about point 966. (action nil)

All Brigades have rendered NIL Casualty returns

I have the honour to be,

Sir,

Your obedient Servant,

Brigadier General R.A.,

28/5/15. G.O.C.R.A. 49th (W.R.) Division.

Office Copy

No. 134.

FIRST ARMY INTELLIGENCE SUMMARY.

OPERATIONS.

22nd May.—Four German counter-attacks at the Lorette plateau and at Neuville St. Vaast were repulsed with heavy loss on the night 22nd/23rd.

The French captured a few more houses in the northern portion of Ablain St. Nazaire.

A counter-attack to the north of Ypres on the eastern side of the canal was repulsed with heavy loss.

23rd May.—An attack delivered yesterday by the Germans towards K.4 was stopped by our artillery fire. The enemy suffered heavy loss from artillery and machine-gun fire.

A house between M.9 and M.10 not marked on the map was secured by a night attack and is being consolidated.

24th May.—K.5 was captured and an advance made for some 100 yards towards L.8. J.3 was also captured. Operations are proceeding.

Reports have been received of an attack with asphyxiating gas on our front near Ypres.

INTELLIGENCE.

Air reconnaissance :—

Air reconnaissance about mid-day reported a considerable decrease in stock in the Lille—Douai area. A corresponding increase in stock was noticed at stations north of the Lys especially at Staden, Cortemarck and Ostend.

About 1 battalion was seen marching into Commines from the east at 12 noon.

A movement of motor transport and about 1 battalion of infantry was observed from north to south in the La Bassée—Haisnes area late yesterday afternoon.

The area La Bassée—Lorgies—Marquillies—Fournes—Haubourdin is reported clear of movement this morning.

DISTRIBUTION OF THE ENEMY'S FORCES.

The 78th Reserve Regiment, 37th Reserve Infantry Brigade, 19th Reserve Division, X. Reserve Corps was identified near Metzeral in Alsace on the 22nd May.

The 73rd Reserve Regiment of the same Brigade was also identified in the same area on the 18th May. This Brigade has therefore not accompanied the 2nd Guard Reserve Division. The remaining Brigade of the 19th Reserve Division has not been identified recently. It appears probable that the X. Reserve Corps is split up, the XIX. Reserve Division remaining in Alsace when the 2nd Guard Reserve Division moved north.

According to a deserter, drafts from the 111th Reserve Regiment, XIV. Reserve Corps have been moved northward, probably to make good some of the casualties in the XIV. Corps.

MISCELLANEOUS.

According to recent information the Germans are withdrawing heavy guns from the Belgian coast.

J. CHARTERIS, Major,
General Staff, 1st Army.

Monday, 24th May, 1915.
Sun rises 3.44 a.m., sets 7.38 p.m.
Moon rises 2.5 p.m., sets 1.13 a.m.

1st Army Printing Section, R.E. (128).

8th Division Artillery Report
from 6 a.m. 24th May, to 6 a.m. 25th, 1915.

1.(a) No.22 Anti Aircraft Section reports -

9.15 a.m. AVIATIK Biplane approached from S. and travelled S.E. Engaged.
9.40 a.m. Two AVIATIK Biplanes cruising about in front of Section. Engaged.
11.30 a.m. AVIATIK Biplane. Approached from E. and retired S.E. Engaged.
Ammunition expended - 90 rounds.

(b) 9 a.m. Road from CROIX BLANCHE to CROIX LESCORNEX shelled by 5.9 Howitzers working in conjunction with aeroplanes. The aeroplane was engaged by the Anti Aircraft Section and retired, when the shelling ceased.
9.25 a.m. Flashes of Anti Aircraft guns at FOURNES, probably O 31 C 9.0
9.30 - 10 a.m. 10 rounds from field gun behind AUBERS on RUE MASSELOT.
9.30 a.m. Observation station M 21 c 9.0 shelled . 4 direct hits obtained.
9.30 - 9.45 a.m. Cross roads in M 18 A shelled by enemy Howitzer.
10 - 11 a.m. Observation station M 21 C 9.0 shelled.
11 - 11.10 a.m. N 13 a and M 18 b shelled by enemy Howitzer.
11.40 a.m. 6 or 8 quich salvoes of H.E. fired at RUE MASSELOT by Field Howitzer.
1.45 p.m. Road junction between RUE DELVAS and RUE PETILLON shelled by Field Battery.
11.55 a.m. - 2 p.m. Trench Mortars, one at Pt. 324, and one between 319 and 321 fired repeatedly.
2 p.m. Cross roads N 2 C shelled by Field Battery.
2.50 p.m. Road junction M 15 c shelled.
5 p.m. Two 5.9 howitzers fired 6 rounds between our own trenches in N 13 a and RUE TILLELOY.
5 - 5.15 p.m. Field Howitzer fired 6 rounds at N 13 central.
5.45 - 6 p.m. 5.9 Howitzer fired about N 13 a, apparently from LA PLOUICH.
9 - 9.15 p.m. A few shell fired about the Junction of 1 P and 1 Q. No flashes visible.
6.40 a.m. Cross roads N 2 C shelled by Field Battery.

Gun flashes located as follows :-
(1) 4 gun battery Mag. bearing 178)
(2) One or two Heavy guns Mag. bearing 187) taken from house 50 yds.N.W. of RUE TILLELOY at a pt. 220 yds N.E. of X.rds. in M 23 d.

It is reported that both these batteries were firing at 12 mn. in the direction of NEUVE CHAPELLE.
(3) Anti Aircraft guns flashes measured as 10 degrees left of FROMELLES church from H 34 a 5.1
(4) Flashes of field guns seen from H 34 a 5.1 to be 5½ degrees Right of LE MAISNIL church. Time from flash to report 9 secs. Observation taken from near BOUTILLERIE places these guns about N 18 b 0.8 or O 13 c 4.5

P.T.O.

Genoral.

A holio was being used at 4.30 a.m. at RADINGHEM.
Parapet at Pt. 321 made some two feet higher.

2. 3rd Battery fired 15 rounds at Houso Pt.159
32nd Battery continuod registration and fired during bombardment as ordered.

33rd Battery fired at trench mortars at Pts. 321, 324, 319 at roquest of Infantry, also at a working party near 321.
Highland Heavy Battery continued registration with aeroplano.
118th and 119th Batteries fired during bombardment as ordered.
112th Heavy Battery. fired during bombardment as ordered.

C. E. Stranack
Capt for Major. R.A.

11 a.m. Brigade Major 8th Division Artillery.

LVIX.

War Diary file

G.O.C.R.A.

49th (W.R.) Division.

The G.O.C. desires me to inform you that the Corps Commander expressed himself as well satisfied with the arrangements for the bombardment of the enemy's lines yesterday evening and this morning.

The G.O.C. desires that you will express to all units which assisted on that occasion under your command his appreciation of the skill and precision with which your orders were carried out. It was largely due to the fire of the batteries under your command that the infantry were enabled to establish themselves on the desired position.

C H Harington Lieut.Colonel.

25/5/15. General Staff. 49th (W.R.) Division.

To be a special order, to be attached to DAO

Copies of this order to be sent also to the following

5th Battery R.F.A.

36th " "

55th " How. R.G.A.

No. 3 Gun 12" Siege battery

1/40 11

DIVISIONAL ARTILLERY ORDERS

by

Brigadier General C.T.Caulfeild R.A.,
Commanding R.A. 49th (W.R.) Division.

France,
26/5/15.

GENERAL STAFF.

1.OPERATIONS, 24th, 25th May, 1915.

With reference to Special Order of todays date, the C.R.A., wishes to thank all ranks for their work on 24th, 25th May 1915. The precise and accurate shooting of the guns shows that the laying and Fuze setting during the stress and excitement of action was very good and that Officers and men carried out orders efficiently, thereby the operations were successfully carried out with very small loss.

2.LINES OF COMMUNICATION.

On no account are units to use the cable laid out direct to their H.Qrs., from this office for communication between neighbouring units. Any communication necessary between units must be carried out on lines laid down by units.

3. TELEPHONE COMMUNICATION.

Officers of units requiring to speak over the telephone to any Staff Officer of the H.Qrs.,R.A. 49th (W.R.)Division will invariably be at the end of the telephone when the Staff Officer concerned arrives. Much time and annoyance will thus be saved if consideration is given to this matter.

(sd) L.W.Lewer. Major R.A.,
Brigade Major R.A.,49th (W.R.) Division.

No 11 Bde Major

DIVISIONAL ARTILLERY ORDERS

by

Brigadier General C.T.Caulfeild R.A.,

Commanding R.A. 49th (W.R.) Division.

France
26/5/1

GENERAL STAFF.

1.OPERATIONS, 24th, 25th May, 1915.

With reference to Special Order of todays date, the C.R.A., wishes to thank all ranks for their work on 24th, 25th May 1915. The precise and accurate shooting of the guns shows that the laying and Fuze setting during the stress and excitement of action was very good and that Officers and men carried out orders efficiently, thereby the operations were successfully carried out with very small loss.

2.LINES OF COMMUNICATION.

On no account are units to use the cable laid out direct to their H.Qrs., from this office for communication between neighbouring units. Any communication necessary between units must be carried out on lines laid down by units.

3. TELEPHONE COMMUNICATION.

Officers of units requiring to speak over the telephone to any Staff Officer of the H.Qrs.,R.A. 49th (W.R.)Division will invariably be at the end of the telephone when the Staff Officer concerned arrives. Much time and annoyance will thus be saved if consideration is given to this matter.

(sd) L.W.Lewer. Major R.A.,
Brigade Major R.A.,49th (W.R.) Division.

OPERATIONS on the BOIS GRENIER – BRIDOUX Road
22 – 25 May.

22nd May. On the night of the 22/23rd May a new line of trench about 400 yards in length was marked out halfway between the British and German lines just North of the ruined house on the BOIS GRENIER – BRIDOUX Road.

23rd May. On the night of the 23/24th May a commencement was made with the entrenchment of this line. There were a few casualties. The working party was withdrawn before daybreak.

24th May. At dusk on the evening of the 24th the new trench was found to be occupied by a strong German patrol. Machine gun and rifle fire was opened.

The 4th K.O.Y.L.I. advanced with the bayonet and the enemy retired. Considerable progress was made with the trench line and wire entanglements during the night.

During the day our batteries carried out registration and the enemy replied by shelling the trench line and generally all the area occupied by the division including Divisional Headquarters. There were several casualties.

From 8 p.m. to 8.50 p.m. the enemy's trenches were bombarded and subjected to heavy rifle and machine gun fire. The artillery of the Division had been reinforced by a number of heavy guns and by batteries lent by the 6th and 8th and Highland Divisions. 2 Machine Gun detachments were also lent by the 8th Division.

At 8.50 p.m. the 4th K.O.Y.L.I. advanced over the old parapet, occupied the new trench and the ruined house and by morning were strongly entrenched and wired along the whole front. Casualties, 1 Officer wounded, other ranks 9 killed 31 wounded.

25th May. Further bombardments were carried out at 10 p.m. 12 midnight 2 a.m. 25th May, 2.20 a.m., 3 a.m. and 12 noon.

During the morning the 4th K.O.Y.L.I. were withdrawn and replaced by the 5th K.O.Y.L.I.

The enemy has shelled the new line during the day with guns and trench mortars.

The new line is now strongly established and connected up with the old parapet.

The G.O.C. IVth Corps has asked that his high appreciation should be conveyed to Officers and men of the 4th K.O.Y.L.I. on the gallantry and precision with which the operation was carried out.

49th (W.R.) DIVISION.

PROGRESS REPORT. NOON 23rd May to NOON 24th May.

Work. Right Section. (Trenches 1S and 2)

Parapet and parados repaired, dug-outs improved. Communication Trench from Post 1S to rear carried on. Posts 1A and 10 improved. Shallow well made in rear of parapt and passed by Medical Officer for drinking if boiled.

Centre Section. (Trenches 3 and 4).

New parapetin front of Convent wall continued. Communication trench, parapet and parados improved. New Store shelter made in 4S.

Left Section. (Trenches 5 and 6.

Communication trenchmade from old trench to new advanced trench in 6. New support trenches dug and old ones repaired. New traverse begun in Salient in 5. Work on new breastwork continued. Railway from 5J to new breastwork behind Salient completed.

Information. Officers patrol at dusk reported new advanced trench held by enemy. Enemy was driven out by machine gun fire.

Workingparties went out and made considerable improvement to the new trench and wire in front of it.

Casualties 1 killed and 6 wounded.

Enemy's snipers were very active opposite 1S and 2 last night.

Enemy shelled as follows :-

Time.	Objective.	Remarks.
3 p.m.	Convent Wall.	H.E.
11.30 p.m.	trench 1S.	Trench Mortar. Ceased fire when replied to by 5" Howitzers.
9 a.m.	Croix Blanche CROIX MARECHAL.	15 centimetre working with Aeroplane which was driven off by Anti-aircraft gun.
10 a.m.	RUE DE QUESNE.	About 40 H.E.
10.30 a.m.	Yorkshire Hussars lines at FORT ROMPU and 49th (W.R.) Division Headquarters.	15 centimetre H.E. and shrapnel. Possibly aimed at Armoured Train.
11.20 to 11.35 a.m.	FLEURBAIX.	A biplane was up over CROIX BLANCHE at the time with British markings.
During morning.	6M and 5Y.	

[signature]

Captain.
for Major-General.
Commanding. 49th (W.R.) Division.

24/5/15.

S E C R E T.

Officer Commanding,

4th W.Rid: (How:) Bde,

At 9.15 pm tonight 28th instant one Section of 11th W.Rid: Battery will move to new position at H 34 a 8-4;the other Section will be laid on Pt.976, BOIS GRENIER - BRIDOUX road, ready to open fire if called on.

28/5/15.

Major,R.A.,

Brigade Major,R.A.,49th W.Rid:Division,T.F.

LXI

From,

The Officer Commanding,

1/3rd West Riding Brigade R.F.A.(T)

To,

Headquarters R.A.

28th May 1915.

MEMORANDUM.

Herewith as requested in your letter No ——
of yesterday's date, please.

Major R.F.A.
Adjutant for
Commanding 1/3rd West Riding Bde R.F.A.(T).

SECRET.

ACTION TO BE TAKEN BY THE 3rd WEST RIDING BRIGADE R.F.A. IN THE EVENT OF A SUDDEN ATTACK ON ANY SECTION OF THE PRESENT 49th (W.R.) DIVISION LINE.

In all cases S.O.S. Signal will be passed at once through Brigade Headquarters to Headquarters R.A. and to adjoining Units.

(a) ACTION.

In case of attack upon section covered by left Brigade, Batteries will fire as under :-

"S.O.S." No. 4 SECTION.

7th Battery on hostile trenches N 5 d 10.3 - N 6 d 2.5 (Night line)

9th Battery covers approaches in N 12 a

8th Battery covers approaches in N 12 b

"S.O.S." No. 5 SECTION.

7th Battery on hostile trenches N 5 d 10.3 - N 6 d 2.5 (Night line)

9th Battery hostile trenches N 6 d 2.5 - O 1 a 6.9 (Night line)

8th Battery searches down road O 1 b or a

"S.O.S." No. 6 SECTION.

7th Battery N 6 d and search 400 yards

9th Battery hostile trenches N 6 d 2.5 - O 1 a 6.9 (Night line)

8th Battery hostile trenches O 1 a 6.9 - I 31 d 9.7 (Night lines)

12th Brigade R.F.A. 6th Division covers approaches

I 32 c   O 1 b   O 2 a

"S.O.S." 6th DIVISION (RIGHT SECTION).

7th Battery N 6 d 2.5 - O 1 a 3.7 and search 200 yards

9th Battery O 1 a 3.7 - I 31 d 5.9 and search 200 yards

8th Battery I 31 d 5.4 to I 26 c 10.5

(b) ACTION IN CASE TRENCHES ARE CAPTURED.

(1) CAPTURE OF NO. 4 SECTION.

7th Battery fires on captured trenches No. 4 Section

9th Battery fires on N 12 a

8th Battery fires on N 12 b

(2) CAPTURE OF NO. 5 SECTION.

7th and 9th Batteries fire on captured trenches No. 5 Section.

8th Battery on approaches O 1 a b

(3) CAPTURE OF NO. 6 SECTION.

7th Battery fire on N 6 d and search back to road junction N 12 d9,6
8th and 9th Batteries on captured trenches.

LXII

<u>49th (West Riding) Divisional Artillery.</u>

Progress Report from 12 Mid-night 27th to 12 Mid-night 28th May, 1915.

(a) The situation remains normal.

(b) Registration was carried out by the O.C. 10th W.R. Battery.

(c) O.C. 1st W.R. F.A. Bde. reports 12 German Howitzer shell as falling around the 1st Battery gun position and billet. The position of hostile battery is thought to be near DUBEM WOOD.

(d) The O.C. 11th W.R. Battery reports the move of his right Section to new position.

(e) An enemy's balloon was observed yesterday afternoon at 5.15 p.m. S.W. of FROMELLES.

(f) Nil Casualtu Reports are returned.

(g) A further report from O.C. 11th W.R. Battery states an Infantry request for help about 3 p.m. to silence a trench mortar, this mortar was located by Capt. Dust F.O.O. 8th Battery as being 50 yards West of BOIS GRENIER - BRIDOUX road and 100 yards in rear of hostile front trench.

29/5/15.

Major R.A.,
Brigade Major R.A.49th (W.R.) Division.

49th (West Riding) Divisional Artillery.

Progress Report from 12 Mid-night 27th to 12 mid-night 28th May, 1915.

===========================

(a) The situation remains normal.

(b) Registration was carried out by the O.C. 10th W.R. Battery.

(c) O.C. 1st W.R. F.A. Bde., reports 12 German Howitzer shell as falling around the 1st Battery gun position and billet. The position of hostile battery is thought to be near DUBEM WOOD.

(d) The O.C. 11th W.R. Battery reports the move of his right Section to new position.

(e) An enemy's balloon was observed yesterday afternoon at 5.15 p.m. S.W. of FROMELLES.

(f) Nil Casualty Reports are returned.

(g) A further report from O.C. 11th W.R. Battery states an Infantry request for help about 3 p.m. to silence a trench mortar, this mortar was located by Capt. Dust F.O.O. 8th Battery as being 50 yards West of BOIS GRENIER - BRIDOUX road and 100 yards in rear of hostile front trench.

L W Lewer

29/5/15.

Major R.A.,
Brigade Major R.A.49th (W.R.) Division.

"C" Form (Duplicate). Army Form C. 2123.

MESSAGES AND SIGNALS. No. of Message

Sm. Recd 2.15pm LXIII FBW

Charges to Pay. £ s. d.

Office Stamp. FBW 29.5.15

Service Instructions.

FBW.

Handed in at ... Office ... m. Received ... m.

TO Bde Major R.A. 49th (W.R.) Div Arty

Sender's Number FBW 161 | Day of Month 29th | In reply to Number | AAA

Enemy Field gun fired at Infy Hdqtrs at N.13.c.6.1 this morning and magnetic Bearing of strike of shell N.13.c.6.1 was 145 deg aaa A fuze head was ~~recovered~~ recovered set at 2500. metres aaa The Battery fires daily at the Infy Bde Hdqrs It would appear to be at about N.14.c.5.7

Arranged with Aeronautics 2 for a wireless plane + in conjunction with AT to endeavour to knock out battery at 3 Pm

FROM 2nd W.R. Bde. R.F.A.

PLACE & TIME 2.5 p.m.

(24932). M.R.Co.,Ltd. Wt.W9668/1672. 50,000 Pads—1/15. Forms/C.2123.

"C" Form (Duplicate). Army Form C. 2123.

MESSAGES AND SIGNALS. No. of Message 28

Recd. 3.5 pm

	Charges to Pay. £ s. d.	Office Stamp.

Service Instructions.

Handed in at 146th Bde Office 2.47 p m. Received 2.52 p m.

TO Goc RA 49 WR Divn

Sender's Number	Day of Month	In reply to Number	AAA
SC 508	29		

Following information gathered by gunner observation officer it would appear that battery which shelled Headquarters N3C6.1 this morning is the same which shelled Headquarters No 2 section on 24th aaa Bearing 145 degrees magnetic from N3C6.1 aaa Damaged fuse head recovered setting appears to be 2500 metres approximately aaa can this battery be silenced please

FROM PLACE & TIME 146 Bde 2.40 pm

(24932). M.R.Co.,Ltd. Wt.W9668/1673. 50,000 Pads—1/15. Forms/C.2123.

"C" Form (Duplicate). Army Form C. 2123.

MESSAGES AND SIGNALS. No. of Message

Prefix / Code: Recd 6.5pm — A T Churchill

Charges to Pay. £ s. d.

Office Stamp. LWR 29-5-15

Service Instructions.

Handed in at ... Office ... m. Received ... m.

TO Brigade Major. WR Artd

Sender's Number	Day of Month	In reply to Number	AAA
C B 45	29th		

Operations Report

Engaged Battery No 18 b 5.5 with Aeroplane at 4.30pm fired 10 rounds of 6" and obtained 2 direct hits. aaa Aeroplane then went home.

FROM PLACE & TIME: O.C. A Y Churchill 5.33 pm

(24932). M.R.Co.,Ltd. Wt.W9668/1672. 50,000 Pads—1/15. Forms/C.2123.

"C" Form (Duplicate). Army Form C. 2123.

MESSAGES AND SIGNALS. No. of Message

Sm. 87
Recd 3.27 pm 24
LXIII
FAW

	Charges to Pay. £ s. d.	Office Stamp. FWR 29.5.15

Service Instructions.

Handed in at FAW Office m. Received m.

TO 49 WR D Arty

Sender's Number	Day of Month	In reply to Number	AAA
174	29th		

A new German emplacement built during last night at n6C4.4½ aaa Emplacement built about 4 feet above level of old parapet, seven large loopholes about 3 feet by 2 observed immediately on left of new emplacement and reported by FOO 3rd WR Batty

Telephoned message to HQ Div. at 3.45pm

FROM PLACE & TIME: 1st WR FA Bde
3-30pm

(24932). M.R.Co.,Ltd. Wt. W9668/1672. 50,000 Pads—1/15. Forms/C.2123.

"C" Form (Duplicate). Army Form C. 2123.

MESSAGES AND SIGNALS. No. of Message

	Charges to Pay. £ s. d.	Office Stamp.
3.37 pm 7 Bty		
Service Instructions. LXIV		

Handed in at Office m. Received m.

TO C R A

Sender's Number	Day of Month	In reply to Number	AAA
	29/7		

Enemy observation balloon up at 165 deg magnetic from House at H31a22

To for

FROM
PLACE & TIME OC 4th WR Bty 3.30.

(24932). M.R.Co.,Ltd. Wt.W9668/1672. 50,000 Pads—1/15. Forms/C.2123.

"C" Form (Duplicate). Army Form C. 2123.

MESSAGES AND SIGNALS. No. of Message

Sm 40 10 pm

FCW

Charges to Pay. £ s. d.

Office Stamp. FWR 29 5 15

Service Instructions.

Handed in at Office m. Received m.

TO Hdqrs RA 49th Div

Sender's Number 141/W. Day of Month 29th In reply to Number AAA

Balloon magnetic bearing H29 b 7.6 187 deg

Bad observation

FROM 3rd FA Bde

PLACE & TIME 3-50 pm

(24932). M.R.Co.,Ltd. Wt.W9668/1672. 50,000 Pads—1/15. Forms/C.2123.

"C" Form (Duplicate). Army Form C. 2123.

MESSAGES AND SIGNALS. No. of Message

	Charges to Pay. £ s. d.	Office Stamp.
Recd 4 30 pm		FWR 29-5-15
Service Instructions.		

Handed in at .... Office .... m. Received .... m.

TO Hdqrs RA 49th WR Div

Sender's Number	Day of Month	In reply to Number	AAA
180	29th		

F.O.O. 1st Batty reports German observation balloon aaa bearing from FOO post 177 deg aaa FOO position N4A2.4 aaa

Too far

FROM PLACE & TIME 1st WR FA Bde 4.20 pm

(24932). M.R.Co.,Ltd. Wt.W9668/1672. 50,000 Pads—1/15. Forms/C.2123.

LXVY

"C" Form (Duplicate). Army Form C. 2123.

MESSAGES AND SIGNALS.

No. of Message

Sn

Recd 4.15 pm

LXY

7 [illegible]

Charges to Pay.
£ s. d.

Office Stamp.
29.5.15

Service Instructions.

Handed in at .... Office .... m. Received .... m.

TO C R A 49th Div Art

Sender's Number	Day of Month	In reply to Number	AAA
	29th		

I have examined an uncommon looking object immediately in rear of enemy's trench about 45 yds W of point E 83 The true reading from 4th Bty gun position H 31a 3 3 is 113 deg and the object is dome shaped and glistens like steel and there is a round shaped attachment approximately 6" in diameter aaa In my opinion this should be fired upon and I am remaining in the trenches in case I am required for observation

FROM Adjt 3rd W R Bde

PLACE & TIME 3.18 pm

(24932). M.R.Co.,Ltd. Wt.W9668/1672. 50,000 Pads—1/15. Forms/C.2123.

1/3rd West Riding Brigade R.F.A.(T)

SITUATION REPORT No. 29.

From 12 midnight 28/5/1915 to 12 midnight 29/5/1915.

Approximate time.	
4.p.m.	O. C. 8th Battery reports "A conflagration was seen about 279 deg. EAST possibly at HOUPLANES"

Otherwise normal.

S E Earnshaw

Captain R.F.A.(T)
Adjutant for
Commanding 1/3rd West Riding Brigade R.F.A.(T)

Recd 4.25 pm

Observation report AAA. I have examined an uncommon looking object immediately in rear of enemy's trench about 75 yards West of pt 883, the true reading from the 4th Battery Gun position @ H 31 a 3.3 is 135°, the object is dome shaped and glistens like steel, there is a nozzle shaped attachment approximately 6 inches in diameter AAA In my opinion this should be fired upon and I am remaining in trenches in case I am required for observation AAA.

From Lt St Paer F.O.O 4th W.R. Batty

3.45 pm

From N 9 C 0.5 Bearing 134°

Ordered to fire on this by H.Q. Div

4th How bde ordered to turn 10th W.R. Battery on to this 6 rounds allotted.

4.30 pm

[initials]

"C" Form (Duplicate). Army Form C. 2123.

MESSAGES AND SIGNALS. No. of Message

	Charges to Pay. £ s. d.	Office Stamp.
on pcr FAW Parker		FWR 30/5/15
Service Instructions.		

Handed in at FAW Office m. Received 10.20 pm.

TO 49 Div. (WR) R.A. (2)

Sender's Number	Day of Month	In reply to Number	AAA

Last	night	the	enemy	cutting
their	wire	etc	The	F
O.	O.	10th	Battery	reports
having	seen	a	V	shaped
hole	in	the	enemy's	parapet
at	the	extreme	left	of
section	S. A.	AAA	Infantry	state
this	gap	is	filled	with
blue	sandbags	AAA	It	would
be	possible	to	remove	the
sandbags	and	replace	with	field
gun	without	being	observed	away
to	background	being	dark	AAA

FROM PLACE & TIME: First (W.R.) F.A. Bde 10.15 pm

(24932). M.R.Co.,Ltd. Wt.W9668/1672. 50,000 Pads—1/15. Forms/C.2123.

"C" Form (Duplicate). Army Form C. 2123.

MESSAGES AND SIGNALS. No. of Message

Service Instructions. Parkin

Charges to Pay. £ s. d.

Office Stamp. FWK 30-5-15

Handed in at FAW Office 10.15 p.m. Received 10.20 p.m.

TO 49th (W.R.) Divisional Arty.

Sender's Number	Day of Month	In reply to Number	AAA
194	20th		

1st	Battery	F.O.O.	reports	that
infantry	in	section	3 P.	saw
timber	being	carried	into	small
cottage	about	200	yds	E.
of	Point	869	at	11 am.
today	AAA	The	bearing	taken
from	4	E.	shell	holes
made	during	bombardment of		1st
Battery	this	afternoon	is	169
degrees	magnetic	and	from	fuze
holes	of	shrapnel 170		magnetic
AAA	The	B.	C.	Estimates
the	line	of	H.	E
shells	to	be	midway	between
HAYEM	WOOD	and	DUBEM	wood
AAA	Reference	your	message	of

FROM

PLACE & TIME

(24932). M.R.Co.,Ltd. Wt.W9668/1672. 50,000 Pads—1/15. Forms/C.2123.

LXVI

1/3rd West Riding Brigade R.F.A.(T)

SITUATION REPORT NO. 28.

From 12 midnight 27/5/1915 to 12 midnight 28/5/1915.

Approximate time.	
3.3 0.p.m.	Enemy's Trench Mortar fired on in Section 6. Silenced but not knocked out.

[signature]

Major R.F.A.
Adjutant for
Commanding 1/3rd West Riding Brigade R.F.A.(T).

"A" Form. Army Form C. 2121.

MESSAGES AND SIGNALS. No. of Message 13

Prefix R Sh 6 Code 7 W 78 m. | Words | Charge | This message is on a/c of: LXVII Service | Recd. at 18 m.

Office of Origin and Service Instructions. Y. J. J. | Sent At m. To By | (Signature of "Franking Officer.") | Date From By

TO GOC R.A.

Sender's Number	Day of Month	In reply to Number	
G 779	twenty ninth		AAA

Following is copy of wire recd from 4th Corps. G 3885 29/5/15 G point 2 at present attached to you will move to join 2nd Army tonight AAA Instructions as to route and destination follow. from 4th Corps

From 49 Divn

Place

Time 6.5 pm

The above may be forwarded as now corrected. (Z) H. J. Nicholl

Censor. Signature of Addressor or person authorised to telegraph in his name

* This line should be erased if not required.

8350 S. B. Ltd. Wt. W4843/541—50,000. 9/14. Forms C2121/10.

(1390) Wt. W 9044-1194. 12/14. 40,000 Pads. S. B. Ltd.

"B" Form. Army Form C 2122

Recd 7.17pm

MESSAGES AND SIGNALS.

No. of Message ______

Prefix: Sm Code ______ m.	Received	Sent	Office Stamp.
Office of Origin and Service Instructions: LXVII / Words:	At 7.15pm. From How. By JC	At ______ m. To ______ By ______	JCS

TO — Major Lewes. Bde Major R.A. HQ W.R.D.

Sender's Number	Day of Month	In reply to Number	AAA

The 10th Battery have rung up the adjutant of this Brigade that German Aeroplane passed over South + South East between 6.45pm and 7pm

From: adjutant 4th (How) Bde RA

Place:

Time: 7.15pm

* This line should be erased if not required.

"C" Form (Original). Army Form C. 2123.

MESSAGES AND SIGNALS. No. of Message

Prefix Code Words	Received	Sent, or sent out	Office Stamp.
£ s. d. Charges to collect	From 17/55 By 1/30	At m.	
Service Instructions.		To	
		By	

Handed in at Office m. Received m.

TO H. Q. RA

*Sender's Number	Day of Month	In reply to Number	AAA
65	29	aaa	

Ref. your Orders to fire on point near 883 aaa 10th Battery fired 2 rounds in conjunction with F.O.O. 4th Bty the latter was unable to observe shots but O.C. 10th Bty was able to observe from tree nearby aaa

FROM

PLACE & TIME

*This line should be erased if not required.

(24932). M.R.Co.,Ltd. Wt.W9668/1672. 50,000 Pads—1/15. Forms/C.2123.

"C" Form (Original). Army Form C. 2123.

MESSAGES AND SIGNALS. No. of Message

Prefix ... Code ... Words ...	Received	Sent, or sent out	Office Stamp.
£ s. d. Charges to collect	From ... By ...	At ... m.	
Service Instructions.		To ... By ...	

Handed in at ... Office ... m. Received ... m.

TO

*Sender's Number	Day of Month	In reply to Number	AAA

The second shot was approximately on point but observation was difficult firing was hampered by hostile Aero plane

FROM PLACE & TIME: Adjutant 1st W R Bde

*This line should be erased if not required.

(24932). M.R.Co.,Ltd. Wt.W9668/1672. 50,000 Pads—1/15. Forms/C.2123.

LXVIII

"C" Form (Duplicate). Army Form C. 2123.

MESSAGES AND SIGNALS. No. of Message

LXIX

Charges to Pay. £ s. d.	Office Stamp.
	FLOX 28th

Service Instructions.

Handed in at FLOX Office m. Received 8.50a m.

TO 149 Bde (WR) Brigade Arty

Sender's Number	Day of Month	In reply to Number	AAA
176	28th	—	

Summary	report	aaa	The	first
battery	was	shelled	at	5.15 pm
yesterday	aaa	12	shell	were
fired	3	fell	on	the
battery	positions	and	9	close
around	the	farm	aaa	an
enemy	balloon	was	observed	S
W	of	FROMELLES	at	the
same	time			

FROM PLACE & TIME 1st (WR) FA Bde 8.45am

(24932). M.R.Co.,Ltd. Wt.W9668/1672. 50,000 Pads—1/15. Forms/C.2123.

LXIX

Headquarters RA.

FIRST WEST RIDING BRIGADE
Date 28.5.15
No. 217
R.F.A. (T.)

Report on the shelling of the 1st W.R. Battery by the Germans at 5.45pm 28th May 1915

I beg to report that this afternoon 12 German howitzer shell fell in and around the 1st Battery gun position and billet, 4 of these shell being within 10 yards of the Farm.

I am of the opinion that owing to the large amount of mounted traffic which passes down this road usually at the trot, this shelling took place this afternoon.

At about 3.30pm this afternoon two [illegible] motor cars drew up outside this farm and as there happened to be at this time an observation balloon in the neighbourhood of FROMELLES I am convinced that this was the cause of the shelling which took place later.

I respectfully beg that steps may be taken to prevent unnecessary mounted traffic passing down this road at high speed.

Bearings were taken from shell holes

(2).

which showed the hostile Battery to be situated somewhere on the line of squares N.3.b N.17.d..

The O.C. 1st Battery is of the opinion that this battery is situated in ~~the neighbourhood of~~ DUBEM WOOD as previously reported.

[signature] LIEUT. COLONEL
COMMDG. 1st WEST RIDING Bde. R.F.A. (T)

LXIX

(1390) Wt. W 9044-1494. 12/14. 40,000 Pads. S. B. Ltd.

"B" Form. Army Form C 2122

MESSAGES AND SIGNALS. No. of Message

Prefix B.G. Code m.

Office of Origin and Service Instructions. | Words. | Received At m. From By | Sent At m. To By | Office Stamp.

TO { Brigade Major RA 146

Sender's Number | Day of Month | In reply to Number | AAA

Suspicious machine have been removed aaa Heavy work going on between pt 883 & 884 aaa Between these points 7 new squares opening have been made covered with sheets aaa Wire appears to be cut in one place for a few yards by pt 883 aaa

Telephoned to Div H.Q. 9.25pm who told us to stand fast

From 1/8 West Yorks (1.6).

Place

Time

* This line should be erased if not required.

"A" Form. Army Form C. 2121.

MESSAGES AND SIGNALS.

P

No. of Message

Prefix	Code K1p m.	Words	Charge	This message is on a/c of:	Recd. at m.
Office of Origin and Service Instructions. PRIORITY 4 D I		Sent At m. To By		Service (Signature of "Franking Officer.")	Date From By

TO GOCRW

Sender's Number	Day of Month	In reply to Number	AAA
G 785	29th		

A	very	careful	watch	should
be	kept	tonight	on	the
point	in	the	enemy's	line
between	883	and	884	and
opposite	45	and	5P	where
you	suspect	the	wire	has
been	cut	and	there	have
loopholes	made	in	his	parapet
aaa	Lights	should	be	used
frequently	and	artillery	called	on
instantly	If	required	aaa	Special
attention	to	be	paid	to
masks	aaa	Your	machine	guns
should	be	arranged	to	bring
cross	fire	to	bear	on
the	suspected	place	and	make

From

Place

Time

The above may be forwarded as now corrected. (Z)

Censor. Signature of Addressor or person authorised to telegraph in his name

* This line should be erased if not required.

158 S. B. Ltd. Wt. W5673/619—50,000. 10/14. Forms C2121/10.

"A" Form. Army Form C. 2121.

MESSAGES AND SIGNALS.

No. of Message

Prefix Code m. | Words | Charge

Office of Origin and Service Instructions.

Sent

At m.

To

By

This message is on a/c of:

Service.

(Signature of "Franking Officer.")

Recd. at m.

Date 23.V.17

From

By

TO

Sender's Number	Day of Month	In reply to Number	AAA

aaa. The artillery is NOT to be called on merely to shoot at where the suspected places are but only in case of emergency

All units informed to be prepared.

11.15pm

From

Place

Time 10.40pm

The above may be forwarded as now corrected. (Z)

Censor. Signature of Addressor or person authorized to telegraph in his name

* This line should be erased if not required.

158 S. B. Ltd. Wt. W5673/619—50,000. 10/14. Forms C2121/10.

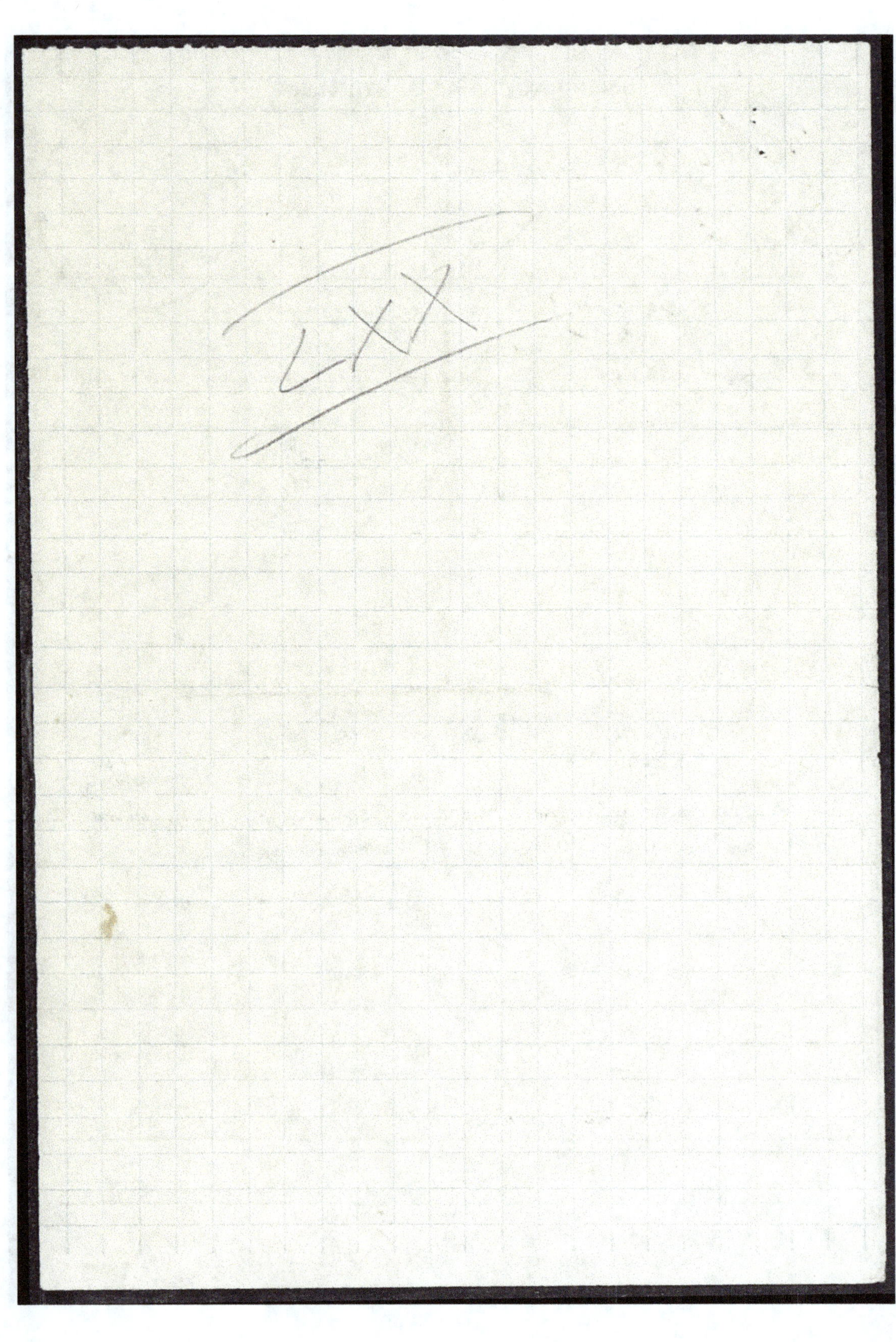
LXX

"C" Form (Duplicate). Army Form C. 2123.

MESSAGES AND SIGNALS. No. of Message

Sm — 7.10 a.m. — O.C.

Service Instructions.

Charges to Pay.			Office Stamp.
£	s.	d.	FWR.

Handed in at .... Office .... m. Received .... m.

TO C.R.A.

Sender's Number	Day of Month	In reply to Number	AAA
X 11	30	aaa	

Continuations		of	my	X 10
O.C.	10th Bty	reports	fire	in
front	of	2 S.	continuing	aaa
Its	outbreak	was	very	sudden
it	appeared	either	due	to
explosion	or	soaking	of	object
in	petrol			

FROM
PLACE & TIME Adjutant 4th Bde.

[illegible]

(24932). M.R.Co.,Ltd. Wt.W9668/1672. 50,000 Pads—1/15. Forms/C.2123.

"C" Form (Duplicate). Army Form C. 2123.

MESSAGES AND SIGNALS. No. of Message

	Charges to Pay. £ s. d.	Office Stamp.
Mr 7C.		[illegible]
Service Instructions.		

Handed in at ... Office ... m. Received ... m.

TO C R A

Sender's Number	Day of Month	In reply to Number	AAA
X 10.	30.	[illegible]	

O.C	10th Bty	reports	as	follows
aaa	[illegible]	observed	behind	wood
[illegible]	enemy's	lines	opposite	C R
and	3.S.	aaa	These	can
be	saw	above	wood	and
[illegible]	under-	growth	aaa	[illegible]
report	[illegible].	aaa		

FROM
PLACE & TIME Adjutant [illegible] W R Hor[illegible]

(24932). M.R.Co.,Ltd. Wt.W9668/1672. 50,000 Pads—1/15. Forms/C.2123.

LXXI

"C" Form (Duplicate). Army Form C. 2123.

MESSAGES AND SIGNALS. No. of Message

Sm. ... FAW

Service Instructions.

Charges to Pay. £ s. d.

Office Stamp. FWR 30 ...

Handed in at FAW Office m. Received m.

TO 49th WR Div Art

Sender's Number	Day of Month	In reply to Number	AAA
187	30th		

German observation Balloon now visible aaa My position is H24d3.3. aaa Compass bearing to Balloon 185 aaa Balloon very far distant aaa

FROM PLACE & TIME 1st WR FABde

(24932). M.R.Co.,Ltd. Wt.W9668/1672. 50,000 Pads—1/15. Forms/C.2123.

"C" Form (Duplicate). Army Form C. 2123.

MESSAGES AND SIGNALS. No. of Message

Em BJ 50

Jaw 4.45pm

Service Instructions.

Charges to Pay. £ s. d.

Office Stamp. FWR

Handed in at ... Office ... m. Received ... m.

TO 49th WR Divl Arty

Sender's Number	Day of Month	In reply to Number	AAA
192	30	aaa	

German observation balloon is again in position aaa F.O.O. 1st Battery at N4 A 27 and bearing from that point 117° 1st Battery is being shelled with Field Guns.

FROM PLACE & TIME: 1st WR FA Bde. 4.40pm

(24932). M.R.Co.,Ltd. Wt.W9668/1672. 50,000 Pads—1/15. Forms/C.2123.

"C" Form (Duplicate). Army Form C. 2123.

MESSAGES AND SIGNALS. No. of Message

Dm

7 Bn
76

Service Instructions.

Charges to Pay. £ s. d.

Office Stamp.

FWR

Handed in at Office m. Received m.

TO CRA

Sender's Number	Day of Month	In reply to Number	AAA
X17	30	aa	

10th Battery report that a Balloon has gone up from FROMELLES at 4 pm

FROM
PLACE & TIME 4th WR How Bde
4/5 pm

(24932). M.R.Co.,Ltd. Wt.W9668/1672. 50,000 Pads—1/15. Forms/C.2123.

"C" Form (Duplicate). Army Form C. 2123.

MESSAGES AND SIGNALS. No. of Message

Om Mr

A Bo

A G

Charges to Pay. £ s. d.

Office Stamp.

D WR

Service Instructions.

Handed in at Office m. Received m.

TO Brigade Major R.A.

Sender's Number	Day of Month	In reply to Number	AAA
A.BW 168	30	aaa	

Enemys observation balloon up this morning aaa Bearing from H33a 10.8 168° magnetic aaa bearing from H29c.1 163° magnetic

FROM PLACE & TIME: 2nd W R Bde R F A
12/noon

(24932). M.R.Co.,Ltd. Wt.W9668/1672. 50,000 Pads—1/15. Forms/C.2123.

LXXII

49th (W.R.) Divisional Artillery.

Progress Report from 12 Mid-night 28th to 12 Mid-night 29th May, 1915.

(a) The situation remains normal.

(b) Further Registration is recorded.

(c) The remaining Section of 11th W.R. Battery joined the Section that had already moved to its new position.

(d) O.C. 1st W.R. F.A. Bde. reports a new German empalment built about level of old parapet, seven large holes observed immediately on left of new empalment.

(e) O.C. 4th W.R. Battery reports a hostile balloon up at T 11 d bearing 163 deg: magnetic from House at H 31 a 2.2.

(f) O.C. 2nd W.R. Bde. reports a hostile field gun firing on Infantry H.Qrs., at N 3 c 6.1. Magnetic bearing of the strike of shell at N 3 c 6.1. wasv145 deg:.

A fuze was recovered and found to be at 2500 metres which located the battery in the vicinity of DUBEM.

O.C. Armoured Train engaged Battery with aeroplane at 4.30 p.m., position, M 18 b 5.5. 10 rounds were fired and two direct hits obtained. Observation by Wireless Machine.

(g) F.O.O. 2nd W.R. Bde. reports examined "an uncommon looking object immediately in rear of enemys trench about 75 yards West of Pt 883". The object was dome shaped and glistens like steel, there is nozzle shaped attachment about 6 inch in diameter.

O.C. 8th Battery reports a conflagration was seen about 279 deg: East, possibly at HOUPLANES.

Nill Casualty Reports are received from Units.

[signature]

Major R.A.,

30/5/15. Brigade Major R.A.49th (W.R.) Division.

SECRET.

Officer Commanding,

4th W.R. (How:) F.A. Bde.

The remaining Section 11th W.R. Battery will move tonight to join the section that has already moved to the new position.

Time of start 9 p.m.

L W Lewer

Major R.A.,

29/5/15. Brigade Major R.A.49th(W.R.)Division.

49th (W.R.) Divisional Artillery

Progress Report from 12 Mid-night 28th to 12 Mid-night 29th May, 1915.

=================================

(a) The situation remains normal.

(b) Further Registration is recorded.

(c) The remaining Section of 11th W.R Battery joined the Section that had already moved to its new position.

(d) O.C. 1st W.R. F.A. Bde. reports a new German empalment built about level of old parapet, seven large holes observed immediately on left of new empalment.

(e) O.C. 4th W.R. Battery reports a hostile balloon up at T 11 d bearing 163 deg magnetic from House at H 31 a 2.2.

(f) O.C. 2nd W.R. F.A. Bde. reports a hostile field gun firing on Infantry H.Qrs., at N 3 c 6.1. Magnetic bearing of the strike of shell at N 3 c 6.1. was 145 deg:.

A fuze was recovered and found to be at 2500 metres which located the battery in the vicinity of DUBEM.

O.C. Armoured Train engaged Battery with aeroplane at 4.30 p.m. position, M 18 b 5.5. 10 rounds were fired and two direct hits obtained. Observation by Wireless Machine.

(g) F.O.O. 2nd W.R. Bde. reports examined "an uncommon looking object immediately in rear of enemys trench about 75 yards West of Pt 883". The object was dome shaped and glistens like steel, there is a nozzle shaped attachment about 6 inch in diameter

O.C. 8th Battery reports A conflagration was seen about 279 deg: East, possibly at HOUPLANES.

Nil Casualty reports are received from Units.

[signature]
Major R.A.,
Brigade Major R.A.49th (W.R.)Division.

30/5/15.

49th (W.R.) DIVISION.

PROGRESS REPORT. Noon 28th May to Noon 29th May.

Work. Right Section. (Trenches 1B and 2).

Work on communication Trench in 1S. Parapets strengthened, parados, snipers loopholes and ammunition recesses built.

Centre Section. (Trenches 3 and 4).

Dug-outs for support Company in Trench 3.progressing. Communication Trench in 3 improved. Wire repaired. Washing place made in 4. Communication trenches, parados, and latrines improved.

Left Section. (Trenches 5 and 6).

Work on new trench improved. Work on new breastwork at 6R, and ~~chord~~ in 5 continued.

Operations. 3 p.m. 28/5/15.

11th Battery fired on a trench mortar 50 yards West of BOIS GRENIER - BRIDOUX Road and 100 yards in rear of hostile front trench.

Enemy shelled advanced trench in 6 Section, yesterday afternoon. Little damage.

Information. At 2 a.m. green red andwhite lights were seen in succession near 826 at intervals of 5 minutes.

Special Report. A machine of bright metal, dome shaped, with a bell mouth was reported at 883 at about 12.30 p.m. today. Explosions were heard near this point last night. West Riding Howitzer Brigade shelled this point today.

The machine is reported to be no longer visible but the enemy has made an opening about 3 to 4 fooot square in the parapet between 883 and 884. This is confirmed By Colonel Wood, Commanding 5th West Yorks.

The German wire is reported to be cut near 883.

An epaulment at N.8.c.4.4 was reported 4 ft. above end of old parapet with 7 large loopholes measuring about 3 feet by 2.

[signature] Captain.

29/5/15. General Staff. 49th (W.R.) Division.

8th Division Artillery Report
from 6 a.m. 29th May, to 6 a.m. 30th May, 1915.

---

1. (a) 6.30 p.m. Enemy L.V.G. biplane approached from the SOUTH-EAST, was engaged and retired to the SOUTH.
6.45 p.m. Apparently same machine approached again from the SOUTH was re-engaged and retired to the SOUTH.

Ammunition expended - 70 rounds.

(b) 3.30 p.m. - 5 p.m. RUE TILLELOY near PICANTIN, N 13 a central, and N 7 b shelled by 4.2 and 5.9 howitzers.
(M 22 d 1.4)
4 p.m. Enemy obtained a direct hit on the "MIN"/observation station with a field gun.

5.15 p.m. "E" lines shelled with shrapnel by field howitzers.

7.30 p.m. Enemey shelled RUE BACQUEROT in neighbourhood of the "MIN" (M 22 d 1.4) as G.S. wagons full of troops were proceeding along it.

Hostile field guns active on "C" lines throughout the day.
Sniping reported general.
Indications of work reported as going on about 50 yards right of point 321. Planks observed and sounds of pumping heard.

German sausage balloon reported up to the SOUTH.
Working parties at Pts. 324 and 323 all the afternoon.
Field works located round Pt. 160.
A machine gun emplacement with loopholes located between Pt.310 and TRIVELET road.

C. S. Skamach Capt for Major. R.A.

11 a.m. Brigade Major 8th Division Artillery.

Appendix ....

Casualties.

	Killed.	Wounded.	Missing.	
Officers.	1*	2ø	nil.	* Capt: & Adjt: T. A. Abbott. ø Lieut: S. Blackburn. ø 2nd Lieut: S. B. Howarth.
Other Ranks.	nil	9*	nil.	* one since died of Wounds.

Ammunition Expended.

	Number of Rounds		Rounds per Gun.	
15 pdr B.L.C.	8294.		230·38	
5 in: Howitzer.	1535. Lyddite		—	
4·7 in Gun.	257. Lyddite		201 Shrapnel	197 Common Pointed.
9·2 in Gun	39. Lyddite			

Names forwarded for Gallant Conduct.

No. 1221 Bdr. Elliot. J. for mending telephone wires on 9-5-1[illegible] ...[illegible]

No. 1059 Gnr: Mortimer. G. H. -do- -do-

G.O.C.R.A.

The 49th Division having been transferred to the Indian Corps, the following returns have been called for in lieu of those which hitherto have been rendered to Divisional Headquarters.

(a) Telegraphic "Situation Report" from Infantry Brigades to reach Divisional Headquarters by 5.15 a.m. and 5.15 p.m.

(b) A Tactical Progress Report to cover 24 hours ending 6 p.m. of previous evening, compiled under the following headings :-

To units [illegible]

I. Operations. (a) Action by our own troops.
(b) Action by enemy troops.
II. Information gained.
III. Work done in the trenches.

These reports, compiled by Infantry Brigades, C.R.A., and C.R.E., are to reach Divisional Headquarters in manuscript or typewritten by 10 a.m. daily without fail.
(Samples of reports are attached for guidance which must be returned when noted).

(c) Trench Return.

Brigades finding trench or supporting line garrisons will submit to Divisional Headquarters :-

(1) On the 10th, 20th, and 30th of each month and also on days during which a Brigade relief is in progress, a return on the form attached.

(11) A report to reach Divisional Headquarters at 7 a.m. daily in the following telegraphic form :-

5 Section.	Trenches	500	4/Y.& L.
	In lettered Posts.	150	4/Y.& L.
	For counter-attack.	150	4/Y.& L.
		100	5/Y.& L.
	In numbered Posts.	100	5/Y.& L.
	In Brigade Reserve	600	5/Y.& L.

(or "No Change" asthe case may be).

NOTE. Minor changes of strength need not be reported and the words "NO CHANGE" will be used if there has been no change since last telegraphic report.

The first report on the form attached is to be sent in as soon as possible today. The next return on this form will be due at 7 a.m. on the 10th June.

H. I. Nicholl Captain

31/5/15. General Staff. 49th (W.R.) Division.

Officer Commanding,

As the 49th (W.R.) Divisional Artillery has been transferred to the Indian Corps, the following returns have been called for in lieu of those which hitherto have been rendered to Divisional Artillery Headquarters.

A TACTICAL PROGRESS REPORT, to cover 24 hours ending 6 p.m. ~~of previous evening,~~ compiled under the following headings :-

I. Operations. (a) Action by our own troops.
(b) Action by enemy troops.

II. Information gained.

III. Work done in the trenches.

The above report is required daily by this office and must reach this office not later than 8 p.m. each evening.

The first report is required by 8 p.m. today, May 31st.

[signature]

Major R.A.,
Brigade Major R.A.49th (W.R.) Division.

31/5/15.

Officer Commanding,

As the 49th (W.R.) Divisional Artillery has been transferred to the Indian Corps, the following returns have been called for in lieu of those which hitherto have been rendered to Divisional Artillery Headquarters.

A TACTICAL PROGRESS REPORT, to cover 24 hours ending 6 p.m. of previous evening, compiled under the following headings :-

I. Operations. (a) Action by our own troops.
(b) Action by enemy troops.

II. Information gained.

III. Work done in the trenches.

The above report is required daily by this office and must reach this office not later than 8 p.m. each evening.

The first report is required by 8 p.m. today, May 31st.

Major R.A.,
31/5/15. Brigade Major R.A.49th (W.R.) Division.

On His Majesty's Service.

49th Division

121/5930

Head Quarters R.A. 49th Division

Vol III 1 — 30.6.15.

A2

A/6.

Instructions regarding War Diaries and Intelligence Summaries are contained in F. S. Regs., Part II. and the Staff Manual respectively. Title pages will be prepared in manuscript.

WAR DIARY
or
~~INTELLIGENCE~~ ~~SUMMARY.~~
(Erase heading not required.)

Army Form C. 2118.

I

Place	Date	Hour	Summary of Events and Information	Remarks and references to Appendices
FORT ROMPU	JUNE			
	1		Summary report.	
			1/	
			a/ Machine gun emplacement seen about N.10 b 8.2. This emplacement is a round hole filled with a plate 12 inches across. ---.	
			b/ Trenches about 883 contain several large loop holes closed by canvas curtains	I
			c/ Reference to location of gun cupola --.	
			d/ Rue PETILLON shelled ---	
			e/ Reference to new earth works seen at N 6 C 1.1 ---	
			f/ Reference to amount of traffic seen on road leading to Trenches ----	
			2/ Tactical Progress report.	II
			4th Howitzer Brigade Register.	

1577 Wt. W10791/1773 500,000 1/15 D. D. & L. A.D.S.S./Forms/C. 2118.

Instructions regarding War Diaries and Intelligence Summaries are contained in F. S. Regs., Part II. and the Staff Manual respectively. Title pages will be prepared in manuscript.

WAR DIARY
or
~~INTELLIGENCE SUMMARY.~~
(Erase heading not required.)

Army Form C. 2118.

II

Hour, Date, Place	Summary of Events and Information	Remarks and references to Appendices
Fort Rompu.	Summary report.	
June 2nd 1915 10AM	(a) Fifth WEST RIDING Battery shelled at 10AM.	III
	(b) 6 inch armoured train engaged battery located 50 yards south of L in LE HAYEM	
12-58PM.	(c) Hostile Battery fired at Sec 6. 12,58 PM	
2-30PM.	(d) Cupola registered at 2-30PM.	
4-56PM.	(e) FLEUXBAIX Shelled.	
	(f) BOIS GRENIER Shelled.	
	~~Registration continued.~~	IV
	Tactical Progress Report.	

(9 29 6) W4141—463 100,000 9/14 H W V Forms/C. 2118/10

Instructions regarding War Diaries and Intelligence Summaries are contained in F. S. Regs., Part II. and the Staff Manual respectively. Title pages will be prepared in manuscript.

WAR DIARY
or
~~INTELLIGENCE~~ SUMMARY.
(Erase heading not required.)

Army Form C. 2118.

3

Place	Date June	Hour	Summary of Events and Information	Remarks and references to Appendices
Fort Rompu.	3.		Summary Report:—	V
		8-45 AM	Hostile aeroplane passed over 3rd W. R. F. A. Bde time 8-45 am.	
		9-30 AM.	Hostile Aeroplane over 3rd & 4th Batteries at 9-30 AM.	
		2-20pm.	Two Pigeons flew from BOIS GRENIER towards German Lines	
		3-pm.	Three Pigeons flew from German Lines to BOIS GRENIER.	
		4pm.	11th Battery registered cupolas near Pt. 883.	
		4-20pm.	Hostile Balloon up.	
		4-30pm	RUE DES. LOMBARDS. & 2nd Battery billet shelled.	
		—	SAXON's reported to be in trenches opposite Sect 5.	
		6-30pm	Infantry complaint re 'sniping' — — —, orders given re 'sniping,'— result —	VI
			Tactical Progress report.	VII

1577 Wt. W10791/1773 500,000 1/15 D. D. & L. A.D.S.S./Forms/C. 2118.

Instructions regarding War Diaries and Intelligence Summaries are contained in F. S. Regs., Part II. and the Staff Manual respectively. Title pages will be prepared in manuscript.

WAR DIARY
or
~~INTELLIGENCE SUMMARY.~~

(Erase heading not required.)

Army Form C. 2118.

(4)

Place	Date	Hour	Summary of Events and Information	Remarks and references to Appendices
	June			
FORT Rompu	4.		Summary Report.	VIII
			a/ Trench Mortar at I.S. fired 3 rounds at Cupola near 883 — — — — —	
		11-15AM	b/ Hostile trench mortar's active — — — — —	
		12-40 - 1-45PM	c/ Farm at H33d8.5. set on fire by hostile field battery, one man killed — —	
		4-30PM	d/ Hostile Battery commenced firing on Section 6	
			e/ First Battery fired 12 rounds at FERME DELANGRE. which contained snipers — — — — —	
		6pm.	f/ Hostile aeroplane over Sections 3. 4 & 5., 1st 7. a Bty & How Bty — — —	
		7-26PM	4" gun registered on House in N16 4.6. — — —	IX
			Batteries registered — —	
			Tactical Progress Report — —	X

Army Form C. 2118.

Instructions regarding War Diaries and Intelligence Summaries are contained in F. S. Regs., Part II. and the Staff Manual respectively. Title pages will be prepared in manuscript.

WAR DIARY
or
~~INTELLIGENCE~~ ~~SUMMARY.~~

(*Erase heading not required.*)

5

Place	Date June	Hour	Summary of Events and Information	Remarks and references to Appendices
FORT ROMPU	5,	—	a Hostile aeroplane over Batteries. — —	XI
		8-30AM 9-30AM	b Hostile Field Battery shelled N 3b 2-3.	
		11AM.	c Pair Iron doors reported in German trenches — — —	
		10-30 to 1-20PM	d Captive Balloon up.	
			e Earthworks reported.	
			F Aeroplane seen over 10th Battery, marked with rings on one wing only.	
			Registration of 4" How. Batteries.	
			Tactical Progress report.	XII
				[initials]

Instructions regarding War Diaries and Intelligence Summaries are contained in F. S. Regs., Part II. and the Staff Manual respectively. Title pages will be prepared in manuscript.

WAR DIARY
or
INTELLIGENCE SUMMARY.
(Erase heading not required.)

Army Form C. 2118.

6

Place	Date	Hour	Summary of Events and Information	Remarks and references to Appendices
FORT Rompo	June 6.		Summary report	XIII
		2-55pm	a/ Report received from aeronautics re shelling of 1st + 2nd Line of trenches of MEERUT. DIVISION.	
			Orders issued	
			b/ Iron doors again observed. 70 yards N of Pt 960.	
			Tactical Progress Report.	XIV

KWR

Army Form C. 2118.

Instructions regarding War Diaries and Intelligence Summaries are contained in F. S. Regs., Part II. and the Staff Manual respectively. Title pages will be prepared in manuscript.

WAR DIARY
or
INTELLIGENCE SUMMARY.

(Erase heading not required.)

Place	Date	Hour	Summary of Events and Information	Remarks and references to Appendices
Fort Rompu	June 7.		Summary Report	
		3pm	(a) Infantry & horsemen observed on road ENGLOS to ———	XV
		3-30pm	(b) Magnetic bearing etc report from M Bty	
		2-20 to 4pm	c) Captive balloon up in direction of DUBEM. etc	
			Tactical Progress report.	XVI

1577 Wt. W10791/1773 500,000 1/15 D. D. & L. A.D.S.S./Forms/C. 2118.

Instructions regarding War Diaries and Intelligence Summaries are contained in F. S. Regs., Part II. and the Staff Manual respectively. Title pages will be prepared in manuscript.

WAR DIARY
or
INTELLIGENCE SUMMARY.
(Erase heading not required.)

Army Form C. 2118.

(8)

Place	Date	Hour	Summary of Events and Information	Remarks and references to Appendices
FORT ROMPU.	June 8		Summary report.	
			1	
			(a) 4th W.R. Battery continued registration	
		10.15AM	(b) Hostile aeroplane over 3rd Battery.	
			(c) Three small gaps in parapet, – VIDE Progress Report –	
		5-10pm	(d) Hostile aeroplane over Section 3. 4. & 5 – " " –	XVII
			2 Work in progress round FERME DE MOUQUET.	
			3 Fire in Enemys Lines. –	
			4 Tactical progress report – –	XVIII

1577 Wt. W10791/1773 500,000 1/15 D. D. & L. A.D.S.S./Forms/C. 2118.

Instructions regarding War Diaries and Intelligence Summaries are contained in F. S. Regs., Part II. and the Staff Manual respectively. Title pages will be prepared in manuscript.

WAR DIARY
or
INTELLIGENCE SUMMARY.
(Erase heading not required.)

Army Form C. 2118.

(9)

Place	Date	Hour	Summary of Events and Information	Remarks and references to Appendices
FORT ROMPU.	June			
	9		Summary Report.	
		8-35AM	a. Working parties seen 200 yards EAST of pt 887 ------	XVIII
		[illegible]	b. Hostile trench motor action opposite pts 879-883 & 884.	
		3-35pm	c. FLEUXBAIX shelled.	
		3-45pm to 4-15	d. Armoured train fired on LE MAISNIL ---	
		3-45pm	e. Hostile shell around farm N4A 2½-4	
			e. House at point 904 thought to be an observing station.	
			Tactical Progress Report ---	XIX

Army Form C. 2118.

(10)

Instructions regarding War Diaries and Intelligence Summaries are contained in F. S. Regs., Part II. and the Staff Manual respectively. Title pages will be prepared in manuscript.

WAR DIARY
or
INTELLIGENCE SUMMARY.
(Erase heading not required.)

Place	Date	Hour	Summary of Events and Information	Remarks and references to Appendices
Fort Rompu	10		Summary Report.	
			1	XX
	9.	PM 10-20	a) 10 How. Battery fired 50 yards west of 883 (3 rds) - - - - - - - -	
		~~6pm~~	b) RUE DES LOMBARDES, shelled at (6 pm).	
		2-PM & 3PM	c) Trenches I.S. shelled	
		4 pm	d) Trenches in vicinity of LA BOUTILLERIE shelled	
			e) Work reported on parapet at 976, also party observed - - - -	
			f) Digging between 966 & 969 - - - -	
			g.) Re Cylindrical object on parapet - - - -	
			h) Re Hostile battery firing at mid. S. - - - - - also position	
		7PM	i) Further report gives ~~the~~ position located by flashes. - -	
			2	
			Tactical Progress Report.	XXI

1577 Wt. W10791/1773 500,000 1/15 D. D. & L. A.D.S.S./Forms/C. 2118.

Instructions regarding War Diaries and Intelligence Summaries are contained in F. S. Regs., Part II. and the Staff Manual respectively. Title pages will be prepared in manuscript.

WAR DIARY
or
INTELLIGENCE SUMMARY.
(Erase heading not required.)

Army Form C. 2118.

Place	Date June	Hour	Summary of Events and Information	Remarks and references to Appendices
Fort Rompu	11.		Summary Report	
			1	
		2 pm	(a) S. W. FLEURBAIX shelled.	
			(b)	
		4.20pm	Hostile battery reported active located as near LES POTIERIES — Armoured train opened fire on it.	XXII
			(c)	
		4.55pm	Hostile battery located 150 yds NORTH of Pt 756	
			10 Battery moves to 8th Div on 9th midnight.	
			Initial Progress report.	XXIII

RWR

Instructions regarding War Diaries and Intelligence Summaries are contained in F. S. Regs., Part II. and the Staff Manual respectively. Title pages will be prepared in manuscript.

WAR DIARY
or
INTELLIGENCE SUMMARY.
(Erase heading not required.)

Army Form C. 2118.

(12)

Place	Date	Hour	Summary of Events and Information	Remarks and references to Appendices
Fort Rompu	June 12.		Summary report	
		11.15AM	a) Hostile battery fires 6 shells to left of 2nd Battery. ---	XXIV
		12.10PM	b) Observation balloon up.	
		5.6pm	(c) Hostile aeroplane seen.	
		5.50pm	d) Hostile battery shelled Hq 4th Batt K.O.Y.L.I	
			(e) Digging at 2nd line trench 100 yards W of 969.	
			F) Work being done at 966 & 967.	
			Progress Report	XXV

Instructions regarding War Diaries and Intelligence Summaries are contained in F. S. Regs., Part II. and the Staff Manual respectively. Title pages will be prepared in manuscript.

WAR DIARY
or
INTELLIGENCE SUMMARY.
(Erase heading not required.)

Army Form C. 2118.

13

Place	Date June	Hour	Summary of Events and Information	Remarks and references to Appendices
Fort Rompu.	13.	11 AM & 2 pm.	a – Hostile aeroplane over H 27 d and H 28 a	
		2-5pm	b – Hostile battery opened fire on H 20 d 3.0. 1st W. R.F.A. Bde Wagon Lines. fire directed by plane. 3 men killed and approx 3 injured. Several horses injured & 3 killed.	XXVI
			d – German working party opposite 3 Q.	
			e – Tactical progress report.	XXVII

1577 Wt. W10791/1773 500,000 1/15 D. D. & L. A.D.S.S./Forms/C. 2118.

Army Form C. 2118.

WAR DIARY
or
INTELLIGENCE SUMMARY.
(Erase heading not required.)

Instructions regarding War Diaries and Intelligence Summaries are contained in F. S. Regs., Part II. and the Staff Manual respectively. Title pages will be prepared in manuscript.

14.

Place	Date	Hour	Summary of Events and Information	Remarks and references to Appendices
FORT ROMPO	June 14th		Summary Report.	
		11AM	a/ Hostile battery again shelled old wagon lines of 1st W R Bty	XXVIII
		1-30PM	b/ Fromelles battery shelled BOIS GRENIER	
		1-10PM	c/ 5P + 5Q shelled.	
			a/ W R R G A. fired on LES POTERIES battery (1-15PM)	
		2-8PM	d/ " " " " " FROMELLES " "	
			e/ Hostile battery near LES BAS CHAMPS FARM	
			a/ ENEMY still busy with second line trenches	XXIX
			c/ Tactical Progress Report	

[initials]

1577 Wt. W10791/1773 500,000 1/15 D. D. & L. A.D.S.S./Forms/C. 2118.

Instructions regarding War Diaries and Intelligence Summaries are contained in F. S. Regs., Part II. and the Staff Manual respectively. Title pages will be prepared in manuscript.

WAR DIARY
or
INTELLIGENCE SUMMARY.
(Erase heading not required.)

Army Form C. 2118.

15

Place	Date	Hour	Summary of Events and Information	Remarks and references to Appendices
Fort Rompu	June 15.	2-30AM	1 Trench mortar fired ---	
		11-20AM	2 W. R. R.F.A. fired 12 rounds at Hostile battery --	XXX
		10-12.20 pm	3 Hostile Battery bombarded 119th Battery, & old wagon lines 1st Brig	
			4 Hostile Batteries located during night of 14th-15th from flashes.	
			5 2nd W. R Battery reports the running forward of hostile guns, seen	
			6 Report from 1st W. R. Bde re "rings of smoke & brushwood"	
			7 Re parapet at bend of stream.	
			8 Observation post in tree 300 yards N of BRIJEAUX.	
			9 Observation balloons.	XXXI
			Tactical Progress Report.	

1577 Wt. W10791/1773 500,000 1/15 D. D. & L. A.D.S.S./Forms/C. 2118.

LWB

Instructions regarding War Diaries and Intelligence Summaries are contained in F. S. Regs., Part II. and the Staff Manual respectively. Title pages will be prepared in manuscript.

WAR DIARY
or
INTELLIGENCE SUMMARY.
(Erase heading not required.)

Army Form C. 2118.

16

Place	Date	Hour	Summary of Events and Information	Remarks and references to Appendices
Fort Rompo	June 16.	7-30AM	a Hostile plane over 7th Battery	XXXII
		10.AM	b Re. Observing by German Plane	
		2-30pm	c Enemy shells our trench mortars.	
			d Re Train at FROMELLES.	
			e Re troops along road at O 11 d 5-5.	
			f Our mortars fire on suspicious wire.	
		3PM	g Balloon seen.	
			Tactical Progress Report.	XXXIII

([illegible])

1577 Wt. W10791/1773 500,000 1/15 D. D. & L. A.D.S.S./Forms/C. 2118.

Instructions regarding War Diaries and Intelligence Summaries are contained in F. S. Regs., Part II. and the Staff Manual respectively. Title pages will be prepared in manuscript.

WAR DIARY
or
INTELLIGENCE SUMMARY.
(Erase heading not required.)

Army Form C. 2118.

(17)

Place	Date	Hour	Summary of Events and Information	Remarks and references to Appendices
Fort Rompu	June 17			
		7-40 AM to 8. AM.	(a) Hostile aeroplane over 1st W R Brig Hq.	XXXIV
		4. PM.	b Enemy shelled. Rue Petillon	
			e Battery at Fromelles, probable location	
			F Re observed horsemen & motor car.	
		5-35 pm	e Battery in direction of Feterie started shelling	
			F 11th Battery registered	
			1 Working parties observed	
			F Traffic observed on road running through O 11d. 5-6.	
			g Re building of Flank Parapet	XXXV
			(H) 3rd W R A C moved to new lines.	
			(I) Tactical Progress Report	XXXVI

1577 Wt. W10791/1773 500,000 1/15 D. D. & L. A.D.S.S./Forms/C. 2118.

RWB

Instructions regarding War Diaries and Intelligence Summaries are contained in F. S. Regs., Part II. and the Staff Manual respectively. Title pages will be prepared in manuscript.

WAR DIARY

or

~~INTELLIGENCE SUMMARY.~~

(Erase heading not required.)

Army Form C. 2118.

(18)

Place	Date	Hour	Summary of Events and Information	Remarks and references to Appendices
FORT ROMPU	June 18.		Summary Report	
		10.50AM	(a) Observation balloon up.	XXXVII
			(b) Hostile heavy battery firing on area near LAVENTIE.	
			(c) Hostile Field Battery firing from near pt 887.	
		11AM	(d) Hostile battery shelled H 31 c 8.8.	
			(e) Hostile aeroplane over FLEURBAIX.	
			(f) Moves of Brigade A.C. ----	XXXVIII
			(g) Tactical Progress report.	XXXIX

Instructions regarding War Diaries and Intelligence Summaries are contained in F. S. Regs., Part II. and the Staff Manual respectively. Title pages will be prepared in manuscript.

WAR DIARY

or

~~INTELLIGENCE SUMMARY.~~

(Erase heading not required.)

Army Form C. 2118.

19.

Place	Date	Hour	Summary of Events and Information	Remarks and references to Appendices
Fort Rompu	June 19		Summary Report	XL
		11.45 AM	a Hostile aircraft very active this morning.	
			b Battery (hostile) located.	
			c Traffic observed during the day on road O 11 d 5.5.	
			d Captive balloon up.	
			e Wire entanglements strengthened	
			f Re Parapet at 32	
			g. Tactical Progress Report.	XLI

1577 Wt. W10791/1773 500,000 1/15 D. D. & L. A.D.S.S./Forms/C. 2118.

Instructions regarding War Diaries and Intelligence Summaries are contained in F. S. Regs., Part II. and the Staff Manual respectively. Title pages will be prepared in manuscript.

WAR DIARY

or

~~INTELLIGENCE SUMMARY.~~

(Erase heading not required.)

Army Form C. 2118.

(20)

Place	Date	Hour	Summary of Events and Information	Remarks and references to Appendices
FORT Rompu	June 20th	9-20 AM	a RGA firing on N 23. a. 10. 3	
			b Ten 77 mm shells fell about cross roads H 31. c. 8. 1.	XLII
			c Captive balloons up most of day.	
		2-55 pm	d FLEURBAIX shelled	
		4-30 pm	e 2nd W R Battery billets shelled at 4-30. Also near H Q 1st Bn.	
			F German seen on roof of House at Pr 975.	
			g Look out man at H 29 c. 8. 7.	
			H. Tactical Progress Report.	XLIII

1577 Wt. W10791/1773 500,000 1/15 D. D. & L. A.D.S.S./Forms/C. 2118.

Army Form C. 2118.

Instructions regarding War Diaries and Intelligence Summaries are contained in F. S. Regs., Part II. and the Staff Manual respectively. Title pages will be prepared in manuscript.

WAR DIARY

or

~~INTELLIGENCE SUMMARY.~~

(Erase heading not required.)

(21)

Place	Date	Hour	Summary of Events and Information	Remarks and references to Appendices
Fort Rompu	June 21		Summary Report	
		9 A.M.	a) 7 or 77 mm shell fell at N8c 2.2.	
			b) Trench mortar fired.	
		11 AM & 2 PM	c) Hostile battery located near N 16 b 5.2 shells 1st W.R.F.A. Bde HQ & farm. 1st W. R Battery [illegible] & [illegible] fire ceased	XLIV
		11-20 AM	d) FLEURBAIX shelled.	
			e) Captive balloon up near Fournes.	
			f) Working parties seen	
			g) Large conflagration seen east night over [illegible].	
		5-50 pm to 6 pm	h) Hostile plane seen with markings (sketch VIDE APPENDICES).	
			Progress Report	XLV

Instructions regarding War Diaries and Intelligence Summaries are contained in F. S. Regs., Part II. and the Staff Manual respectively. Title pages will be prepared in manuscript.

WAR DIARY

or

~~INTELLIGENCE SUMMARY.~~

(Erase heading not required.)

Army Form C. 2118.

22

Place	Date	Hour	Summary of Events and Information	Remarks and references to Appendices
Fort Rompu	June 22			
	21	8PM 21st	a 4th W. R. Battery fired at German working party	
		9-15	b Enemy's 5.9" Howitzers fired on LA CROYX LESCORNEX and anti aircraft gun.	LXVI
		9-50	c Captive balloon up.	
		10-30.	d Hostile aircraft very active.	
			e Germans cut grass between trenches.	
			(E) Two small trenches observed	
			(F) Isolated digging observed.	
			Progress Report.	
			Armoured Train returned to this Div. at 11-15 pm	LXVII
			10th Battery " " at [illegible]	

Instructions regarding War Diaries and Intelligence Summaries are contained in F. S. Regs., Part II. and the Staff Manual respectively. Title pages will be prepared in manuscript.

WAR DIARY

or

~~INTELLIGENCE SUMMARY.~~

(Erase heading not required.)

Army Form C. 2118.

23.

Place	Date	Hour	Summary of Events and Information	Remarks and references to Appendices
Fort Rompu	June 23rd		a) Trench mortar at junction 2 p. & 2 q. fired at 7-15 pm.	LXVIII
			b) 4th W.R. Battery fired 3 rounds at 7 pm.	
			c) Hostile " " fired 5 rounds in vicinity of 1st & 2nd W R batteries at 6-25 pm.	
			d) Hostile Parapet raised.	
			e) Reference to fires — — —	
			f) Swing board visible.	
			g) Movement of men round the field & house near 934.	
			h) Men seen going from 0.4. d.9.4.	
			i) Searchlight seen —	
			j) Men & horses observed in vicinity of farm on LE MAISNIL FROMELLES ROAD. Near LA HAUTE LOGE	

Progress Report.

Army Form C. 2118.

Instructions regarding War Diaries and Intelligence Summaries are contained in F. S. Regs., Part II. and the Staff Manual respectively. Title pages will be prepared in manuscript.

WAR DIARY

or

~~INTELLIGENCE SUMMARY~~.

(Erase heading not required.)

24

Place	Date	Hour	Summary of Events and Information	Remarks and references to Appendices
Fort Rempr.	June 24th		Nil —	~~24~~ ~~7418~~
			Report. —	L
				[illegible]

1577 Wt. W10791/1773 500,000 1/15 D. D. & L. A.D.S.S./Forms/C. 2118.

Instructions regarding War Diaries and Intelligence Summaries are contained in F. S. Regs., Part II. and the Staff Manual respectively. Title pages will be prepared in manuscript.

WAR DIARY

or

~~INTELLIGENCE SUMMARY.~~

(Erase heading not required.)

Army Form C. 2118.

25

Place	Date	Hour	Summary of Events and Information	Remarks and references to Appendices
Fort Rompu.	June 26.		Summary. Report.	LI
			NIL.-	
			Progress. Report. NIL.	LII

1577 Wt. W10791/1773 500,000 1/15 D. D. & L. A.D.S.S./Forms/C. 2118.

Army Form C. 2118.

WAR DIARY

or

~~INTELLIGENCE SUMMARY~~.

(Erase heading not required.)

Instructions regarding War Diaries and Intelligence Summaries are contained in F. S. Regs., Part II. and the Staff Manual respectively. Title pages will be prepared in manuscript.

(26)

Place	Date June	Hour	Summary of Events and Information	Remarks and references to Appendices
Fort Rompu	26.			
		A.M. 10.45	a 3 Hostile shells fell near Top of Communication trench 2.	LIII
			b Five Hostile Captive balloons up.	
		P.M. 5-10	c Hostile How. Battery in 27th Div area shell FLEURBAIX - ARMENTIERS Rd	
			(d) Re pennant seen at pt 969.	
			(e) Progress Report.	
			Re move of Artillery. (2nd Brigade + 3rd Brigade.) March Table	LIV LV

1577 Wt. W10791/1773 500,000 1/15 D. D. & L. A.D.S.S./Forms/C. 2118.

Instructions regarding War Diaries and Intelligence Summaries are contained in F. S. Regs., Part II. and the Staff Manual respectively. Title pages will be prepared in manuscript.

WAR DIARY
or
~~INTELLIGENCE SUMMARY.~~
(Erase heading not required.)

Army Form C. 2118.

27

Place	Date	Hour	Summary of Events and Information	Remarks and references to Appendices
FORT ROMPU	June			
	27. & 28.			
		11AM.	Hostile batteries from near 784 & 837 shelled LA BOUTILLERIE & N36-4-2.	LXI
			1st W.R. Battery fired 12 rounds at 837.	
			11th How Battery fired at 784.	
		1-pm.	H.Q. Battalion at N 3.c.8-2 burnt out by hostile shell.	
			Progress Report. R.A. Div Ord. 8. & table of moves.	LXII

1577 Wt. W10791/1773 500,000 1/15 D. D. & L. A.D.S.S./Forms/C. 2118.

Army Form C. 2118.

Instructions regarding War Diaries and Intelligence Summaries are contained in F. S. Regs., Part II. and the Staff Manual respectively. Title pages will be prepared in manuscript.

WAR DIARY

or

~~INTELLIGENCE SUMMARY.~~

(Erase heading not required.)

Place	Date	Hour	Summary of Events and Information	Remarks and references to Appendices
PROVEN.	June 29. & 30.		Nil. 49th Div. R.A. Resting Ammunition Expended. & Casualties. Final. for Month of June	

1577 Wt. W10791/1773 500,000 1/15 D. D. & L. A.D.S.S./Forms/C. 2118.

Appendices
to
War Diary
for
Month of June

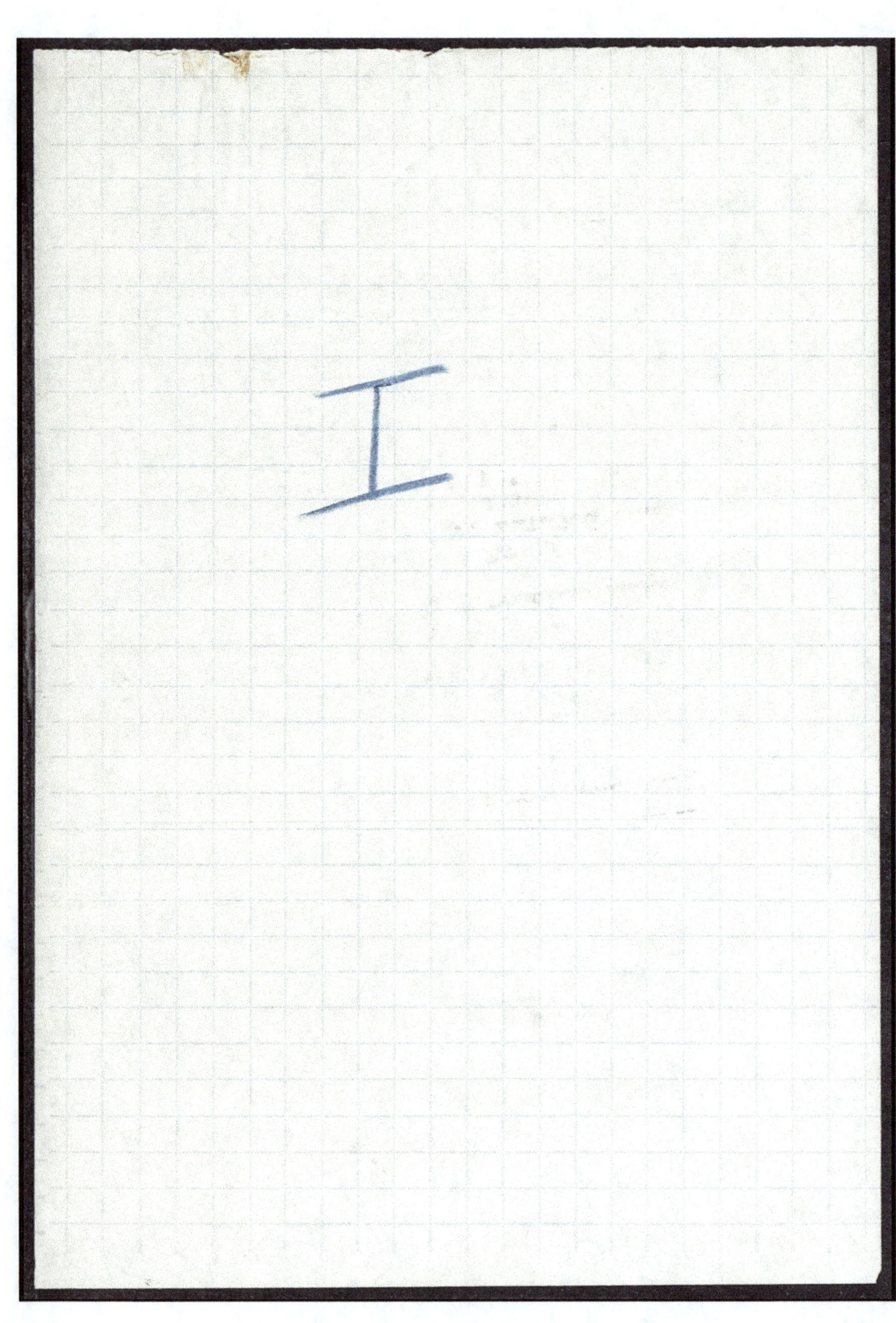
I

"A" Form. Army Form C. 2121.

MESSAGES AND SIGNALS.

No. of Message

Prefix ____ Code ____ m.	Words	Charge	This message is on a/c of:	Recd. at ____ m.
Office of Origin and Service Instructions.	Sent		Service.	Date
	At ____ m.			From
	To			By
	By		(Signature of "Franking Officer.")	

TO 2

* Sender's Number	Day of Month	In reply to Number	AAA

[illegible] [illegible] [illegible] trenches ok

N [illegible] [illegible] [illegible] ok N [illegible]

From 4th [illegible] R [illegible]

Place

Time

The above may be forwarded as now corrected. (Z) [illegible signature]

Censor. Signature of Addressor or person authorised to telegraph in his name

* This line should be erased if not required.

158 S. B. Ltd. Wt. W3673/619—50,000. 10/14. Forms C2121/10.

"A" Form. Army Form C. 2121.

MESSAGES AND SIGNALS.

No. of Message

Prefix Code m.	Words	Charge	This message is on a/c of:	Recd. at m.
Office of Origin and Service Instructions.	Sent		[illegible] Service.	Date
	At m.		[illegible]	From
	To		(Signature of "Franking Officer.")	By
	By			

TO	[illegible]	W	R	DIVN

* Sender's Number	Day of Month	In reply to Number	AAA
[illegible]	1	G 839	

[illegible]		Summary	Recd at	AAA
Machine	Gun	emplacement	seen	at
about	N 6 8.2	[illegible]	emplacement	[illegible]
[illegible]	[illegible]	[illegible]	[illegible]	[illegible]
[illegible]	[illegible]	[illegible]	[illegible]	[illegible]
[illegible]	[illegible]	[illegible]	[illegible]	parapet.
AAA	Trenches	about	[illegible] 3	contain
several	large	loop	holes	about
big	canvas	Curtains.	AAA	Gun
Circular	not	exactly	located	but
somewhere	about	374	AAA	RUE
PETILLON	shelled	1 am	this	morning
&	shells	AAA	New	earthworks
seen	at	N 6 C.1.1	and	some
50 yards	East	of	that	point,
AAA	Good	deal	of	traffic
seen	on	road	[illegible]	[illegible]

From

Place

Time

The above may be forwarded as now corrected. (Z)

Censor. Signature of Addressor or person authorised to telegraph in his name

* This line should be erased if not required.

158 S. B. Ltd. Wt. W3673/619—50,000. 10/14. Forms C2121/10.

Ammunition Expended.

15 pdr B.L.C.	5 in How:	4.7 in: Gun. L.	4.7 in: Gun. S.	4.7 in: Gun. C.P.
146	443	-	48	12.

Casualties

	Killed	Wounded	Missing.
Officers	nil.	nil.	nil.
Other Ranks.	6	13	nil.

49th (W.R.) Divisional Artillery

TACTICAL PROGRESS REPORT.

6 p.m. 31st May to 6 p.m, 1st June, 1915.

1. OPERATIONS. (a) (1) 4th W.R. (HOW:) Bde. Registration continued.

(2) W.R., R.G.A. fired 8 rounds of time shrapnel at German Battery in HYEN WOOD.
True bearing 141½ Map Range 5,700, Gun Range reduced charge 6,600, Battery silenced 3 p.m.

(b) (1) Enemy dropped four shells on RUE PETILLON at 1 a.m. this morning.

(2) German Battery fired at the Lines of W.R., R.G.A. from HYEN WOOD. at 2.30 p.m.

2. INFORMATION GAINED.

(1) F.O.O. 4th W.R. Battery reports that Infantry BG have observed a revolving gun in enemy's trenches opposite Pt 376.

(2) Large gaps are noticeable in enemy's parapet. These are covered by canvas curtains. About Pt 383, a 50 yard length of trench contains at least 5 of these loopholes.

(3) O.C. 9th W.R. Battery after an enquiry made in Section 5 re epaulment, can discov r no special characteristics as attaching to it.

3. WORK DONE BY BATTERIES. Gun epaulments and dug outs improved.

RW Lewen

2/6/15.

Major, R.A.,
Brigade Major, R.A., 49th (W.R.) Division.

"A" Form — Army Form C. 2121.

MESSAGES AND SIGNALS.

No. of Message

Prefix ___ Code ___ m.	Words	Charge	This message is on a/c of:	Recd. at ___ m.
Office of Origin and Service Instructions.	Sent		O H M Service.	Date
	At ___ m.			From
	To		Rl Wharncliffe [?] Maj	
	By		(Signature of "Franking Officer.")	By

TO — 49th W R DIVN

Sender's Number	Day of Month	In reply to Number	AAA
*BM 77/9	2nd		

Fifth	WEST	RIDING	Battery	shelled
at	10.30 am	by	4.2	with
Howitzer	from	direction	of	HAYEM
Wood	AAA	Hostile	aeroplane	directed
the	fire	AAA	ANTI-AIRCRAFT	
guns	fired	at	plane	with
little	effect	AAA	6 inch	Armoured
train	engaged	the	above	battery
which	was	located	by	Wireless
machine	as	being	50	yards
[illegible] South	of	LE in	LE	HAYEM
14	rounds	fired	5	direct
hits	AAA	Same	hostile	battery
fired	at	Section	6	12.58 pm
AAA.	Cupola	registered	at	2.30 pm
one	track	hit	damage	slight

From

Place

Time

The above may be forwarded as now corrected. (Z)

Censor. — Signature of Addressor or person authorised to telegraph in his name

* This line should be erased if not required.

158 S. B. Ltd. Wt. W5673/619—50,000. 10/14. Forms C2121/19.

"A" Form. Army Form C. 2121.

MESSAGES AND SIGNALS.

No. of Message

Prefix Code m.	Words / Charge	This message is on a/c of:	Recd. at m.
Office of Origin and Service Instructions.	Sent At m. To By	Service. (Signature of "Franking Officer.")	Date From By

TO (9)

* Sender's Number	Day of Month	In reply to Number	AAA

AAA	FLEURBAIX	shelled	from	4
to	6 pm	AAA	BOIS	GRENIER
shelled	by	FROMELLE	Battery	AAA
LA	BOUTILLERIE	building	shelled	NORTH
&	WEST	of	BOIS	GRENIER
AAA				

From 49th W R ARTY

Place

Time 4.40 pm

The above may be forwarded as now corrected. (Z) [illegible]

Censor. Signature of Addressor or person authorised to telegraph in his name

* This line should be erased if not required.

158 S. B. Ltd. Wt. W5673/619—50,000. 10/14. Forms C2121/10.

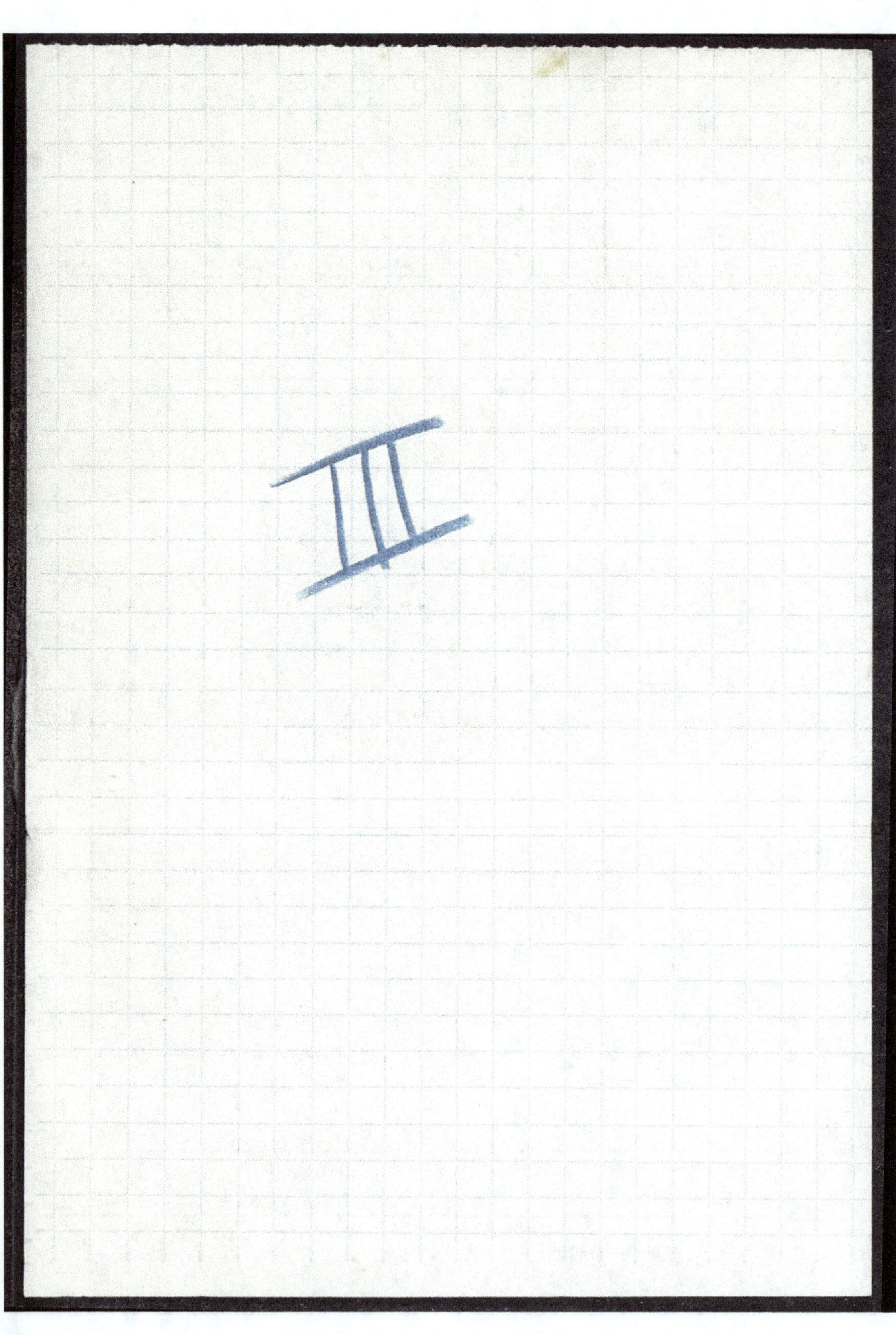
III

49th (W.R.) Divisional Artillery.

TACTICAL PROGRESS REPORT.

6 p.m. June 1st to 6 p.m. June 2nd 1915.

1. OPERATIONS.

(a) (1) 6 inch Armoured Train fired at Battery located 50 yards South of "L" in LE HAYEM.

(b) (1) Enemy shelled RUE DE BOIS about 500 yards West of 1st Battery position which is H 33 d 3.3.
This shelling commenced at 10.30 ~~this~~ yesterday morning and continued till 10.55 a.m.
Hostile Aeroplane hovered over this area at the same time.
The shell were High Explosive, probably about 5-9" calibre.

(2) Two H.E. shells fell in FLEUXBAIX at 4.55 p.m. this afternoon.

(3) Artillery directed by aeroplane shelled 5th W.R. Battery. No Casualties, but two limbers smashed.

2. INFORMATION GAINED.

NIL.

3. WORK DONE BY BATTERIES. Gun pits and dug outs improved.

3/6/15.

R W Lewer
Major R.A.,
Brigade Major R.A. 49th (W.R.) Division.

"A" Form. Army Form C. 2121.

MESSAGES AND SIGNALS.

No. of Message

Prefix	Code	m.	Words	Charge	This message is on a/c of:	Recd. at	m.
Office of Origin and Service Instructions.			Sent		37th Service.	Date	
			At	m.	[illegible]	From	
			To		(Signature of "Franking Officer.")	By	
			By				

TO: 49th W R DIVN.

Sender's Number	Day of Month	In reply to Number	AAA
* BM/2/9	3rd		

[illegible]	report	aaa	8.45	am
hostile	aeroplane	passed	[illegible]	[illegible]
[illegible]	[illegible]	[illegible]	A	[illegible]
[illegible]	[illegible]	direction	[illegible]	[illegible]
BOUTILLERIE	AAA	hostile	aeroplane	over
3rd	[illegible]	7th	Balloons	at
German	AAA	12	pigeons	flew
from	BOIS	GRENIER	towards	German
lines	at	2.20pm	AAA	2
pigeons	flew	from	German	lines
to	BOIS	GRENIER	at	3pm
AAA	11th	Battery	registered	cupola
near	PT	883	4pm	AAA
German	observation	balloon	up	at
Magnetic	235°	from	H 28 a 1.2	time
4.20pm	AAA	RUE	DES	LOMBARDS
and	2nd	Battery	billet	H 33 b 2.5

From

Place

Time

The above may be forwarded as now corrected. (Z)

Censor. Signature of Addressor or person authorised to telegraph in his name

* This line should be erased if not required.

158 S. B. Ltd. Wt. W5673/619—50,000. 10/14. Forms C2121/10.

"A" Form. Army Form C. 2121.

MESSAGES AND SIGNALS.

No. of Message

Prefix Code m.	Words	Charge		Recd. at m.
Office of Origin and Service Instructions.	Sent		This message is on a/c of:	Date
	At m.		Service.	From
	To			By
	By		(Signature of "Franking Officer.")	

TO (2)

* Sender's Number	Day of Month	In reply to Number	AAA

Shelled	at	4.30 pm	AAA	5 Rounds
[illegible]	reported	6	[illegible]	[illegible]
[illegible]	6 [illegible]	[illegible]	Section	[illegible]

From 49th W R Art.

Place

Time 7.24 pm

The above may be forwarded as now corrected. (Z) [illegible signature]

Censor. Signature of Addressor or person authorised to telegraph in his name

* This line should be erased if not required.

158 S. B. Ltd. Wt. W5673/619—50,000. 10/14. Forms C2121/10.

"C" Form (Duplicate). Army Form C. 2123.

MESSAGES AND SIGNALS. No. of Message 9

	Charges to Pay. £ s. d.	Office Stamp.

Service Instructions. aeronautics 2 Recd by phone from Indian Corps

Handed in at .... Office .... m. Received 7 ... m.

TO WR Royal Artillery

Sender's Number	Day of Month	In reply to Number	AAA
S/2 129	3		

An	aeroplane	will	be	out
to	work	with	WR	Artillery
and	Armoured	Train	at	7.30
am				

Telephone R.G.A and Armoured train at 7.35 am

FROM PLACE & TIME Aeronautics 2 7.0 am

(24932). M.R.Co.,Ltd. Wt.W9668/1672. 50,000 Pads—1/15. Forms/C.2123.

rec. 7.25 am

"C" Form (Duplicate). Army Form C. 2123.

MESSAGES AND SIGNALS. No. of Message 5

Sm. Pg	FOW 06	Charges to Pay. £ s. d.	Office Stamp. 9 WR
Service Instructions.			

Handed in at .... Office .... m. Received .... m.

TO Headquarters R. G.

Sender's Number	Day of Month	In reply to Number	AAA
	3		

O6 10th Bty reports German aeroplane flying in a westerly direction at 9.15 am.

FROM PLACE & TIME O/C WR 9 a Bde 9/20

(24932). M.R.Co.,Ltd. Wt.W9668/1672. 50,000 Pads—1/15. Forms/C.2123.

"C" Form (Duplicate). Army Form C. 2123.

MESSAGES AND SIGNALS. No. of Message

Sm.

4B10

Charges to Pay. £ s. d.

Office Stamp. 4WR 3.6.15

Service Instructions.

Handed in at Office m. Received m.

TO Bde Mjr 49th W R Div

Sender's Number	Day of Month	In reply to Number	AAA
G 10	3rd		

Infantry complain that they are being sniped from FERME DE MOUQUET and they have lost a few men in the trenches about junction of 3P + 2S

1st W R Bde ordered to fire on this house, 12 rounds allotted.

7.10pm

FROM PLACE & TIME Adjt 2nd W R Bde 6.30pm

(24932). M.R.Co.,Ltd. Wt. W9668/1672. 50,000 Pads—1/15. Forms/C.2123.

"C" Form (Duplicate). Army Form C. 2123.

MESSAGES AND SIGNALS. No. of Message

Sm KO 46

Charges to Pay. £ s. d.

Office Stamp. FWR 3.6.15

Service Instructions.

Handed in at FAW. Office m. Received m.

TO 49th WR Div Art

Sender's Number	Day of Month	In reply to Number	AAA
051	3rd		

OC 1st Batt reports that he obtained four direct hits on ~~on~~ ~~of~~ FERME DE MOUQUET aaa he then under orders from the infantry fired time shrapnel on a line pointed ~~pointed~~ out to him by them aaa Infantry express complete satisfaction with the result of this fire aaa Sniping ceased at once aaa

FROM PLACE & TIME 1st WR FABde 1010Pm

(24932). M.R.Co.,Ltd. Wt.W9668/1672. 50,000 Pads—1/15. Forms/C.2123.

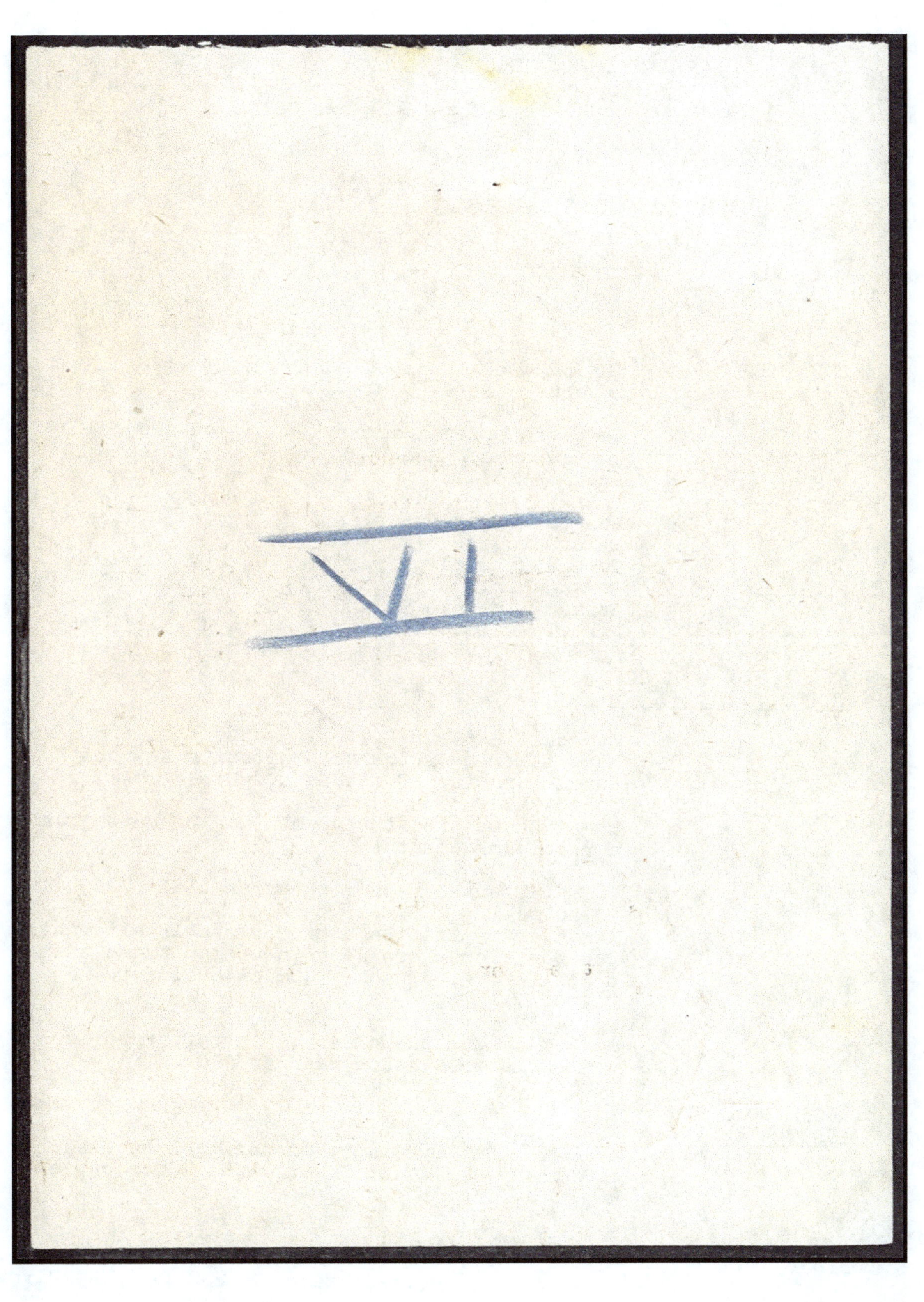

49th (W.R.) Divisional Artillery.

TACTICAL PROGRESS REPORT.

6 p.m. June 2nd to 6 p.m. June 3rd 1915.

1. OPERATIONS.

(a) (1) 2nd W.R. Battery expended 8 rounds in registration.

(2) 5th W.R. Battery registered trenches and FERME DELANGRE.

(b) (1) Hostile aeroplane flew over 3rd W.R. Battery position at 9.30 a.m. yesterday morning (Position H 28.c.4.4.)
RUE DES LOMBARDS shelled by enemy yesterday afternoon at 4.30 p.m.

(2) Complaint from Infantry that they are being sniped from FERME DE MOUQUET, a few casualties are recorded.

(3) Hostile aeroplane over 3rd and 7th W.R. Batteries at 9.30 a.m.
Two pigeons flew from BIOS GRENIER towards German lines at 2.20 p.m. 3 Pigeons flew from German lines to BOIS GRENIER at 3 p.m.
Hostile Balloon observed up at Magnetic 235 from H 28.a.1.2 time 4.20 p.m.

2. INFORMATION GAINED.

(1) 3rd W.R. Battery F.O.O. reports that the Saxons have taken over trenches opposite Section 5.
Cupola and top of a pair of wheels observed at N 5.d.3.1 from N 5.b.0.1.
The idea is that the cupola may be cover for a revolving cannon.

(2) Enemy observed repairing parapet at Pt 969 (1/5000).
A number of loop holes for probable alternative gun positions were seen in German front trench opposite 5 Q, 5 R, 5 S and extending to LE BRIDOUX.

(3) A Machine Gun was observed in rafters of small white thatched house near Pt.975.

3. WORK DONE BY BATTERIES.

5th W.R. Battery improved position vacated by O Battery R.H.A. at H 33.c.4.8. and occupied same.

4/6/15.

[signature] Major R.A.,
Brigade Major R.A.49th (W.R.)Divn.

"C" Form (Duplicate). Army Form C. 2123.

MESSAGES AND SIGNALS. No. of Message

Sm. Aam 26.

FCW

Charges to Pay. £ s. d.

Office Stamp.

Service Instructions.

Handed in at FCW Office m. Received m.

TO Hdqtrs RA 49th W R Div.
Bde Mjr.

Sender's Number	Day of Month	In reply to Number	AAA
13/E	19th		

Enemy's	Artillery	opened	fire	12.40pm
firing	on	121	Brigade	They
have	set	on	fire	2
farm	house	&	buildings	
close	to	~~that~~ 1st	Battery	

12.4P

FROM PLACE & TIME: 1/3rd W R Bde RFA
1.5pm.

(24932). M.R.Co.,Ltd. Wt.W9668/1672. 50,000 Pads—1/15. Forms/C.2123.

"C" Form (Duplicate). Army Form C. 2123.

MESSAGES AND SIGNALS. No. of Message

Gm.

FBW

Charges to Pay. £ s. d.

Office Stamp. FWR 4-6-15

Service Instructions.

Handed in at Office m. Received m.

TO Bde Mjr RA 49 (WR) Div

Sender's Number	Day of Month	In reply to Number	AAA
GL 15	4th		

4th Batt Y.O.O reports enemy using Trench Mortar from point behind and between 882 & 884 aaa exact position not located aaa It was firing between 11.15 am & 11.45 am and again from 12.30 pm to 12.35 pm.

FROM PLACE & TIME 2nd WR Bde RFA 1.58 pm

(24932). M.R.Co.,Ltd. Wt.W9668/1672. 50,000 Pads—1/15. Forms/C.2123.

"A" Form. Army Form C. 2121.

MESSAGES AND SIGNALS.

No. of Message

Prefix ____ Code ____ m.	Words	Charge	This message is on a/c of:	Recd. at ____ m.
Office of Origin and Service Instructions.	Sent		[illegible] Service.	Date
	At ____ m.			From
	To			
	By		[illegible] (Signature of "Franking Officer.")	By

TO { 49th W R DIVN

Sender's Number	Day of Month	In reply to Number	AAA
* BM[illegible]	fourth		

Summary	Report	AAA	~~The~~	
Trench	mortar	~~battery~~	at	1 S[?]
f[illegible]	3	rounds	at	[illegible]
[illegible]	883	one	did	not[?]
explode	other	two	rounds	effective
AAA	Hostile	trench	mortars	between
883	and	884	active	at
intervals	AAA	Farm	at	H33d8.5
set	on	fire	by	hostile
field	battery	from	direction	of
LE	MAISNIL	one	man	1st
Battery	killed	between	12.40pm	and[?]
1.45pm	AAA	Hostile	battery	~~fired~~
commenced	firing	on	Section	6
at	4.30pm.	AAA	First	Battery
fired	12	rounds	at	FERME
DELANGRE	which	contained	snipers	there

From

Place

Time

The above may be forwarded as now corrected. (Z)

Censor. Signature of Addressor or person authorised to telegraph in his name

* This line should be erased if not required.

158 S. B. Ltd. Wt. W3673/619—50,000. 10/14. Forms C2121/10.

"A" Form. Army Form C. 2121.

MESSAGES AND SIGNALS.

No. of Message

Prefix	Code	m.	Words	Charge	This message is on a/c of:	Recd. at	m.
Office of Origin and Service Instructions.			Sent			Date	
			At	m.	Service.	From	
			To			By	
			By		(Signature of "Franking Officer.")		

TO (2)

* Sender's Number	Day of Month	In reply to Number	AAA

[illegible]	[illegible]	AAA	Hostile	aeroplane
[illegible]	[illegible]	[illegible]	[illegible]	[illegible]
5	[illegible]	7	a	Bde
and	4th	[illegible]	Bde.	[illegible]
6 pm.				

From	49th	W	R	ARTY
Place				
Time	4. 6 pm			

The above may be forwarded as now corrected. (Z) [illegible signature] Maj RA

Censor. Signature of Addressor or person authorised to telegraph in his name

* This line should be erased if not required.

158 S. B. Ltd. Wt. W5673/619—50,000. 10/14. Forms C2121/10.

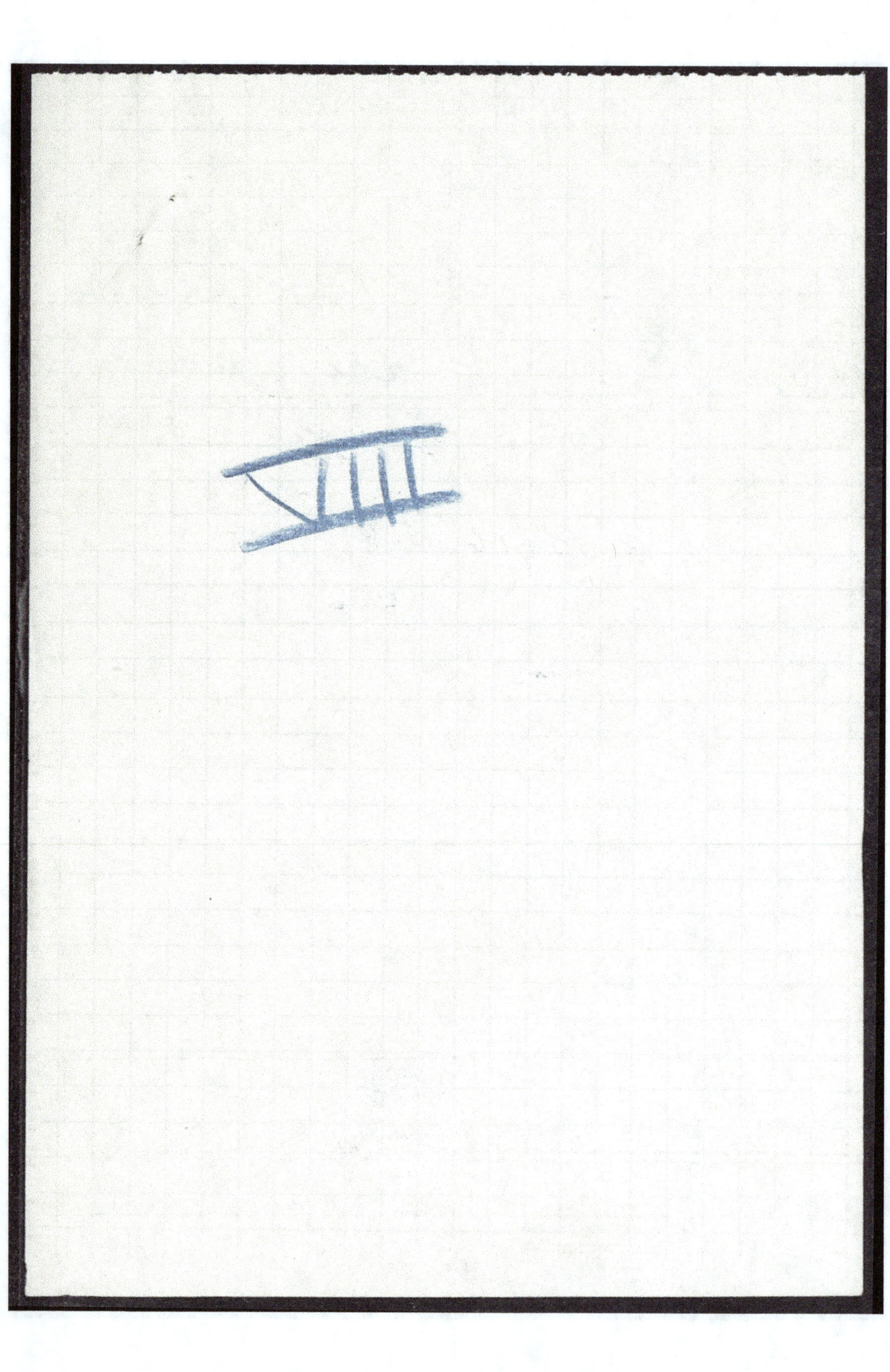

"A" Form. Army Form C. 2121.

MESSAGES AND SIGNALS.

No. of Message

Prefix SM Code GK m. | Words | Charge

Office of Origin and Service Instructions: A.N.

Sent At m. To By

This message is on a/c of: Service.

(Signature of "Franking Officer.")

Recd. at m. Date From By

TO Brigade Major W. R. Arty

Sender's Number.	Day of Month.	In reply to Number	AAA
C119.	4	aac	

Registered with 4" Gun on House in N16 4.6 with good results

From O/C A. T. Churchill

Place

Time 11/20 pm

The above may be forwarded as now corrected. (Z)

Censor. Signature of Addressor or person authorised to telegraph in his name.

* This line should be erased if not required.

(75644). Wt. 11400-2045. 50,000. 2-15. B., M. & S., Ltd.

49th (W.R.) Divisional Artillery,

TACTICAL PROGRESS REPORT.

6 p.m. June 3rd to 6 p.m. June 4th 1915.

1. OPERATIONS.

(a) (1) At 3.25 p.m. yesterday 1st Battery opened fire on FERME DELANGRE. Three direct hits obtained.

(2) At 7.12 p.m. on June 3rd 1st Battery fired on FERME DE MOUQUET, occupied at the time by Snipers. Twelve rounds were fired and four direct hits obtained.

(3) Trench Mortar at 1 S, fired 3 rounds at Cupola near 883. One did not explode. Two rounds effective.

(b) (1) Hostile trench mortars used at intervals during the day between 883 and 884.

(2) PETILLON Corner shelled at 3 p.m. yesterday.

(3) Enemy's aeroplane up at 6.30 p.m. and 7 p.m. driven off by anti air-craft guns.

(4) Farm at H.33.a.8.5 set on fire by hostile field battery from direction of LE MAISNIL. One man 1st Battery killed. This took place between 12.40 p.m. and 1.45 p.m.

(5) Hostile battery commenced firing on Section 6 at 4.30 p.m.

(6) Hostile Aeroplane flew backwards and forward over Sections 3, 4 and 5 and 1st Brigade Gun positions at 6 p.m. yesterday.

2. INFORMATION GAINED.

(1) Bearing taken from unexploded hostile shell, which gave a true bearing of 131 degrees 30 minutes.

(2) Infantry in Section 3 suspect Machine Gun is concealed in Bushy Trees about 100 - 200 yards behind German lines.

3. WORK DONE BY BATTERIES. Batteries improve gun pits and dug-outs and destroy traces of old paths.

5/6/15.

M H Calvert-Jones for Major R.A.,
Brigade Major R.A.49th (W.R.) Division.

"A" Form. Army Form C. 2121.

MESSAGES AND SIGNALS.

No. of Message ______

Prefix ___ Code ___ m.	Words	Charge	This message is on a/c of:	Recd. at ___ m.
Office of Origin and Service Instructions.	Sent		[illegible] Service.	Date
	At ___ m.			From
	To		[illegible]	
	By		(Signature of "Franking Officer.")	By

TO	49th	W	R	DIVN

Sender's Number	Day of Month	In reply to Number	AAA
* BM/16/9	Fifth		

Summary	Report	AAA	~~[illegible]~~	[illegible]
Aeroplane	[illegible]	Between	[illegible] 30 a.m.	
9.30 am	AAA	hostile	[illegible]	Battery
[illegible]	N 6 0 2 3	[illegible]	[illegible]	AAA
[illegible]	[illegible]	does	reported	[illegible]
German	[illegible]	located	[illegible]	[illegible]
[illegible]	magnetic	bearing	from 20 yards	[illegible]
100°	AAA	Captive	balloon	magnetic
bearing	170°	from	H 25 b 1-9	up
from	10.30am	to	1.20pm	AAA
Earthworks	reported	250	yards	N E
of	point	782	possibly	communication
trench	AAA	Aeroplane	seen	over
10th	Battery	H 34 a 5-6	with	rings
marked	on	one	wing	only

From	49th	W	R	ARTY
Place				
Time	7 2.20pm			

The above may be forwarded as now corrected. (Z) [illegible signature]

Censor. Signature of Addressor or person authorised to telegraph in his name

* This line should be erased if not required.

158 S. B. Ltd. Wt. W5673/619—50,000. 10/14. Forms C2121/10.

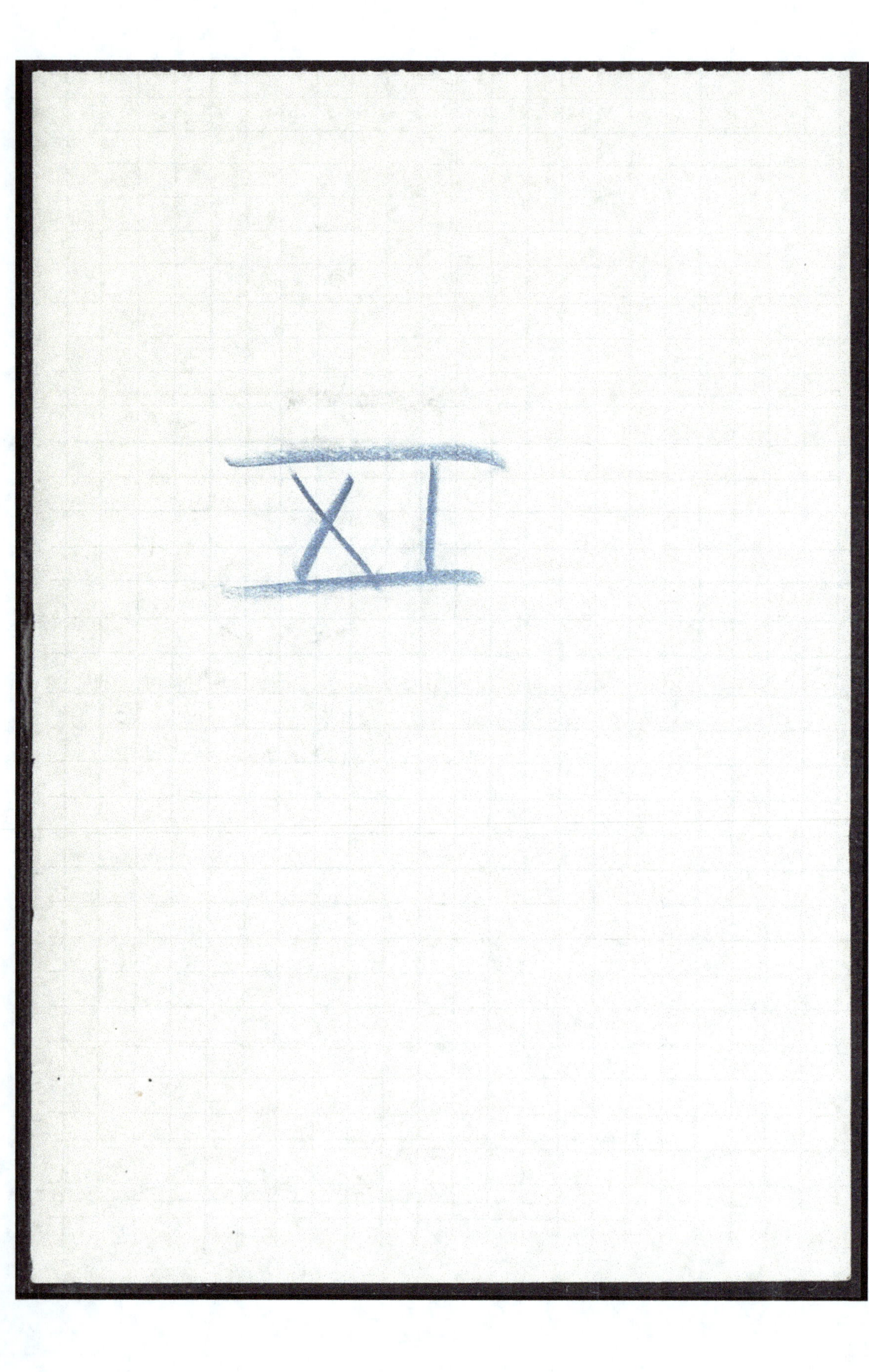
XI

40th (W.R.) Divisional Artillery.

TACTICAL PROGRESS REPORT.

6 p.m. June 4th to 6 p.m. June 5th 1915.

1. OPERATIONS.

(a) (1) 10th Battery registered trenches 900 - 896.

(2) 11th Battery registered on House O 7.b.4.9.

(b) (1) Hostile aeroplane hovered over Sections 3, 4 & 5 and 1st W.R. Brigade Guns.

(2) Six Pigeons flew from FROMELLES to FLEURBAIX at noon.

(3) Hostile Field Battery shelled N.3.b.2.3 at 11 a.m.

(4) Captive balloon, Magnetic bearing 170 from H.25.b.1.9. up 10.30 a.m. to 1.20 p.m.

(5) Aeroplane seen over 10th Battery H.34 a 5.6 with rings marked on one wing only.

2. INFORMATION GAINED.

(1) Pair iron doors reported in German trenches, located near point 960.

(2) 6 Earthworks reported 250 yards N.E. of point 782, possibly communication trench.

3. WORK DONE BY BATTERIES.

5th W.R. Battery changed position of gun pit of No.1 gun to avoid being marked by some trees at extreme right of Zone. Work completed.

New dug out started and gun pits improved by 1st W.R. F.A. Bde.

Major R.A.,
Brigade Major R.A.49th(W.R.) Division.

6/6/15.

"C" Form (Duplicate). Army Form C. 2123.

MESSAGES AND SIGNALS. No. of Message

Sm 9 pm

FCW

Charges to Pay. £ s. d.

Office Stamp. FWR 6-6-15

Service Instructions.

Handed in at FCW. Office m. Received m.

TO H Q RA 49th W R Div Art
Brigade Major.

Sender's Number	Day of Month	In reply to Number	AAA
71	6th		

OC 8 th Batty reports having located by flashes at least 2 3 inch Enemy field guns near to point O 7 b 0 6

A.T. Want to search Square O 7 b 0.6

7.30 pm

FROM PLACE & TIME: O C 3rd W R R F A 7.5 pm.

(24932). M.R.Co.,Ltd. Wt.W9668/1673. 50,000 Pads—1/15. Forms/C.2123.

"A" Form. Army Form C. 2121.

MESSAGES AND SIGNALS.

No. of Message

Prefix ___ Code ___ m.	Words / Charge	This message is on a/c of:	Recd. at ___ m.
Office of Origin and Service Instructions.	Sent		Date
	At ___ m.	Service.	From
	To		
	By	(Signature of "Franking Officer.")	By

TO { 49th W. R. DIVISION

Sender's Number	Day of Month	In reply to Number	AAA
* BM [illegible]	[illegible]	—	AAA

Shelling	Report	AAA	Report	received
from	Aeronautics	[illegible]	[illegible]	[illegible]
[illegible]	shelling	of	1st	[illegible]
2	lines	trenches	of	[illegible]
DIVISION	at	2.55	pm	AAA
VIII	DIV	wanted	[illegible]	[illegible]
[illegible]	to	W R	Heavy	B[illegible]
HQ	stand	by	for	action
AAA	1st	W R	Brigade	R F A
report	that	an	iron	plate
3'	by	3'	with	double
doors	was	observed	in	hostile
trench	70	yards	N	of
Pt	960			

From 49th W R ARTILLERY

Place

Time 6.50 pm

The above may be forwarded as now corrected. (Z) [illegible] Major R.F.A. [illegible]

Censor. Signature of Addressor or person authorised to telegraph in his name

* This line should be erased if not required.

158 S. B. Ltd. Wt. W5673/619—50,000. 10/14. Forms C2121/10.

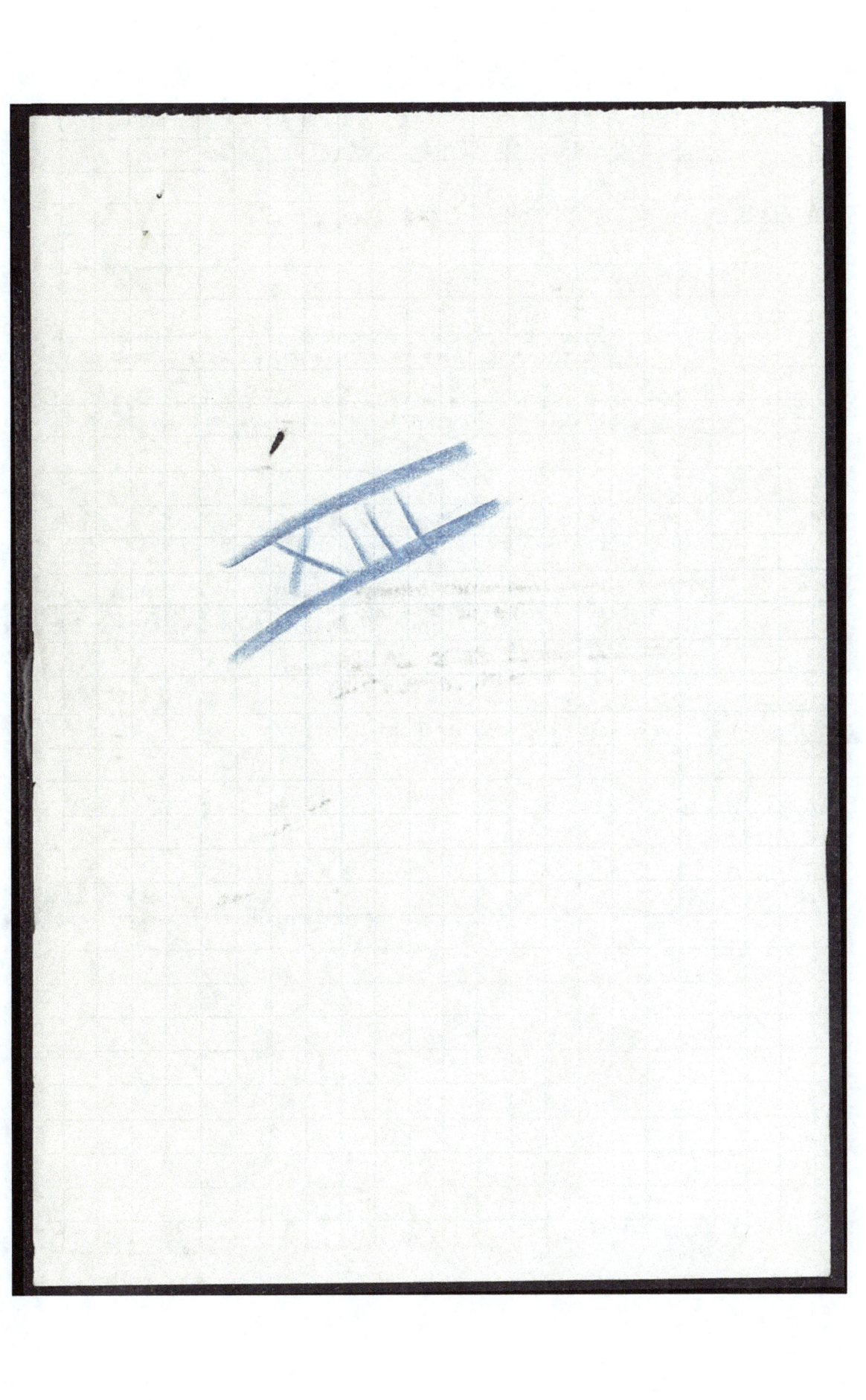

49th (W.R.) Divisional Artillery,

TACTICAL PROGRESS REPORT.

6 p.m. June 5th to 6 p.m. June 6th 1915.

1. OPERATIONS.

(a) Nil.

(b) (1) Report received that enemy are heavily shelling 1st and 2nd Line trenches of MEERUT Divn. at 2.55 p.m.

(2) A Shrapnel shell fell at Mid-day today on road N.3.b.2.0. Magnetic bearing of strike of shell 162°.

2. INFORMATION GAINED.

(1) 1st W.R. F.A. Bde. report that an Iron Plate 5' by 3' with double doors was observed in hostile trench 70 yards N of Pt 960.

(2) O.C. 8th Battery reports having located by flashes at least two 3 inch hostile Field guns near to point O.7.b.0.6.

3. WORK DONE BY BATTERIES. Gun pits and dug-outs improved.

7/6/15.

Major R.A.,
Brigade Major R.A.49th (W.R.) Division.

MESSAGES AND SIGNALS. No. of Message

Prefix ______ Code ______ m.	Words	Charge	This message is on a/c of:	Recd. at ______ m.
Office of Origin and Service Instructions.	Sent		[illegible] Service.	Date
	At ______ m.		[illegible]	From
	To		(Signature of "Franking Officer.")	By
	By			

TO { 49th W R Div

* Sender's Number	Day of Month	In reply to Number	AAA
[illegible]	Seventh		

S[illegible]	[illegible]	AAA	S[illegible]	[illegible]
[illegible]	[illegible]	and	[illegible]	[illegible]
[illegible]	[illegible]	[illegible]	[illegible]	[illegible]
[illegible]	[illegible]	EN[illegible]	to	EN[illegible]ES
0b[illegible]	to	0b[illegible]	[illegible]	[illegible]
3pm	and	[illegible]	[illegible]	[illegible]
3.30pm?	[illegible]	leaving	1.12	[illegible]
H.5.d.	1-6	[illegible]	by	1st
F	A	Rides?	Confirmed	by
3rd	F	A	Ride	AAA
Captive	balloons	up	[illegible]	direction
of	DUREM	2.30pm	to	4pm
down	4pm	to	4.20pm	up
again	4.20pm	to	4.40pm	

From 4[illegible]
Place
Time 4.[illegible]

The above may be forwarded as now corrected. (Z) [illegible]

Censor. Signature of Addressor or person authorized to telegraph in his name

* This line should be erased if not required.

158 S. B. Ltd. Wt. W5673/619—50,000. 10/14. Forms C2121/10.

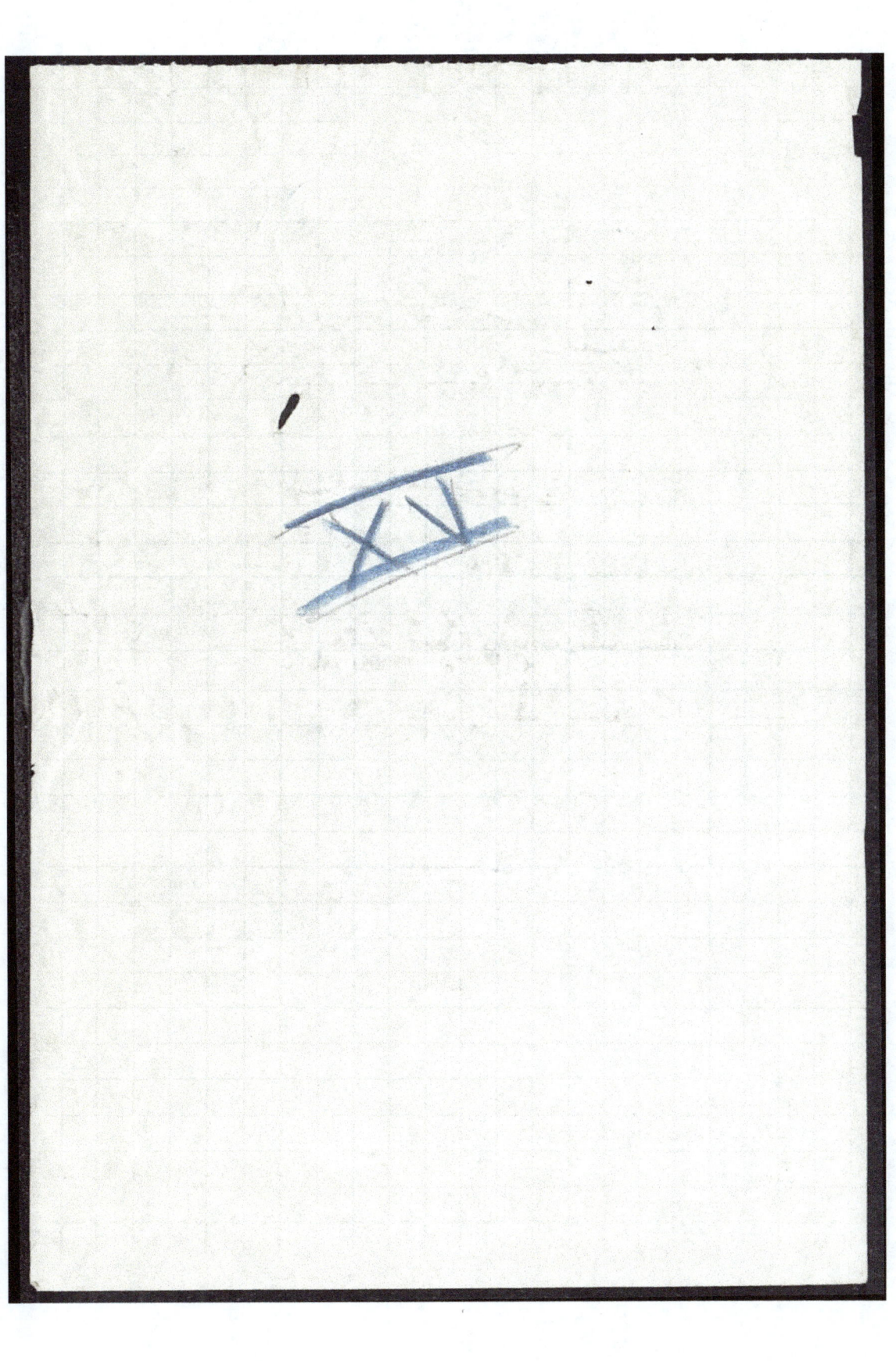

49th (W.R.) Divisional Artillery.

TACTICAL PROGRESS REPORT.

From June 6th 6 p.m. to 6 p.m. June 7th 1915.

1. OPERATIONS.

(a) (1) W.R. R.G.A. fired 10 rounds on road at O.8.c & d.

(b) (1) 77 mm opened on front trench about 600 yards East of BRIDOUX - BOIS GRENIER.

(2) Small bodies of Infantry and a few horsemen passed at short intervals along road ENGLOS to ENNETIERES - O.6.d.10.2 to O.6.d.7.7. Seen at 5 p.m. and continued till about 8.30 p.m.
Magnetic bearing 112 from H 31.d.1.6 reported by 1st Artillery Bde and confirmed by 3rd W.R. F.A. Bde.

(3) Captive balloon up at 2.30 p.m. to 4 p.m. in direction of DOREM. DUREM

(4) On June 6th time 7,50 p.m. Infantry are reported moving along road in front of LES POTERRIE in a N.E. direction. It is estimated that the Troops seen composed 1 Battalion of Infantry and Transport and 2 Squadrons of Cavalry. The above road runs through O.8.c & d.

2. INFORMATION GAINED.

(1) Working party of about 6 men observed about N 6.d.3.6 filling sand bags.

(2) Men also seen collecting clothes behind parapet about N.6.d.4.8.

(3) At about pt 0.1 a 5.5 there is a considerable amount of new wire staked in between front and rear trench.

3. WORK DONE BY BATTERIES. Gun pits and dug outs improved.

8/6/15.

Major R.A.,
Brigade Major R.A. 49th (W.R.) Division.

49th (W.R.) Divisional Artillery.

TACTICAL PROGRESS REPORT.

From June 6th 6 p.m. to 6 p.m. June 7th 1915.

1. OPERATIONS.

(a) (1) W.R. R.G.A. fired 10 rounds on road at O.8.c & d.

(b) (1) 77 mm opened on front trench about 600 yards East of BRIDOUX - BOIS GRENIER.

(2) Small bodies of Infantry and a few horsemen passed at short intervals along road ENGLOS to ENNETIERES - O.6.d.10.2 to O.6.d.7.7. Seen at 3 p.m. and continued till about 3.30 p.m.
Magnetic bearing 112 from H 31.d.1.6 reported by 1st Artillery Bde and confirmed by 3rd W.R. F.A. Bde.

(3) Captive balloon up at 2.30 p.m. to 4 p.m. in direction of DOREM.

(4) On June 5th time 7.50 p.m. Infantry are reported moving along road in front of LES POTERRIE in a N.E. direction. It is estimated that the Troops seen composed 1 Battalion of Infantry and Transport and 2 Squadrons of Cavalry. The above road runs through O.8.c & d.

2. INFORMATION GAINED.

(1) Working party of about 6 men observed about N 6ad.8.6 filling sand bags.

(2) Men also seen collecting clothes behind parapet about N.6.d.4.8.

(3) At about pt O.1 a 5.5 there is a considerable amount of new wire staked in between front and rear trench.

3. WORK DONE BY BATTERIES. Gun pits and dug outs improved.

8/6/15.

Major R.A.,
Brigade Major R.A.49th (W.R.) Division.

49th (W.R.) Divisional Artillery.

TACTICAL PROGRESS REPORT&

6 p.m. June 7th to 6 p.m. June 8th 1915.

1. OPERATIONS.

(a) (1) 4th (W.R. (How) Bde. continued Registration.

(b) (1) FLEURBAIX bombarded at 5 p.m. 6 shells in all.

2. INFORMATION GAINED.

(1) Hostile aeroplane over 3rd Battery - H.28.c.4.3 at 10.15 a.m.

(2) Three small gaps seen in enemy's parapet about Pt 882. Centre gap has headcover, possibly for Machine Gun. One hundred yards S.E. of point 882, row of pale blue sand bags, about 15 yards long and 10 yards from enemy's trench.

(3) Hostile aeroplane over Sections 3, 4 and 5 at 5.10 p.m., also another of enemy's aeroplanes flew South to North over H.28, apparently directing hostile gun fire at 6.55 p.m.
8th Division informed at 6.55 p.m. and asked to inform Anti aircraft.

(4) A great deal of work appears to be in progress round FERME DE MOUQUET.

(5) A fire observed in enemy's lines, bearing 118° Magnetic from H 35.d.1.6.

3. WORK DONE BY BATTERIES&

1st Battery improved false hedge.
Dug-out at H.35.d.1.6 improved.

[signature]

Major R.A.,
Brigade Major R.A.49th (W.R.) Division.

9/6/15

49th (W.R.) Divisional Artillery.

TACTICAL PROGRESS REPORT.

6 p.m. June 7th to 6 p.m. June 8th 1915.

1. OPERATIONS.

(a) (1) 4th (W.R. (How) Bde. continued Registration.

(b) (1) FLEURBAIX bombarded at 5 p.m. 6 shells in all.

2. INFORMATION GAINED.

(1) Hostile aeroplane over 3rd Battery - H.28.c.4.3 at 10.15 a.m.

(2) Three small gaps seen in enemy's parapet about Pt 882. Centre gap has headcover, possibly for Machine Gun. One hundred yards S.E. of point 882, row of pale blue sand bags, about 15 yards long and 10 yards from enemy's trench.

(3) Hostile aeroplane over Sections 3, 4 and 5 at 5.10 p.m., also another of enemy's aeroplanes flew South to North over H.28, apparently directing hostile gun fire at 6.55 p.m.
8th Division informed at 6.55 p.m. and asked to inform Anti aircraft.

(4) A great deal of work appears to be in progress round FERME DE MOUQUET.

(5) A fire observed in enemy's lines, bearing 118° Magnetic from H 35.d.1.6.

3. WORK DONE BY BATTERIES.

1st Battery improved false hedge.
Dug-out at H.35.d.1.6 improved.

[signature]

Major R.A.,
Brigade Major R.A.49th (W.R.) Division.

9/6/15

MESSAGES AND SIGNALS.

No. of Message

Prefix ______ Code ______ m.	Words	Charge	This message is on a/c of:	Recd. at ______ m.
Office of Origin and Service Instructions.	Sent			Date
	At ______ m.		[illegible] Service.	From
	To			
	By		[illegible] (Signature of "Franking Officer.")	By

TO 49th W R DIVN

Sender's Number	Day of Month	In reply to Number	AAA
* [illegible]	8th		

Summary report :-		AAA	Hostile	aeroplane
[illegible]	[illegible]	Battery	H [illegible] 4.3	at
11.15 am	AAA	The [illegible]	[illegible]	[illegible]
[illegible]	[illegible]	Ranging	[illegible]	[illegible]
[illegible]	882	AAA	Centre	of
[illegible]	[illegible]	formerly	for	working
[illegible]	AAA	100	yards	SE
of	point	882	new	of
parts	blue	Sandbags	about	15
yards	long	and	10 yards	forward
[illegible]	trench	AAA	FLEURBAIX	at
5 pm	6	Shells	in	all
AAA	Hostile	aeroplane	of	Sections
3	4	+	5	at
5.10 pm	AAA	Hostile	aeroplane	flying
SOUTH	to	NORTH	over	H 28

From

Place

Time

The above may be forwarded as now corrected. (Z)

Censor. Signature of Addressor or person authorised to telegraph in his name

* This line should be erased if not required.

158 S. B. Ltd. Wt. W5673/619—50,000. 10/14. Forms C2121/10.

"A" Form. Army Form C. 2121.

MESSAGES AND SIGNALS.

No. of Message

Prefix Code m.	Words	Charge	This message is on a/c of:	Recd. at m.
Office of Origin and Service Instructions.	Sent		Service.	Date
	At m.			From
	To			
	By		(Signature of "Franking Officer.")	By

TO (2)

* Sender's Number	Day of Month	In reply to Number	AAA

[illegible] 6 [illegible]

AIRCRAFT

From

Place

Time

The above may be forwarded as now corrected. (Z)

Censor. Signature of Addressor or person authorised to telegraph in his name

* This line should be erased if not required.

158 S. B. Ltd. Wt. W5673/619—50,000. 10/14. Forms C2121/10.

XVII

49th (W.R.)' Divisional Artillery.

TACTICAL PROGRESS REPORT.

6 p.m. June 8th to 6 p.m. June 9th 1915.

1. OPERATIONS.

(a) (1) Armoured Train fired at LE MAISNIL and Pt.757 in retaliation. This bombardment took place between 3.45 p.m. and 4.15 p.m.

(b) (1) Working parties seen 200 yards EAST of Pt.887 and forty yards from hostile trench.

(2) FLEURBAIX shelled from direction of FROMELLES at 3.35 p.m. 8 shells in all fell.

(3) Twenty four hostile shell around Farm N.4.a.2½.4 at 3.45 p.m. Two stacks set on fire. One blind shell fell at H.27.c.10.6.

(4) Hostile Aeroplane over H.28 at 8.35 a.m.

2. INFORMATION GAINED.

(1) Hostile trench mortar very active between 2 a.m. and 3 a.m. opposite Pt.879, 883 and 884.

(2) Infantry in 5 P have seen a man on roof of house at Pt. 904 BAS MAISNIL and conclude the same as being used for observation purposes.

3. WORK DONE BY BATTERIES.

4th Battery continued work on alternative position. Gun pits and dug-outs improved.

10/6/15.

H F. Calvert-Jones for Major R.A.,
Brigade Major R.A. 49th (W.R.) Division.

19.
XIX

"A" Form. Army Form C. 2121.

MESSAGES AND SIGNALS.

No. of Message

Prefix ___ Code ___ m.	Words	Charge		Recd. at ___ m.
Office of Origin and Service Instructions.	Sent		This message is on a/c of: ___ Service.	Date
	At ___ m.			From
	To			
	By		(Signature of "Franking Officer.")	By

TO 49th [illegible] Div[illegible]

*Sender's Number	Day of Month	In reply to Number	AAA
[illegible]	9		

[illegible] AAA [illegible] ... [illegible] AAA FLEURBAIX [illegible] from [illegible] of FROMELLES at 3.35 pm [illegible] AAA [illegible] ... LE MAISNIL and [illegible] between 3.45 pm and 4.15 pm retaliation AAA [illegible] hostile shells [illegible] farm N 4 A 2½.4 two [illegible] on fire 3.45 pm. one blind shell [illegible] 10-6

From	[illegible]
Place	[illegible]
Time	[illegible] AAA 49th [illegible] R [illegible] ARTY

The above may be forwarded as now corrected. (Z) [illegible]

Censor. — Signature of Addressor or person authorised to telegraph in his name

* This line should be erased if not required.

158 S. B. Ltd. Wt. W3673/619—50,000. 10/14. Forms C2121/10.

XVIII

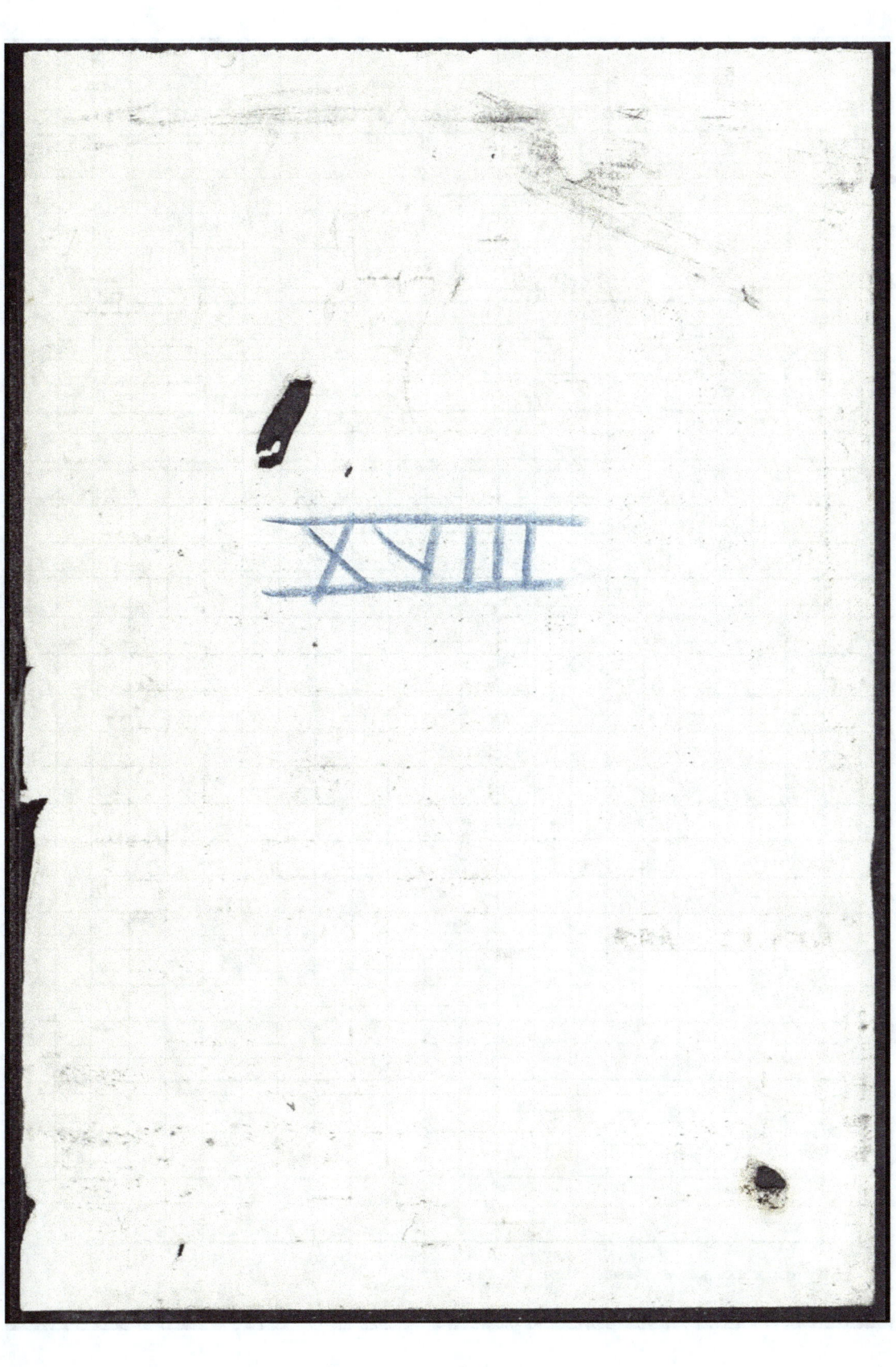

"A" Form. Army Form C. 2121.

MESSAGES AND SIGNALS.

No. of Message ______

Prefix ______ Code ______ m. Office of Origin and Service Instructions.	Words.	Charge.	This message is on a/c of: ______ Service. (Signature of "Franking Officer.")	Recd. at ______ m
	Sent At ______ m. To ______ By ______			Date ______ From ______ By ______

TO (2)

Sender's Number *	Day of Month	In reply to Number	AAA

AAA	[illegible]	between	766	and
769	[illegible]	area	AAA	[illegible]
766	[illegible]	cylindrical	object	[illegible]
[illegible]	[illegible]	[illegible]	was	cylinder
as	it	appears	[illegible]	have
a	handle	protruding	upwards	AAA
Hostile	battery	which	[illegible]	at
fire	S	appears	to	be
in	vicinity	of	FROMELLES	AAA
Hostile	battery	howitzer	at	N22d 1.9
and	N23b 5½.3	AAA	further	report
at	7pm	gives	hostile	battery
firing	from	about	N22d 3.7	flashes
being	seen	185°	magnetic	from
N10c 6.8				

From [illegible]

Place

Time [illegible]

The above may be forwarded as now corrected. (Z)

Censor. Signature of Addressor or person authorised to telegraph in his name

* This line should be erased if not required.

(24473). M.R.Co.,Ltd. Wt.W4848/541. 50,000. 9/14. Forms C2121/10.

"A" Form. Army Form C. 2121.

MESSAGES AND SIGNALS.

No. of Message

Prefix ___ Code ___ m.	Words.	Charge.	This message is on a/c of:	Recd. at ___ m.
Office of Origin and Service Instructions.	Sent		[illegible] Service.	Date
	At ___ m.		[illegible] Major	From
	To		(Signature of "Franking Officer.")	By
	By			

TO { 49th | W | R | DIVN

Sender's Number	Day of Month	In reply to Number	AAA
* BM/309	10th		

Summary	Report	AAA	[illegible]	[illegible]
[illegible]	[illegible]	[illegible]		[illegible]
[illegible]	[illegible]	[illegible]		
and	[illegible]	[illegible]		
[illegible]	[illegible]	[illegible]	[illegible]	[illegible]
[illegible]	[illegible]	[illegible]	[illegible]	[illegible]
9th	[illegible]	[illegible]	[illegible]	[illegible]
examined	[illegible]	[illegible]	[illegible]	[illegible]
in	character	[illegible]	[illegible]	[illegible]
it	AAA	Trenches	[illegible]	[illegible]
shelled	at	2 pm	and	3 pm
light	Shrapnel	and	H E	AAA
Trenches	in	vicinity	[illegible]	[illegible]
[illegible]	shelled	4 pm	[illegible]	[illegible]
H E	AAA	Works	reported	on
parapet	at	9 r 6	and	party
observed	between	9 5 b	[illegible]	[illegible]

From			
Place			
Time			

The above may be forwarded as now corrected. (Z)

Censor. Signature of Addressor or person authorised to telegraph in his name

* This line should be erased if not required.

(24473). M.R.Co.,Ltd. Wt.W4843/541. 50,000. 9/14. Forms C2121/10.

49th (W.R.) Divisional Artillery.

TACTICAL PROGRESS REPORT.

6 p.m. June 9th to 6 p.m. June 10th 1915.

1. OPERATIONS.

(a) (1) At 10.20 p.m. 10th W.R. Battery fired 3 rounds at Pt.880 and three rounds 50 yards West of Pt.883 Trench Mortars silenced.

(2) Armoured Train fired on N.22.d.1.8 (100 yards N of Pt.756) and 50 yards North of Pt.714 (N.28.b.5½.3.).

(b) (1) RUE DES LOMBARDES shelled at 6 p.m. (on 9th) mostly blind, one shell examined and found to be 4-7" in diameter, no fuze in it.

(2) Trenches 1 S shelled at 2 p.m. and 3 p.m. by light shrapnel and high explosive.

(3) Trenches in vicinity of LA BOUTILLERIE shelled at 4 p.m. with small H.E.

2. INFORMATION GAINED.

(1) Work reported on parapet at 976 and party observed between 956 and 957.

(2) Digging between 968 and 969.

(3) At 966 a cylindrical object on parapet. This may prove to be a gas cylinder as it appears to have a handle protruding upwards.

(4) Hostile Battery firing at trench 1 S, thought to be located at N.22.d.1.8 or N.28.b.5½.3., as batteries have fired from these positions previously.
A further report at 7 p.m. gives hostile battery firing from about 100 yards N of Pt.756 (N.22.d.3.7.) flashes being seen 185° Magnetic from N.10.c.6.8. Armoured Train having swept 100 yards each side of N.22.d.1.8 at 7.0 p.m. silenced this battery.

(5) Machine Gun alternative position was observed N.E. of Pt. 976.

3. WORK DONE BY BATTERIES.

4th Battery continued work on alternative position. Gun pits and dug-outs improved.

10/6/15.

H F Calvert Jones for W.A.B.C. Major R.A.,
Brigade Major R.A.49th (W.R.) Division.

XXI

"A" Form. Army Form C. 2121.

MESSAGES AND SIGNALS.

No. of Message

Prefix ___ Code ___ m.	Words.	Charge.	This message is on a/c of:	Recd. at ___ m
Office of Origin and Service Instructions.	Sent		[illegible] Service.	Date
	At ___ m.			From
	To		[illegible] RA	By
	By		(Signature of "Franking Officer.")	

TO	49th	W	R	DIVN

Sender's Number	Day of Month	In reply to Number	AAA
* [illegible]	[illegible]		

[illegible]	report	AAA	3	W
Corner	FLEURBAIX	shelled	2 pm	two
shells	AAA	Hostile	battery	located
[illegible]	2.0 pm	located	[illegible]	near
[illegible]	BATTERIES	Armoured	Train	opened
fire	on	it	at	4.42 pm
[illegible]	battery	ceased	firing	at 4.57 pm
report	was	received	here	at
4.40 pm	AAA	Hostile	battery	located
150 yards	NORTH	of	PR 756	opened
fire	on	FLEURBAIX	at	4.55 pm
Armoured	Train	replied	at	4.59 pm
battery	ceased	at	5.3 pm	AAA
10th	Battery	moved	to	VIIIth
DIVN	Area	during	the	night

From	49th	[illegible]	[illegible]	[illegible]
Place				
Time	7.?? pm		[illegible]	

The above may be forwarded as now corrected. (Z)

Censor. Signature of Addressor or person authorised to telegraph in his name

* This line should be erased if not required.

(24473). M.R.Co.,Ltd. Wt.W4848/341. 50,000. 9/14. Forms C2121/10.

XXII

49th (W.R.) Divisional Artillery.

TACTICAL PROGRESS REPORT.

6 p.m. June 10th to 6 p.m. June 11th 1915.

1. OPERATIONS.

(a) (1) Armoured Train opened fire on an enemy's battery located near LES POTERIES at 4.42 p.m. The above hostile battery ceased firing 4.45 p.m.

(2) Armoured Train also fired on Hostile battery located 150 yards North of Pt.756, time 4.58 p.m. the German battery ceased firing at 5.3 p.m.

(3) 10th Battery moved to VIIIth Division during the night.

(b) (1) The S.W. corner of FLEURBAIX was shelled at 2 p.m. Two shells in all fell.
FLEURBAIX was again shelled at 4.55 p.m., by a hostile battery located 150 yards North of Pt.756. Time 4.55 p.m.

2. INFORMATION GAINED.

(1) Hostile battery located 150 yards North of Pt.756.

(2) A cloud of smoke was observed coming from House at O.1.d.6.3.

(3) Hostile battery located at O.8.a.7.6 220 yards E of LES POTERIES

3. WORK DONE BY BATTERIES. Observation Stations and dug outs improved.

L.W. Lewer
Major R.A.,
Brigade Major R.A.49th (W.R.) Division.

12/6/15.

"A" Form. Army Form C. 2121.

MESSAGES AND SIGNALS.

No. of Message

Prefix Code m.	Words.	Charge.	This message is on a/c of:	Recd. at m.
Office of Origin and Service Instructions.	Sent		Service.	Date
	At m.			From
	To			
	By		(Signature of "Franking Officer.")	By

TO	49th	W	R	Div

Sender's Number	Day of Month	In reply to Number	AAA
* [illegible]	[illegible]		

Summary	report	[illegible]	[illegible]	[illegible]
[illegible]	[illegible]	[illegible]	[illegible]	[illegible]
[illegible]	[illegible]	[illegible]	[illegible]	battery
H [illegible] 3.6	11 15 am	AAA	[illegible]	[illegible]
[illegible]	[illegible]	REPORTS	[illegible]	[illegible]
[illegible]	[illegible]	[illegible]	H 29 C 8.9	[illegible]
[illegible]	AAA	at	[illegible]	[illegible]
AAA	hostile	aeroplane	[illegible]	[illegible]
[illegible]	[illegible]	distinguishing	marks	[illegible]
[illegible]	like	BRISTOL	TRACTOR	[illegible]
[illegible]	shape	AAA	hostile	aeroplanes
very	active	at	4 pm	AAA
Hostile	battery	shelled	[illegible]	[illegible]
[illegible]	4th	Battalion	1 31 a 5.1	at
5.50pm	AAA	digging	at	2nd
line	trench	100	yards	W
of	[illegible]	[illegible]	[illegible]	[illegible]

From			
Place			
Time			

The above may be forwarded as now corrected. (Z)

Censor. Signature of Addressor or person authorised to telegraph in his name

* This line should be erased if not required.

(24473). M.R.Co.,Ltd. Wt.W4848/341. 50,000. 9/14. Forms C2121/10.

XXIV

"A" Form. Army Form C. 2121.

MESSAGES AND SIGNALS.

No. of Message ________

Prefix ____ Code ____ m.	Words.	Charge.	This message is on a/c of:	Recd. at ____ m.
Office of Origin and Service Instructions.	Sent		________ Service.	Date ____
	At ____ m.			From ____
	To ____			
	By ____		(Signature of "Franking Officer.")	By ____

TO

Sender's Number	Day of Month	In reply to Number	AAA
*			

From				
Place				
Time				

The above may be forwarded as now corrected. (Z)

Censor. Signature of Addressor or person authorised to telegraph in his name

* This line should be erased if not required.

(24473). M.R.Co.,Ltd. Wt.W4848/541. 50,000. 9/14. Forms C2121/10.

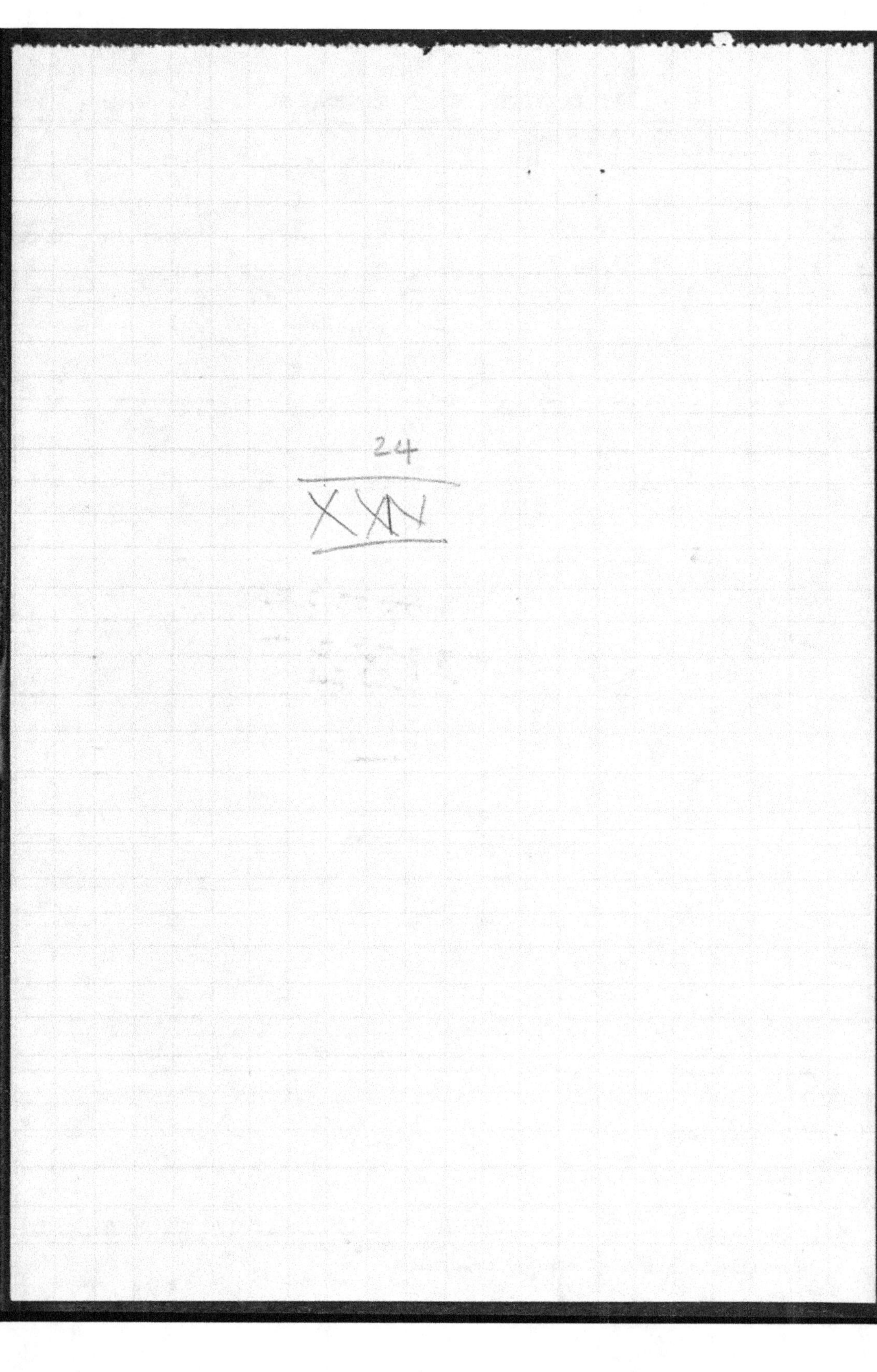
24
XXIV

49th (W.R.) Divisional Artillery.

TACTICAL PROGRESS REPORT.

6 p.m. June 11th to 6 p.m. June 12th 1916.

1. OPERATIONS.

(a) Nil.

(b) (1) Hostile battery fired 5 shells to left of 2nd W.R. Battery (H.35.d.3.8) at 11.15 a.m.

(2) Hostile Aeroplanes very active at 4 p.m.

(3) Hostile battery shelled K.O.Y.L.I. Headquarters (4th Battalion) E.31.a.5.6. at 5.50 p.m.

2. INFORMATION GAINED.

(1) Observation balloon in direction of BERNIERE FARM, observed at 12.10 p.m. Magnetic bearing from H.29.c.8.8. 181 degrees. Out of range.

(2) Hostile aeroplane seen 5.6 p.m. Had no distinguishing marks, but was like Bristol TRACTOR BIPLANE in shape.

Work been done at 900 and 957.

3. WORK DONE BY BATTERIES. Gun pits and dug-outs improved. O.C. 8th Battery has commenced reconstruction of Gun emplacements.

Major R.A.,
Brigade Major R.A.49th (W.R.) Division.

13/6/16.

"A" Form. Army Form C. 2121.

MESSAGES AND SIGNALS.

No. of Message ______

Prefix ______ Code ______ m.	Words.	Charge.	This message is on a/c of:	Recd. at ______ m.
Office of Origin and Service Instructions.	Sent		______ Service.	Date ______
	At ______ m.			From ______
	To ______			
	By ______		(Signature of "Franking Officer.")	By ______

TO	49th	W	R	DIV

Sender's Number	Day of Month	In reply to Number	AAA
* [illegible]	Thirteenth		

Intelligence	summary	AAA	little	plane
[illegible]	H 27 d	and	H 28 a	[illegible]
[illegible]	four	AAA	[illegible]	four
[illegible]	[illegible]	[illegible]	[illegible]	
H 26 d 3.0	[illegible]	[illegible]	[illegible]	
[illegible]	two	[illegible]	[illegible]	[illegible]
rockets	[illegible]	[illegible]	AAA	3
men	killed	and	approx	3
men	injured	AAA	several	horses
injured	and	3	killed	AAA
German	working	party	opposite	3 Q
working	hard	all	day	

From	49th	W	R	DIV
Place				
Time	[illegible]			

The above may be forwarded as now corrected. (Z)

Censor. Signature of Addressor or person authorised to telegraph in his name

* This line should be erased if not required.

(24473). M.R.Co.,Ltd. Wt.W4848/341. 50,000. 9/14. Forms C2121/10.

XXVI

49th (W.R.) Divisional Artillery.

TACTICAL PROGRESS REPORT.

6 p.m. June 12th to 6 p.m. June 13th 1915.

1. OPERATIONS.

(a) Nil.

(b) (1) At 2 p.m. a hostile battery opened fire on H.20.d.3.0, 1st W.R. F.A. Bde. wagon lines.
The fire was directed by plane.
Three men killed and approximately 3 injured.
Several horses were injured and 3 killed.

(2) Hostile aeroplane over H.27.d. and H.28.a. at 11 a.m. and 2 p.m.

2. INFORMATION GAINED.

(1) German working parties observed opposite 3 Q.
Very strenuous work was continued by them all day.

3. WORK DONE BY BATTERIES.

Considerable progress has been made with regard to reconstruction of Gun emplacements by 8th Battery.

R.W. Sewer

Major R.A.,
Brigade Major R.A. 49th (W.R.) Division.

14/6/15

XXVII

"A" Form. Army Form C. 2121.

MESSAGES AND SIGNALS.

No. of Message________

Prefix______ Code______ m. Office of Origin and Service Instructions.	Words.	Charge.	This message is on a/c of: ______ Service. (Signature of "Franking Officer.")	Recd. at______ m.
	Sent			Date______
	At______ m.			From______
	To______			
	By______			By______

TO [illegible]

Sender's Number	Day of Month	In reply to Number	AAA
* [illegible]	[illegible]		

[illegible]	Summary	AAA	Hostile	[illegible]
[illegible]	[illegible]	[illegible]	[illegible]	[illegible]
[illegible]	[illegible]	[illegible]	[illegible]	[illegible]
[illegible]	[illegible]	[illegible]	[illegible]	[illegible]
[illegible]	[illegible]	battery	shelled	[illegible]
[illegible]	[illegible]	AAA	[illegible]	[illegible]
[illegible]	shelled	[illegible]	[illegible]	[illegible]
[illegible]	[illegible]	[illegible]	[illegible]	[illegible]
[illegible]	shelling	ceased	AAA	[illegible]
[illegible]	ceased	on	to	[illegible]
Battery	2.8 pm	shelling	ceased	AAA
Hostile	battery	near	[illegible]	[illegible]
CHAMPS	FARM	shelled	24th	DIVN
from	O9 b 8.9	AAA	Enemy	[illegible]
busy	with	second	line	trenches
near	Point	9 69	AAA	Report
[illegible]	in	[illegible]	in	[illegible]

From			
Place			
Time			

The above may be forwarded as now corrected. (Z)

Censor. Signature of Addressor or person authorised to telegraph in his nam

* This line should be erased if not required.

(24473). M.R.Co.,Ltd. Wt.W4843/541. 50,000. 9/14. Forms C2121/10.

XXVIII

49th (W.R.) Divisional Artillery.

TACTICAL PROGRESS REPORT.

6 p.m. June 13th to 6 p.m. June 14th 1915.

1. OPERATIONS.

(a) (1) W.R. R.G.A. opened fire on LES POTERIES Battery at 1.15 p.m.

(2) W.R. R.G.A. opened fire on FROMELLES Battery at 2.8 p.m. Hostile fire ceased almost instantaneously.

(b) (1). Hostile Battery again shelled old wagon lines 1st W.R. F.A. Bde. at 11 a.m. Three shells in all fell.

(2). FROMELLES Battery shelled BOIS GRENIER at 1.30 p.m.

(3) 5 P and 5 Q shelled at 1.10 p.m. W.R. R.G.A. opened fire on LES POTERIES Battery. 1.15 p.m. shelling ceased.

(4) Hostile battery at LES BAS, CHAMPS FARM shelled 27th Divn., from O.9.b.8.9.

(5) Hostile battery at BEUCAMPS dropped two shells on Battalion Headquarters I.31.a.5.6, and one shell on BRIDOUX Road.

2. INFORMATION GAINED.

(1) F.O.O. 7th Battery reports
Enemy shelled BOIS GRENIER between 1 and 2 p.m. The shells came from the direction of FROMELLES.

The Road crossing the high ground O.6.d.3.5, to O.6.d.2.9 has been under my observation all day and a good deal of traffic proceeds along it in a Northerly direction, about 50 horsemen crossed it about 4 p.m. in groups of 2 or 3.

The enemy are digging a new trench at 200 yards S of 957 apparently with a view to straightening their line a little.

A pipe is located North of 930 near the new trench, it is above the parapet and supported by an upright, probably a pump in conjunction with this work. It is very obvious and easily seen from the trenches.
This information has been verified in conjunction with the Infantry.

(2) Enemy still busy with second line trenches near Pt.969.

3. WORK DONE BY BATTERIES. Gun pits and dug outs improved.

L W Lewer
Major R.A.,
Brigade Major R.A.49th (W.R.) Division.

15/6/15.

XXIX

"A" Form. Army Form C. 2121.

MESSAGES AND SIGNALS.

No. of Message ________

Prefix ____ Code ____ m.	Words.	Charge.	This message is on a/c of:	Recd. at ____ m.
Office of Origin and Service Instructions.	Sent		[illegible] Service.	Date ____
	At ____ m.		[illegible]	From ____
	To ____			
	By ____		(Signature of "Franking Officer.")	By ____

TO { 49th | W | R | DIVN

Sender's Number	Day of Month	In reply to Number	AAA
* [illegible]	[illegible]		

[illegible]	summary	AAA	[illegible]	batteries
located	[illegible]	[illegible]	[illegible]	[illegible]
[illegible]	N 22 b 2.8	N 23 d 5.[illegible]	N 23 c 10.3	N 23 c 3.4
5.9"	[illegible]	N 16 b 5.1	AAA	[illegible]
Hostile	[illegible]	Magnetic	bearings	172½°
188½°	194½°	199°	201°	[illegible] ½°
[illegible] ½°	[illegible]	from	H 25 b 1.9	AAA
another	117°	from	H 34 a 6.1	AAA
one	trench	mortar	at	[illegible]
2 P	fired	at	hostile	mortar
which	was	silenced	at	2.30 am
AAA	119th	Battery	on	[illegible]
wagon	lines	1st	W	R
F	A	Bde	bombarded	by
5.9"	Howitzers	between	10 am	and
12.20 pm	70	shells	fired	AAA
This	hostile	battery	is	[illegible]

From		RK	
Place			
Time			

The above may be forwarded as now corrected. (Z)

Censor. Signature of Addressor or person authorised to telegraph in his name

* This line should be erased if not required.

(24473). M.R.Co.,Ltd. Wt.W4848/541. 50,000. 9/14. Forms C2121/10.

"A" Form. Army Form C. 2121.

MESSAGES AND SIGNALS.

No. of Message______

Prefix______ Code______ m. | Words. | Charge.

Office of Origin and Service Instructions.

Sent
At______ m.
To______
By______

This message is on a/c of:

______ *Service.*

(Signature of "Franking Officer.")

Recd. at______ m.
Date______
From______
By______

TO

Sender's Number	Day of Month	In reply to Number	AAA
*			

[illegible]	[illegible]	[illegible]	[illegible]	[illegible]
[illegible]	[illegible]	[illegible]	[illegible]	[illegible]
[illegible]	[illegible]	[illegible]	[illegible]	[illegible]
[illegible]	[illegible]	[illegible]	[illegible]	[illegible]
[illegible]	forward	[illegible]	[illegible]	[illegible]
[illegible]	[illegible]	[illegible]	[illegible]	[illegible]
[illegible]	forward	[illegible]	O.P.	[illegible]
[illegible]	[illegible]	battery	[illegible]	[illegible]
[illegible]	H 4 a 24.3	from	separate	[illegible]
of	smoke	seen	from	battery
firing	at	19th	battery	[illegible]
bearing	166°	AAA	There	is
a	red	brick	building	behind
left	hand	gun	and	a
building	with	bright	shining	roof
behind	right	hand	gun	AAA
[illegible]	R	[illegible]	battery	[illegible]

From

Place

Time

The above may be forwarded as now corrected. (Z)

Censor. Signature of Addressor or person authorised to telegraph in his name

* This line should be erased if not required.

(24473). M.R.Co.,Ltd. Wt.W4848/541. 50,000. 9/14. Forms C2121/10.

"A" Form. Army Form C. 2121.

MESSAGES AND SIGNALS.

No. of Message ________

Prefix ______ Code ______ m.	Words.	Charge.	This message is on a/c of:	Recd. at ______ m.
Office of Origin and Service Instructions.	Sent		______ Service.	Date ______
	At ______ m.			From ______
	To ______			
	By ______		(Signature of "Franking Officer.")	By ______

TO

Sender's Number	Day of Month	In reply to Number	AAA
*			

[illegible]	[illegible]	at	this	hostile
[illegible]	at	11.20 am	AAA	[illegible]
in	[illegible]	[illegible]	[illegible]	
[illegible]			[illegible]	
[illegible]	[illegible]	[illegible]	[illegible]	
parapet	[illegible]	[illegible]	[illegible]	
[illegible]	[illegible]	being	strengthened	[illegible]
[illegible]	[illegible]	[illegible]	[illegible]	[illegible]
[illegible]	[illegible]	a	sketch	[illegible]
forwarded	[illegible]	AAA	Observation	post
in	tree	300	yards	North
of	PRIDEAUX	about	250	yards
behind	enemy's	line	AAA	This
tree	is	one	in	row
of	poplars	AAA	Two	Germans
entered	house	at	PRIDEAUX	and
there	is	a	heavy	girder

From

Place

Time

The above may be forwarded as now corrected. (Z)

Censor. Signature of Addressor or person authorised to telegraph in his name

* This line should be erased if not required.

(24473). M.R.Co.,Ltd. Wt.W4848/541. 50,000. 9/14. Forms C2121/10.

"A" Form. Army Form C. 2121.

MESSAGES AND SIGNALS. No. of Message ________

Prefix ______ Code ______ m.	Words.	Charge.	This message is on a/c of:	Recd. at ______ m.
Office of Origin and Service Instructions.	Sent		______ *Service.*	Date ______
	At ______ m.			From ______
	To ______			
	By ______		(Signature of "Franking Officer.")	By ______

TO (4)

Sender's Number	Day of Month	In reply to Number	AAA
*			

[illegible]	[illegible]	[illegible]	[illegible]	[illegible]
[illegible]	[illegible]	AAA	[illegible]	[illegible]
[illegible]	[illegible]	[illegible]	170°	[illegible]
A 25 b 1.9	[illegible]	10.30 am	[illegible]	[illegible]
[illegible]	[illegible]	5 pm	AAA	[illegible]
[illegible]	[illegible]	[illegible]	[illegible]	[illegible]
164	[illegible]	A 31 a 2.2	AAA	[illegible]
[illegible]	balloon	[illegible]	HERLIES	[illegible]
[illegible]	579			

From [illegible]
Place
Time [illegible]

The above may be forwarded as now corrected. (Z)

Censor. Signature of Addressor or person authorised to telegraph in his name

* This line should be erased if not required.

(24473). M.R.Co.,Ltd. Wt.W4848/541. 50,000. 9/14. Forms C2121/10.

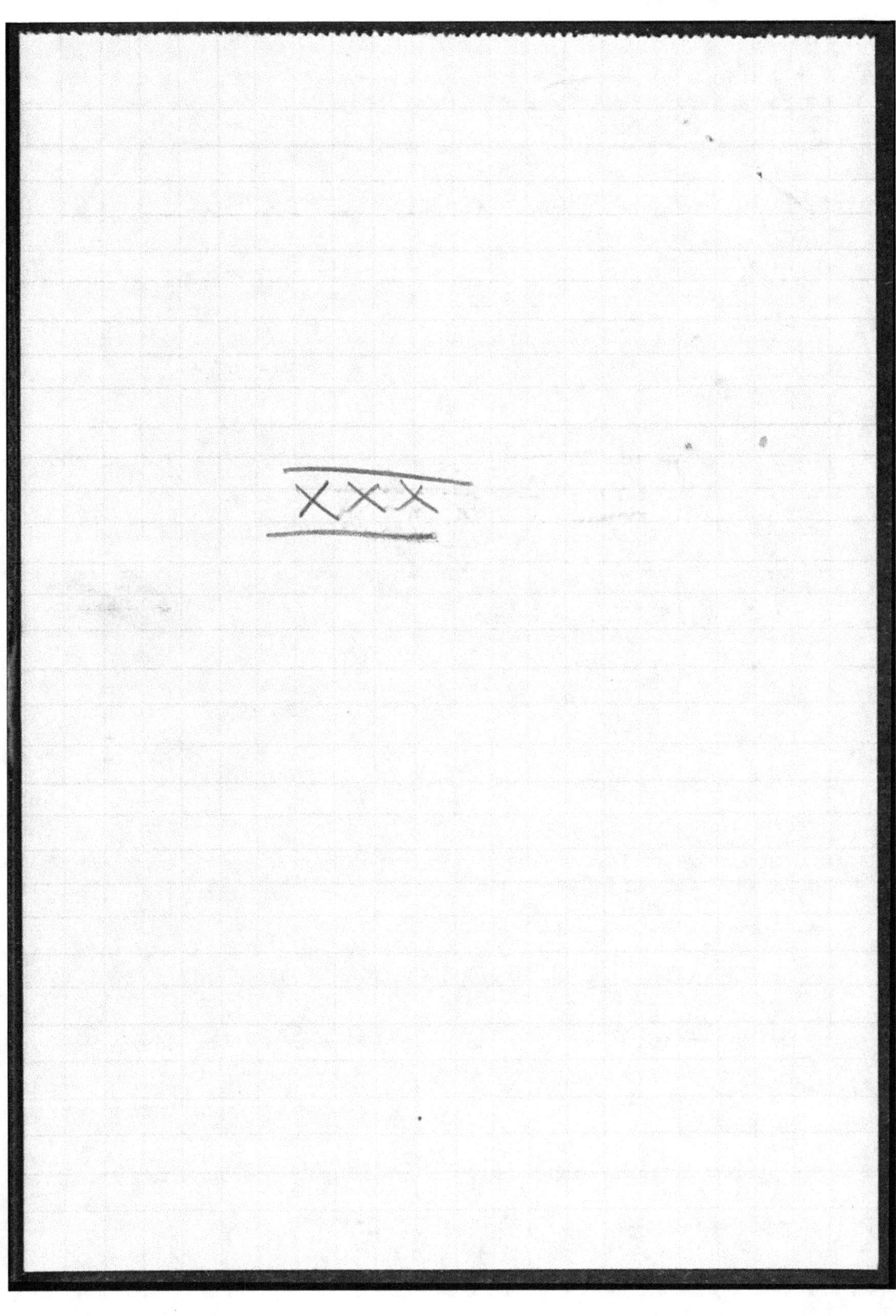

49th (W.R.) Divisional Artillery.

TACTICAL PROGRESS REPORT.

6 p.m. June 14th to 6 p.m. June 15th 1915.

1. OPERATIONS.

(a) (1) Our trench mortar at 2 P fired at hostile mortar which was silenced at 2.30 a.m.

(2) W.R. R.G.A. fired 12 rounds at hostile battery at 11.20 a.m. battery's position is N.23.b.3.4.

(3) 11th W.R. Battery ordered to stand by to fire should battery become active again.

(b) (1) Hostile battery bombarded 119th Battery and old wagon lines of 1st W.R. F.A. Bde., with 5-9" Howitzer(between 10 a.m. & 12.20 p.m.) 70 shell were fired.
Location of this battery is N.23.b.3.4. This is also confirmed by a report given below from 2nd W.R. ~~F.A. Bde.~~ Battery

2. INFORMATION GAINED.

(1) Hostile batteries located during night of 14th - 15th from flashes
(a) N32.b.2.8. 100 yards N.W. Pt.170.
(b) N.33.d.5½.7. 250 yards E. Pt.644.
(c) N.23.a.10.3. 100 yards E. Pt.782.
(d) N.23.b.3.4. (5-9") Just E Pt.784.
(e) N.16.b.5.1. 50 yards S.W. Pt.837.

Other hostile flashes Magnetic bearings
172½°
188½°
194½°
199°
201°
144½°
137½°
The above bearings are all taken from H.25.b.1.9.
Another bearing of 117° was taken from H.34.a.6.1.

(2) 2nd W.R. ~~F.A. Bde.~~ Battery reports that one of the hostile guns was seen to be run forward from a hidden emplacement, it fired and was run back, and hidden by a red screen

(3) A report from 1st W.R. F.A. Bde. gives the following information "From H.4.a.2½.3, four seperate rings of smoke were seen from hostile battery firing at 119th Battery, the Magnetic bearing is 166°. There is a red brick building behind the left hand gun, and a building with a bright shining roof behind the right hand gun.

(4) The parapet at bend of stream (Pt.956) is being strengthened. A new trench is already reported and a sketch is attached herewith.

(5) Observation post in tree 300 yards North of BRIDEAUX and about 250 yards behind enemy's line. This tree is one in row of Poplars.

(6) Two Germans entered house at BRIDEAUX and there is a heavy girder or beam on wheels outside the house.

(7) Observation balloon up Magnetic bearing 170° from H.25.b.1.9, from 10.3 a.m. to 1 p.m. Again up at 5 p.m. Same balloon reported as Magnetic bearing 164½° from H.31.a.2.2.
This gives balloon beyond HERLIES at Pt.519.

3. WORK DONE BY BATTERIES. Gun pits and dug-outs improved.

16/6/15.

H.M. Calvert Jones Lt ADC for Major R.A.,
Brigade Major R.A. 49th (W.R.) Division.

49th (W.R.) Divisional Artillery.

TACTICAL PROGRESS REPORT.

6 p.m. June 15th to 6 p.m. June 16th 1915.

1. OPERATIONS.

(a) (1) Enemy's Biplane observing artillery fire was successfully engaged and driven off by British Monoplane about 10 a.m. The German machine which was attacked from behind, dropped steeply for a time and then made for its own lines.

(b) (1) Hostile aeroplane over 3rd W.R. Battery position at 7.30 a.m. and again at 11.30 a.m.

(2) F.O.O. 6th Battery reports that the enemy shelled our trench mortars to the left of BRIDOUX Road at 2.45 p.m. No damage was done.

2. INFORMATION GAINED.

(1) F.O.O. 6th W.R. Battery reports house at Pt.889 to have a darkened loophole in it. Possibly a Snipers house or artillery observation post.

(2) German troops mounted and dismounted have been seen on Road running N. N.W. through U in ESCOBECQUES.

3. WORK DONE BY BATTERIES. Gun pits improved.
4th W.R. Battery continued work on alternative position.

L W Lever

Major R.A.,
17/6/15. Brigade Major R.A.49th (W.R.) Division.

N.B. Correction to Tactical Progress Report 6 p.m. June 14th to 6 p.m. June 15th 1915.

In 2. INFORMATION GAINED. (d) for "Just to Pt.784" read "Just E. of Pt.784".

"A" Form. Army Form C. 2121.

MESSAGES AND SIGNALS. No. of Message

Prefix	Code	m.	Words	Charge	This message is on a/c of:	Recd. at	m.
Office of Origin and Service Instructions.			Sent At m.		O H M S Service.	Date	
			To			From	
			By		H Calvert Jones for B.M. (Signature of "Franking Officer.")	By	

TO	49th	W	R.	Div.

Sender's Number	Day of Month	In reply to Number	AAA
* ADC to BM/12	Saturday		

Intelligence	Summary	AAA.	Hostile	plane
over	7th	Battery	7.30 AM	AAA
German	Biplane	observing	artillery	fire
engaged	by	British	monoplane	went
away	off	about	10 AM.	AAA
Enemy	shelled	our	Trench	mortars
at	2-30 PM.	to	left	of
BRIDOUX	Road	AAA	no	Damage
AAA.	Train	consisting	of	several
coaches	and	goods	wagon	reported
at	FROMELLES	AAA	Engines	on
train	AAA.	Hammering	&	movements
Germans	observed	in	wood	near
O11a 5.5.	AAA	Our	motors	fired
on	suspicious	work	in	enemys
parapet	AAA.	balloon	seen	in
direction	of	FROMELLES	5 pm	A

From	49th	W.	R.	ARTY
Place				
Time	6-55 PM			

The above may be forwarded as now corrected. (Z) H F Calvert Jones [illegible] for Brigade Major

Censor. Signature of Addressor or person authorised to telegraph in his name

* This line should be erased if not required.

158 S. B. Ltd. Wt. W5673/619—50,000. 10/14. Forms C2121/10.

XXXII

49th (W.R.) Divisional Artillery.

TACTICAL PROGRESS REPORT.

6 p.m. June 15th to 6 p.m. June 16th 1915.

1. OPERATIONS.

(a) (1) Enemy's Biplane observing artillery fire was successfully engaged and driven off by British Monoplane about 10 a.m. The German machine, which was attacked from behind, dropped steeply for a time and then made for its own lines.

(b) (1) Hostile aeroplane over 3rd W.R. Battery position at 7.30 a.m. and again at 11.30 a.m.

(2) F.O.O. 8th W.R. Battery reports that the enemy shelled our trench mortars to the left of BRIDOUX Road at 2.45 p.m. No damage was done.

2. INFORMATION GAINED.

(1) F.O.O. 6th W.R. Battery reports house at Pt.869 to have a darkened loophole in it. Possibly a snipers house or artillery observation post.

(2) German troops mounted and dismounted have been seen on Road running N. N.W. through U in ESCOBECQUES.

3. WORK DONE BY BATTERIES. Gun pits improved, 4th W.R. Battery continued work on alternative position.

17/6/15.

[signature]

Major R.A.,
Brigade Major R.A.49th (W.R.) Division.

N.B. Correction to Tactical Progress Report 6 p.m. June 14th to 6 p.m. June 15th 1915.

In 2.INFORMATION GAINED. (d) for "Just to Pt.784" read "Just E. of Pt.784".

XXXIII

"A" Form. Army Form C. 2121.

MESSAGES AND SIGNALS.

No. of Message

Prefix Code m.	Words / Charge		
Office of Origin and Service Instructions.	Sent At m. To By	This message is on a/c of: O. H. M. S Service. H. F. Calcutt [?] for B.M. (Signature of "Franking Officer.")	Recd. at m. Date From By

TO 49th W. R. Dw

Sender's Number	Day of Month	In reply to Number	AAA
B.M/43/9.	Seventeenth [?].		

Intelligence	Summary.	AAA.	Hostile	plane
over	1st	W	R.	Brigade
7-40 AM.	to	8 AM.	AAA.	Enemy
shelled	RUE	PETILLON	4.0 pm.	AAA.
Probable	position	of	battery	1½
degrees	East	FROMELLES	AAA.	O.
C.	9th	Battery	report	horseman [?]
and	motor	car	seen	111
degrees	magnetic	from	H 35/d 2.6.	AAA
Battery	on	direction	of	FETERIE
Shrapnel [?]	shelling	at	5.35	AAA
Shells	burst	200	yards	right
BOIS	GRENIER	on	BOIS	GRENIER
FLEURBAIX	road.	AAA.	11th	Battery
registered	FME	DELANGRE	during	afternoon
AAA.	Working	parties	observed	on
second	line	trench	at	pt 970

From

Place

Time

The above may be forwarded as now corrected. (Z)

Censor. Signature of Addressor or person authorised to telegraph in his name

* This line should be erased if not required.

158 S. B. Ltd. Wt. W5673/619—50,000. 10/14. Forms C2121/10.

"A" Form. Army Form C. 2121.

MESSAGES AND SIGNALS.

No. of Message

Prefix Code m.	Words	Charge	This message is on a/c of:	Recd. at m.
Office of Origin and Service Instructions.	Sent		Service.	Date
	At m.			From
	To			
	By		(Signature of "Franking Officer.")	By

TO

* Sender's Number	Day of Month	In reply to Number	AAA

AAA.	Traffic	observed	on	road
running	through	O 11 d 5.5.	morning	[illegible]
[illegible]	and	Trains	AAA	Flash.
parapet.	Work	along	communication	trench.
from	957	to	940	AAA
Then	vary	from	~~[illegible]~~ Five	to
Twenty	yards	in	length.	Ten
feet	high	and	three	feet
wide.	AAA			

From	49th	W	R	ARTY
Place				
Time	7-20 PM			

The above may be forwarded as now corrected. (Z) [illegible]

Censor. Signature of Addressor or person authorised to telegraph in his name

* This line should be erased if not required.

158 S. B. Ltd. Wt. W5673/619—50,000. 10/14. Forms C2121/10.

XXXV

[illegible]

"A" Form. Army Form C. 2121.

MESSAGES AND SIGNALS.

No. of Message ________

Prefix ____ Code ____ m. Office of Origin and Service Instructions.	Words. Charge. Sent At ____ m. To ____ By ____	This message is on a/c of: O H M S Service. Cecil Allen (Signature of "Franking Officer.")	Recd. at ____ m. Date ____ From ____ By ____

TO { Third West Riding F.A. Bde.

Sender's Number	Day of Month	In reply to Number	AAA
* SCRA 1	17th		

Your	Brigade	Ammn	Cols	will
move	to	new	billets	shown
on	attached	Sketch	at	4-0 pm.
to-day	AAA	Route	to	be
taken	RUE	BATAILLE	-	RUE
du	QUESNOY	-	Cross	roads
G29a	-	SAILLY	sur	la
LYS	-	SAILLY	BRIDGE	-
Cross	roads	G16a	-	PONT
de la	BOUDRETTE	to	new	billets
at	G10b12	AAA	The	head
of	the	column	is	not
to	be	at	SAILLY	Cross
Roads	before	4.30pm	and	the
rear	of	the	column	is
to	be	clear	of	SAILLY
BRIDGE	by	5.15 pm.		

From SCRA

Place 49th (W.R.) Divn

Time 1-5 pm.

The above may be forwarded as now corrected. (Z) Cecil Allen

Censor. Signature of Addressor or person authorised to telegraph in his name

* This line should be erased if not required.

(24473). M.R.Co.,Ltd. Wt.W4843/541. 50,000. 9/14. Forms C2121/10.

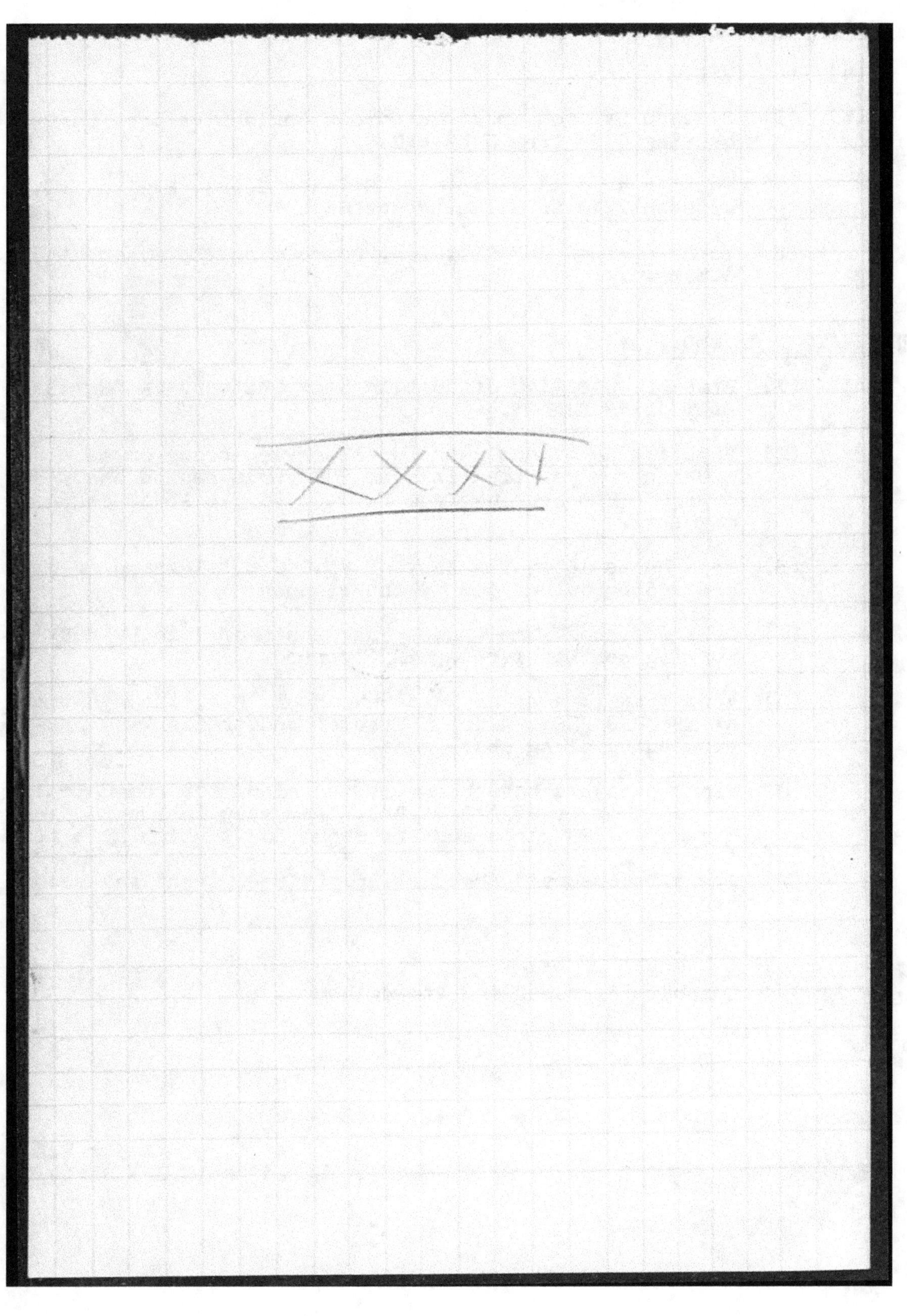

XXXV

49th (W.R.) Divisional Artillery.

TACTICAL PROGRESS REPORT.

6 p.m. June 16th to 6 p.m. June 17th.

1. OPERATIONS.

(a) (Nil.

(b) (1) Sausage balloon up at intervals during the day. Magnetic bearing 163° from H.33.c.3.8.

(2) Hostile aeroplane over 1st Brigade H.Qrs.(H.27.d.2.3.) between 7.40 to 8 a.m. yesterday.

(3) Enemy shelled RUE PETILLON, commencing 4 p.m. and ending 4.30 p.m.

2. INFORMATION GAINED.

(1) Probable position of hostile heavy battery 1½ degrees EAST of FROMELLES.

(2) Haystack doubtless used for observing from, or as a machine gun position is seen 200 yards behind enemy's trench. The bearing from H.35.d.1.6. is 130'5 degrees magnetic.

(3) At a house 150 yards East of Pt.946 a telescope is observed protruding out of one of the windows.

(4) On the second line trench just South of I in BRIDOUX working parties were again observed.

(5) More traffic seen on Road running N. N.W. through the U of ESCOBECQUES. A Motor Tractor and trailer was observed proceeding along above road.

(6) Flank parapets have been erected along the communication trench from Pt.957 to Pt.940, they vary in length from 5 yards to 20 yards and are about 10 ft. high by 3 ft. wide.

(7) New wire observed about Pt.969 between front and second trench.

3. WORK DONE BY BATTERIES. Dug-outs improved and strengthened.

W. Lever

Major R.A.,
Brigade Major R.A.49th (W.R.) Division.

18/6/15.

(...) Divisional Artillery.

__[illegible] D.A. PROGRESS REPORT.__

6 p.m. June 16th to 6 p.m. June 17th.

1. __OPERATIONS.__

(a) Nil.

(b) (1) Sausage balloon up at intervals during the day. Magnetic bearing [illegible]° from [illegible].c.3.3.

(2) Hostile aeroplane over 1st Brigade R.F.A.(R.27.d.3.5.) between 7.40 to 8 a.m. yesterday.

(3) Enemy shelled [illegible], commencing 4 p.m. and ending 4.30 p.m.

2. __INFORMATION GAINED.__

(1) Probable position of hostile heavy battery 1½ degrees EAST of [illegible].

(2) Haystack doubtful [illegible] for observing from, or as a machine gun position is seen [illegible] yards behind enemy's trench. The bearing from [illegible] is 180° degrees magnetic.

XXXVI

(3) At a house 150 yards East of Pt.[illegible] a telescope is observed protruding out of one of the windows.

(4) On the second line trench just south of E in [illegible]ECK working parties were again observed.

(5) More traffic seen on road running N. N.W. through the N of [illegible]. A motor Tractor and trailer was observed proceeding along above road.

(6) Plank parapets have been erected along the communication trench from Pt.[illegible] to Pt.960, they vary in length from 8 yards to 50 yards and are about 10 ft. high by 3 ft. wide.

(7) New wire observed about Pt.[illegible] between front and second trench.

3. __WORK DONE BY BATTERIES.__ Dug-outs improved and strengthened.

Major R.A.,
Brigade Major R.A. [illegible] (...) Division.

[illegible]/6/16.

"A" Form.

Army Form C. 21[illegible]

MESSAGES AND SIGNALS.

No. of Message ______

Prefix ____ Code ____ m.	Words.	Charge.	This message is on a/c of:	Recd. at ____ m
Office of Origin and Service Instructions.	Sent		O H M. Service.	Date ____
	At ____ m.		L W Lewer Maj.	From ____
	To ____		(Signature of "Franking Officer.")	By ____
	By ____			

TO	49th	W	R	DIVN

Sender's Number	Day of Month	In reply to Number	AAA
*BM/46/G	Eighteenth		

Intelligence	Summary	AAA	Observation	balloon
up	10.50 am	to	11.20 am	magnetic
bearing	170½	degrees	from	H25b19
probably	at	T11a7.4	pt	520
AAA	Hostile	heavy	battery	fired
on	area	near	LAVENTIE	from
behind	point	782	11 am	to
1 pm	magnetic	bearing	164½	degrees
from	H33d4.6	AAA	Hostile	field
battery	fired	from	near	pt
837	at	same	time	AAA
Hostile	battery	shelled	H31c88	between
11 am	and	11.30 am	AAA	Hostile
battery	located	by	flashes	near
O9d2.8½	AAA	Hostile	aeroplane	over
FLEURBAIX	5.15 pm			

From	49th	W	R	ARTY
Place				
Time	6.15 pm			

The above may be forwarded as now corrected. (Z) L W Lewer Major RA

Censor. Signature of Addressor or person authorised to telegraph in his name

* This line should be erased if not required.

(24473). M.R.Co.,Ltd. Wt.W4843/541. 50,000. 9/14. Forms C2121/10.

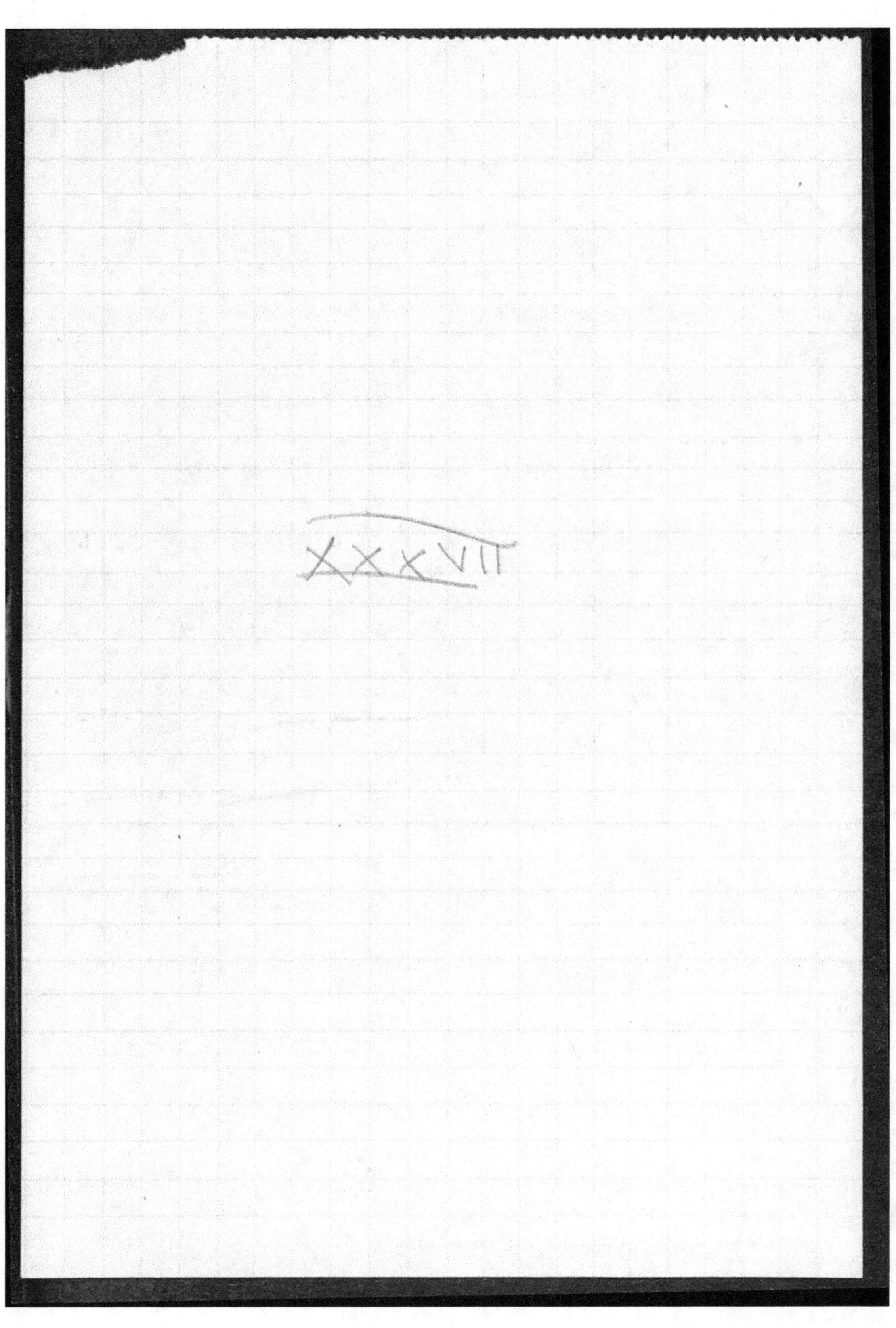

XXXVII

B.M. R.A.

URGENT.

SECRET. Reference Sheet 36 N.W. 1/20000.

Officer Commanding,

The following moves will be completed by 8.0 p.m. June 18th 1915.

1. R.A. Bde. Amm: Columns from present billets to the area vacated by the 49th Divisional Train viz

Roads from Square G.3.d.2.9. to G.9.c.2.9. thence to G.16.a.2.2. thence to G.10.d.3.4. thence to G.10.a.9.5. thence to G.3.d.2.9.
Space within the area bounded by and farms directly accessible from on either side of these Roads, are included in the area allotted.

2. A tracing is attached showing the positions of each Amm:Col: in the area.

3. Time table of moves attached, showing starting point, Route to be taken, time and destination.

4. SAILLY BRIDGE will be available for the passage of these Columns from 4.30 p.m. to 5.45 p.m.
The Head of the Column of 2nd West Rid: Bde. Ammunition Column will be at SAILLY BRIDGE by 4.30 p.m.
The Rear of the Column of the 4th W.R.(H) Bde. A.C. will be clear of SAILLY BRIDGE by 5.45 p.m.

5. In conjunction with the above moves the following will also be made.
(a) 1st W.R. F.A. Bde., wagon lines from present lines to 3rd W.R. Bde. A.C. lines vacated at H.14.a.3.2. Time of move 5.0 p.m. 18/6/15.
(b) 4th W.R. Battery wagon line from present lines to 2nd W.R. Bde. A.C. lines vacated at H.13.d.3.1. Time of move 5.30 p.m. 18/6/15.

6. A report to be sent to this office stating time of arrival at new billets

18/6/15.

Major R.F.A.(T),
Staff Capt.R.A.49th (W.R.) Division.

S E C R E T.

Programme of Moves of Brigade Ammunition Columns

on June 17th and 18th 1915.

Name of Unit.	Starting point.	Route.	Time at Starting point.	Destination.
1st West Rid:Bde. Ammunition Column.	Cross Roads H.19.b.1.9.	RUE du QUESNOY - Cross Roads G.29.d.- SAILLY Sur La LYS - SAILLY BRIDGE Cross Roads G.16.a.	4.0 p.m. 18/6/15.	New Billets at G.9.d.4.5.
2nd West Rid:Bde. Ammunition Column.	Cross Roads H.19.b.1.9.	Rue du QUESNOY - CROSS Roads G.29.d. - SAILLY Sur La LYS - SAILLY BRIDGE - Cross Roads G.16.c. - Pt.de la BOUDRETTE - Road Junction G.10.a.9.4.	3.30 p.m. 18/6/15.	New Billets at G.3.d.3.7.
4th West Rid:Bde. Ammunition Column.	Cross Roads H.19.b.1.9.	RUE du QUESNOY - Cross Roads G.29.d. - SAILLY Sur La LYS - SAILLY BRIDGE - Cross Roads G.16.a. - PONT de la BOUDRETTE- Road Junction G.10.a.9.4.	4.30 p.m. 18/6/15.	New Billets at G.10.a.3.6.

XXXVIII

A. D. C.

49th (W.R.) Divisional Artillery.

TACTICAL PROGRESS REPORT.

6 p.m. June 17th to 6 p.m. June 18th 1915.

1. OPERATIONS.

(a) Nil.

(b) (1) Observation balloon up at 10.50 a.m. to 11.20 a.m. Magnetic bearing 170½ degrees from N.26.b.1.9, probably at T.11.a.7.4. Pt.800.

(2) Hostile heavy battery fired on area near LAVENTIE from behind Pt.782. The firing was between 11 a.m. to 1 p.m. Magnetic bearing 184½ degrees from N.33.d.4.6.

(3) Hostile Field battery fired from near Pt.837 at same time.

(4) Hostile battery shelled N.31.c.8.8. between 11 a.m. and 11.30 a.m.

(5) Hostile aeroplane over FLEURBAIX at 5.15 p.m.

2. INFORMATION GAINED.

(1) Hostile battery located by flashes near O.9.d.2.8½.

(2) Repeated flashes of hostile battery observed at 9 p.m. 17th June from N.25.b.1.9. Magnetic bearing 180 degrees.

3. WORK DONE BY BATTERIES.

Gun pits and dug-outs improved.

Major R.A.,
Brigade Major R.A. 49th (W.R.) Division.

19/6/15.

XXXIX

"A" Form.

MESSAGES AND SIGNALS. No. of Message

Prefix ___ Code ___ m.	Words.	Charge.	This message is on a/c of:	Recd. at ___ m.
Office of Origin and Service Instructions.	Sent At ___ m. To ___ By ___		OTHER Service.	Date ___ From ___ By ___
			Lw Lower Maj (Signature of "Franking Officer.")	

TO	49th	W	R	DIVN

Sender's Number	Day of Month	In reply to Number	AAA
* BM/53/G	nineteenth		

Intelligence	Summary	AAA	Hostile	aircraft
very	active	this	morning	early
AAA	Puffs	of	Smoke	from
hostile	battery	observed	at	11.45 am
magnetic	bearing	117	degrees	from
H 29 C 8.8	approximate	range	5000	yards
AAA	Traffic	of	various	nature
observed	during	the	day	on
road	O 11 d 5.5	moving	northwards	AAA
Captive	balloon	up	5.30 pm	magnetic
bearing	from	H 25 b 1.9	169	degrees
AAA	Wire	entanglements	strengthened	near
point	871	AAA	Hostile	advanced
trench	opposite	3 Q	has	now
low	Sandbagged	parapet	enemy	still
working	hard	on	this	trench

From	49th	W	R	ARTY
Place				
Time	6.15 pm			

The above may be forwarded as now corrected. (Z) Lw Lower Major RA

Censor. Signature of Addressor or person authorised to telegraph in his name

* This line should be erased if not required.

(24473). M.R.Co.,Ltd. Wt.W4848/541. 50,000. 9/14. Forms C2121/10.

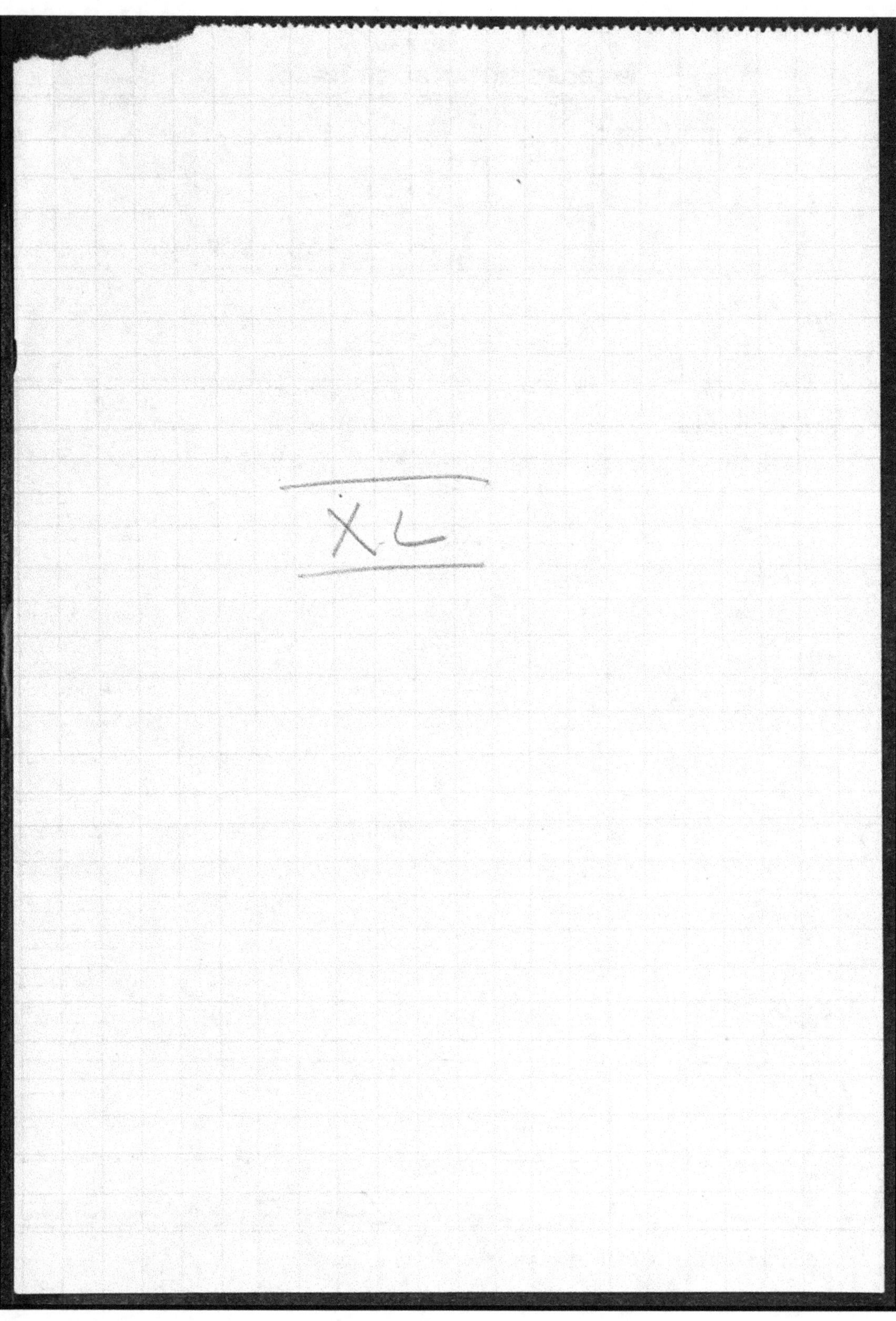
XL

a D C

49th (W.R.) Divisional Artillery.

TACTICAL PROGRESS REPORT.

6 p.m. June 18th to 6 p.m. June 19th 1915.

1. OPERATIONS.

(a) v Nil.

(b) (1) Hostile aircraft very active yesterday morning.

(2) Puffs of smoke from hostile battery observed at 11.45 a.m., Magnetic bearing 117 degrees from H.29.c.8.8. Approximate range 5000 yards.

(3) Captive balloon up at 5.30 p.m. Magnetic bearing from H.25.b.1.9, 169 degrees.

2. INFORMATION GAINED.

(1) Traffic of various nature observed during the day on road C.11.d.5.5. moving northwards.

(2) Wire entanglements strengthened near Pt.871.

(3) Hostile advanced trench opposite 3 Q has now a sand bagged parapet. Enemy still working hard on this trench.

(4) At 4.30 p.m. a party of about 50 Germans were seen carrying tin sheets and white sandbags while passing along bottom of a bank of earth below ENGLOS, Magnetic bearing 116 degrees from H.35.d.2.6.

3. WORK DONE BY BATTERIES.

Dug-outs strengthened and Gun pits improved, and Embrasures covered with sacking.

20/6/15.

Major R.A.,
Brigade Major R.A.49th (W.R.) Division.

X.LI

a D C

49th (W.R.) Divisional Artillery.

TACTICAL PROGRESS REPORT.

6 p.m. June 19th to 6 p.m. June 20th 1915.

1. OPERATIONS&

(a) (1) 9.20 a.m. W.R. R.G.A. fired on N.23.a.10.3 at 77 mm battery in retaliation for firing on Cross Roads H.31.c.8.1, and 146th Infantry Brigade H.Qrs. Hostile battery ceased fire.

(b) (1) From 9 a.m. to 9.30 a.m. about ten 77 mm shell fell about Cross Roads H.31.c.8.1. they were judged as coming from FROMELLES.

(2) Captive balloons up most of the day. Magnetic bearings from H.25.b.1.9.
1 balloon 169 degrees.
5 balloons 181 degrees to 186 degrees.

(3) FLEURBAIX shelled at 2.55 p.m.

(4) 2nd W.R. Battery billets were shelled at 4.30 p.m., the hostile battery ranging back set fire to the farm formerly ~~hut~~ occupied by the 1st W.R. F.A. Bde H.Qrs. A hostile plane was observing results at 5.45 p.m. About 30 shells were fired. The farm has been burnt to the ground.

2. INFORMATION GAINED.

(1) A German was observed on roof of house at Pt.975.

(2) Look Out men at H.29.c.8.7, report black smoke arising from behind trees at a point 112 degrees magnetic.

3. WORK DONE BY BATTERIES.

Progress made by batteries in the construction of alternative Gun emplacements.

L W Lewer
Major R.A.,
Brigade Major R.A.49th (W.R.) Division.

21/6/15.

49th Divisional Artillery.

TACTICAL PROGRESS REPORT.

6 p.m. June 19th to 6 p.m. June 20th 1915.

1. OPERATIONS.

(a) (1) 9.20 am W.R. R.G.A. fired on N.23.a.10.3 at 77 mm battery in retaliation (for firing on Cross Roads H.31.c.8.1 & 146th Inf Bde HQ). Hostile battery ceased fire.

(b) (1) From 9 a.m. to 9.30 a.m. about ten 77 mm shell fell about Cross Roads H.31.c.8.1. they were judged as coming from FROMELLES.

(2) Captive balloons up most of the day. Magnetic bearings from H.25.b.1.9. 1 balloon 169 degrees
5 balloons 181 degrees to 186 degrees.

(3) FLEURBAIX shelled at 2.55 p.m.

(4) 2nd W.R. Battery billets were shelled at 4.30 p.m., the hostile battery ranging back set fire to the farm formerly occupied by the 1st W.R. F.A. Bde. H.Qrs. A hostile plane was observing results at 5.45 p.m.
About 30 shells were fired. The farm has been burnt to the ground.

2. INFORMATION GAINED.

(1) A German was observed on roof of house at ~~O.1.b.3.7~~. Pt 97.5

(2) Look out men at H.29.c.8.7, report black smoke arising from behind trees at a point 112 degrees magnetic.

3. WORK DONE BY BATTERIES.

Progress made by batteries in the construction of alternative Gun emplacements.

21/6/15.

H F Calcutt-Jones 2/Lt RA BC for Major R.A.,
Brigade Major R.A. 49th (W.R.) Division.

43

XLIII

49th (W.R.) Divisional Artillery.

ADC

TACTICAL PROGRESS REPORT.

6p.m. June 20th to 6 p.m. June 21st 1915.

1. OPERATIONS.

(a) (1) From 11 a.m. to 2 p.m. hostile battery located near N.16.b.5.2 shelled 1st W.R. F.A. Bde, H.Qrs., and farm. The 1st W.R. Battery retaliated and hostile fire ceased.

(2) Two rounds were fired from the trench mortar at 6 Q (on the 20th) at 6.45 p.m. Objective, machine gun position in enemy's parapet. Both shells seemed to find the enemy's trench and there was no hostile reply.

(b) (1) At 9 a.m. 10 shells from 77 mm fell at (N.3.c.2.2.) Magnetic bearing of groove 150 degrees.

(2) Trench mortar reported as fired from 130 yards N.W. of Pt.828.

(3) Hostile aeroplane over 1st W.R. Battery at 5.50 p.m. to 6.5.p.m. (20th) markings, a large red ring on white ground with black spots in centre.

(4) Hostile aircraft very active from 6 a.m. to 10 a.m.

(5) FLEURBAIX shelled 11.20 a.m., three shells in all.

(6) Captive balloon up near FOURNES several times during the day.

2. INFORMATION GAINED.

(1) Working parties seen in communication trench S.E. Pt.965.

(2) Large conflagration seen last night over crest. Magnetic bearing 192½ degrees from H.24.a.8.4.

(3) A ruined white house near Pt.837 is thought to be used for observing purposes. Small dark blue and white flags seen moving 4 feet above ground at east end of house between shots when hostile battery was firing.

(4) Red house observed on skyline, magnetic bearing 104 degrees from H.35.c.8.3., horizontal, rectangular slit in wall about 3 feet X 6 inches observed.

(5) At 6.27 p.m. hostile aeroplane dropped one white smoke ball over LE TROU (N.9.a.).
At 6.29 p.m. another white smoke ball was dropped over LA CORDONNERIE FME (N.10.a.).

(6) Working party of at least 20 Germans working on communication trench 200 yards W of Pt.883 and about 100 yards behind the enemy's trenches. 4th W.R. Battery fired 6 rounds at the above party at 8 p.m.

3. WORK DONE BY BATTERIES.

Improvement to dug outs and Embrasures.

R W Lewer

Major R.A.,
Brigade Major R.A.49th (W.R.) Division.

22/6/15.

LXV

"C" Form (Duplicate). Army Form C. 2123.

MESSAGES AND SIGNALS. No. of Message 31.

Sm. Gpm. 39. [illegible]

Charges to Pay. £ s. d.	Office Stamp.
7.8p Staff	[illegible] 21-6-15

Service Instructions.

Handed in at [illegible] Office ... m. Received ... m.

TO HQRA 49th WRDiv.

Sender's Number	Day of Month	In reply to Number	AAA
400.	21st.		

Hostile aeroplane dropped white smoke ball on LETROU N9a 3.7 at 6.27pm and another on LA CORDONNERIE FARM N10a 8.4 at 6.29 pm

FROM PLACE & TIME: 1st WRFA Bde 7.0pm

(24932). M.R.Co.,Ltd. Wt.W9668/1672. 50,000 Pads—1/15. Forms/C.2123.

"A" Form. Army Form C. 2121.

MESSAGES AND SIGNALS.

No. of Message

Prefix Code m. | Words. | Charge.

Office of Origin and Service Instructions.

Sent
At m.
To
By

This message is on a/c of: OTHM Service.

[illegible] Maj

(Signature of "Franking Officer.")

Recd. at m.
Date
From
By

TO { 49th W R DIVN

Sender's Number	Day of Month	In reply to Number	AAA
* BM/56/G	Twentyfirst		

Summary	intelligence	AAA.	9 am	ten
Shells	77 mm	N 3 C 2.2	[illegible]	bearing
of	grove	150	degrees	AAA
Trench	mortar	reported	as	firing
from	130 yards	N W	point	828
AAA	Hostile	aeroplane	over	1st
Battery	5.50 pm	to	6.5 pm	20th
markings	large	red	ring	on
white	ground	with	black	spots
in	centre	AAA	Hostile	aircraft
very	active	6.0 am	to	10.0 am
AAA.	11 am	to	2.0 pm	hostile
battery	located	near	N 16 b 5.2	shelled
1st	W	R	F	A
Bde	HQ	+	farm	1st
Battery	retaliated	and	fire	ceased
AAA	FLEURBAIX	shelled	11. 20 am	3

From

Place

Time

The above may be forwarded as now corrected. (Z)

Censor. Signature of Addressor or person authorised to telegraph in his name

* This line should be erased if not required.

(24473). M.R.Co.,Ltd. Wt.W4848/541. 50,000. 9/14. Forms C2121/10.

"A" Form. Army Form C. 2121.

MESSAGES AND SIGNALS. No. of Message

Prefix ___ Code ___ m. Office of Origin and Service Instructions.	Words.	Charge.	This message is on a/c of: ___ Service. (Signature of "Franking Officer.")	Recd. at ___ m Date ___ From ___ By ___
	Sent At ___ m. To ___ By ___			

TO (2)

Sender's Number	Day of Month	In reply to Number	AAA
*			

Shells	in	all	AAA	Captive
balloon	ups	near	FOURNEL	Several
times	during	the	day.	AAA
Working	parties	seen	in	communication
trench	SE	of	965	AAA
Large	conflagration	seen	last	night
over	crest	~~trees~~	magnetic	bearing
~~100~~ 99	193½°	from	H 24 a 8.4	

From 49th	W	R	ARTY
Place			
Time 6.30 pm			

The above may be forwarded as now corrected. (Z) C Glover Major RA

Censor. Signature of Addressor or person authorised to telegraph in his name

* This line should be erased if not required.

(24473). M.R.Co.,Ltd. Wt.W4848/541. 50,000. 9/14. Forms C2121/10.

XLV

"A" Form. Army Form C. 2121.

MESSAGES AND SIGNALS.

No. of Message ______

Prefix ____ Code ____ m. / Office of Origin and Service Instructions.	Words.	Charge.	This message is on a/c of:	Recd. at ____ m.
	Sent At ____ m. To ____ By ____		O H M Service. Lt Col Lewer Maj (Signature of "Franking Officer.")	Date ____ From ____ By ____

TO: 49th W R DIVN

Sender's Number	Day of Month	In reply to Number	AAA
*BM/59/G	22nd		

Summary	Intelligence	AAA	4th	Battery
fired	at	German	working	party
in	communicatn	trench	near	pt
883	about	8 pm	21st	AAA
4th	Battery	fired	at	trench
mortar	near	884 at 3 am	mortar	silenced
AAA	5.9	howitzers	fired	on
LA	CROIX	LESCORNEY	and	anti-
aircraft	gun	9.15 am	to	10.30 am
AAA	10 am	11th	Howitzer	battery
fired	12	rounds	at	this
hostile	battery	about	N23d7.7	with
apparently	good	effect	AAA	Captive
balloon	up	9.50 am	magnetic	bearing
183°	from	H29c8.7	AAA	Germans
cut	grass	between	trenches	S E
point	969	AAA	Two	small

From ____
Place ____
Time ____

The above may be forwarded as now corrected. (Z)

Censor. Signature of Addressor or person authorised to telegraph in his name

* This line should be erased if not required.

(24473). M.R.Co.,Ltd. Wt.W4843/341. 50,000. 9/14. Forms C2121/10.

"A" Form. Army Form C. 2121.

MESSAGES AND SIGNALS.

No. of Message

Prefix ___ Code ___ m.	Words.	Charge.	This message is on a/c of:	Recd. at ___ m.
Office of Origin and Service Instructions.	Sent		___ Service.	Date
	At ___ m.			From
	To			By
	By		(Signature of "Franking Officer.")	

TO (2)

Sender's Number	Day of Month	In reply to Number	AAA
*			

hostile	trenches	observed	in	front
of	their	front	line	at
966	and	976	occupied	by
a	few	men	AAA	Isolated
digging	at	966	and	a
party	digging	2nd	line	trench
at	965	AAA	Hostile	aircraft
very	active	9.30am	to	10.30am

From	49th	W	R	ArtY
Place				
Time	6.25 pm			

The above may be forwarded as now corrected. (Z) [illegible]

Censor. Signature of Addressor or person authorised to telegraph in his name

* This line should be erased if not required.

(24473). M.R.Co.,Ltd. Wt.W4848/341. 50,000. 9/14. Forms C2121/10.

LXVI

Officer Commanding,

IOth. West Riding Howitzer Battery.

No. B.M. 281 date 22.6.15.

The Section o f your Battery at M 6 a 7.10 will march at 9.30 p.m. to-day via ROUGE de BOUT - RUE du QUESNE - FLEURBAIX and reoccupy its old position.

The section of your battery at M IO d 5.5 will march at 9-30 p.m. to-day via LAVENTIE - ROUGE de BOUT-RUE du QUESNE - FLEURBAIX ahd reoccupy its old position.

Copies to IO th. West Riding Howitzer Battery, detached Section IOth. West Riding Howitzer Battery at M IO d 5.5, 8th. Division ahd West Riding Division Artillery.

R H Johnson

6 a.m. Major R.A.

B rigade Major 8th. Division Artillery.

"A" Form. Army Form C. 2121.

MESSAGES AND SIGNALS. No. of Message ________

Prefix ______ Code ______ m. | Words. | Charge.

Office of Origin and Service Instructions.

Sent
At ________ m.
To ________
By ________

This message is on a/c of:
O H M Service.
R W Lewer Maj.
(Signature of "Franking Officer.")

Recd. at ________ m.
Date ________
From ________
By ________

TO	4th	Hows	Bde	

Sender's Number	Day of Month	In reply to Number	AAA
* BM/58/G	22nd		

10th	Battery	returns	to	position
LA	CROIX	MARESHAL	tonight	AAA
leading	section	reaches	ROUGE	DE
BOUT	9.35 pm	AAA	Rear	section
reaches	ROUGE	DE	BOUT	10 pm
AAA	ROUTE	to	be	followed
by	both	sections	RUE	DU
QUESNE	– FLEURBAIX	AAA	10th	Battery
has	been	informed		

From 49th Div. RA

Place

Time 10.15 am

The above may be forwarded as now corrected. (Z) R W Lewer Maj RA

Censor. Signature of Addressor or person authorised to telegraph in his name

* This line should be erased if not required.

(24473). M.R.Co.,Ltd. Wt.W4843/541. 50,000. 9/14. Forms C2121/10.

E C R A

49th (W.R.) Divisional Artillery.

TACTICAL PROGRESS REPORT.

6 p.m. June 21st to 6 p.m. June 22nd 1915.

1. OPERATIONS.

(a) (1) 4th W.R. Battery fired at German working party in communication trench near Pt.883, about 8 p.m. on the 21st.

(2) The above battery also fired at trench mortar near Pt.884 at 3 a.m. Hostile mortar silenced.

(3) Enemy's 5-9" Howitzers fired on LA CROIX LESCORNEX and anti aircraft gun from 9.15 a.m. to 10.30 a.m. At 10 a.m. 11th Howitzer battery ordered to open fire 12 rounds at this hostile battery about N.23.d.7.7, with apparently good effect.

(b) (1) Captive balloon up at 9.50 a.m. magnetic bearing 183 degrees from H.29.c.8.7.

(2) Hostile aircraft very active from 7.30 a.m. to 10.30 a.m.

2. INFORMATION GAINED.

(1) Germans cut grass between trenches S.E. of Pt.969.

(2) Two small trenches observed in front of their front line at Pt.966 and 976. These are occupied by a few men.

(3) Isolated digging on 2nd line trench at Pt.965.

3. WORK DONE BE BATTERIES.

Dug outs and gun pits improved.

R.W. Lamer

23/6/15.

Major R.A.,
Brigade Major R.A.49th (W.R.) Division.

A. D. C.

49th (W.R.) Divisional Artillery.

TACTICAL PROGRESS REPORT.

6 p.m. June 22nd to 6 p.m. June 23rd 1915.

1. OPERATIONS.

(a) (1) Trench Mortar at Junction 2 P and 2 Q fired at 7.15 p.m. and 7.20 p.m. in retaliation to hostile mortars. Mortar at 6 S also fired.

(2) 4th W.R. Battery fired 5 rounds at 7 p.m. at hostile mortar between 883 and 884. Mortar silenced.

(b) (1) Hostile battery fired 5 shell in vicinity of 1st and 2nd W.R. Batteries at 6.25 p.m. also 5 more near 1st W.R. F.A. Brigade H.Qrs., at 6.30 a.m.

2. INFORMATION GAINED.

(1) Hostile parapet raised at 976 and 969 with fresh earth on latter.

(2) Tall poles about 20 feet apart extending from German parapet of salient near 966 towards disused British trench.

(3) What appears to be a switch board is visible at Pt.956.

(4) Movement of men round the fields and house near 934 at 8.10 p.m.

(5) Men seen going from O.7.d.9.4, to LES POTERIES at 9.45 p.m.

(6) 10.15 p.m. Searchlight seen magnetic bearing 115 degrees from H.28.b.3.8.

(7) Men and horses observed in vicinity of farm on LE MAISNIL - FROMELLES Road near LA HAUTE LOGE.

3. WORK DONE BY BATTERIES.

(1) 5th W.R. Battery registered.

(2) Footpaths and Tracks rendered less conspicuous.

(3) Alternative gun positions proceeded with.

(4) Dug outs improved.

L.W. Lewer
Major R.A.,
Brigade Major R.A.49th (W.R.) Division.

24/6/15.

"A" Form. Army Form C. 2121.

MESSAGES AND SIGNALS. No. of Message ______

Prefix ______ Code ______ m.

Office of Origin and Service Instructions.

Words.	Charge.

Sent
At ______ m.
To ______
By ______

This message is on a/c of: Other Service.

[illegible] for B.M.
(Signature of "Franking Officer.")

Recd. at ______ m
Date ______
From ______
By ______

TO { 49th W. | R. | Div. | }

Sender's Number	Day of Month	In reply to Number	AAA
* B.M. 9	24		

AAA	Action	nil	AAA	Information
Gained	nil	AAA	Position	[illegible]
[illegible]	gun pts			

From: B.M. 49th Div. [illegible]
Place
Time

The above may be forwarded as now corrected. (Z) [illegible]

Censor. Signature of Addressor or person authorised to telegraph in his name

* This line should be erased if not required.

(24473). M.R.Co.,Ltd. Wt.W4848/341. 50,000. 9/14. Forms C2121/10.

XLIX

A.D.C

49th (W.R.) Divisional Artillery.

TACTICAL PROGRESS REPORT.

6 p.m. June 23rd to 6 p.m. June 24th 1915.

1. OPERATIONS.

(a) Nil.

(b) Nil.

2. INFORMATION GAINED.

Nil.

3. WORK DONE BY BATTERIES.

(1) Emplacements prepared for re occupation by Section of 36th Battery by 9th W.R. Battery.

(2) Pathways rendered less conspicuous.

(3) Physical Drill, Gun Drill.

(5) Laying competition.

L.W. Lewer

Major R.A.,
Brigade Major R.A.49th (W.R.) Division.

25/6/15.

"A" Form. Army Form C. 2121.

MESSAGES AND SIGNALS. No. of Message

Prefix ... Code ... m.	Words.	Charge.	This message is on a/c of:	Recd. at ... m
Office of Origin and Service Instructions.	Sent At ... m. To ... By ...		O.H.M.S. Service. (Signature of "Franking Officer.")	Date ... From ... By ...

TO	49	W.	R.	Div.

Sender's Number	Day of Month	In reply to Number	AAA
*BM 63/9	25.		

Summary	Report.	AAA	[illegible]	[illegible]
AAA	Information	Nil.	AAA	[illegible]
[illegible]	[illegible]			

From	49th	Div	R	A
Place				
Time	0-20			

The above may be forwarded as now corrected. (Z) [illegible]

Censor. Signature of Addressor or person authorised to telegraph in his name

* This line should be erased if not required.

(24473). M.R.Co.,Ltd. Wt.W4843/341. 50,000. 9/14. Forms C2121/10.

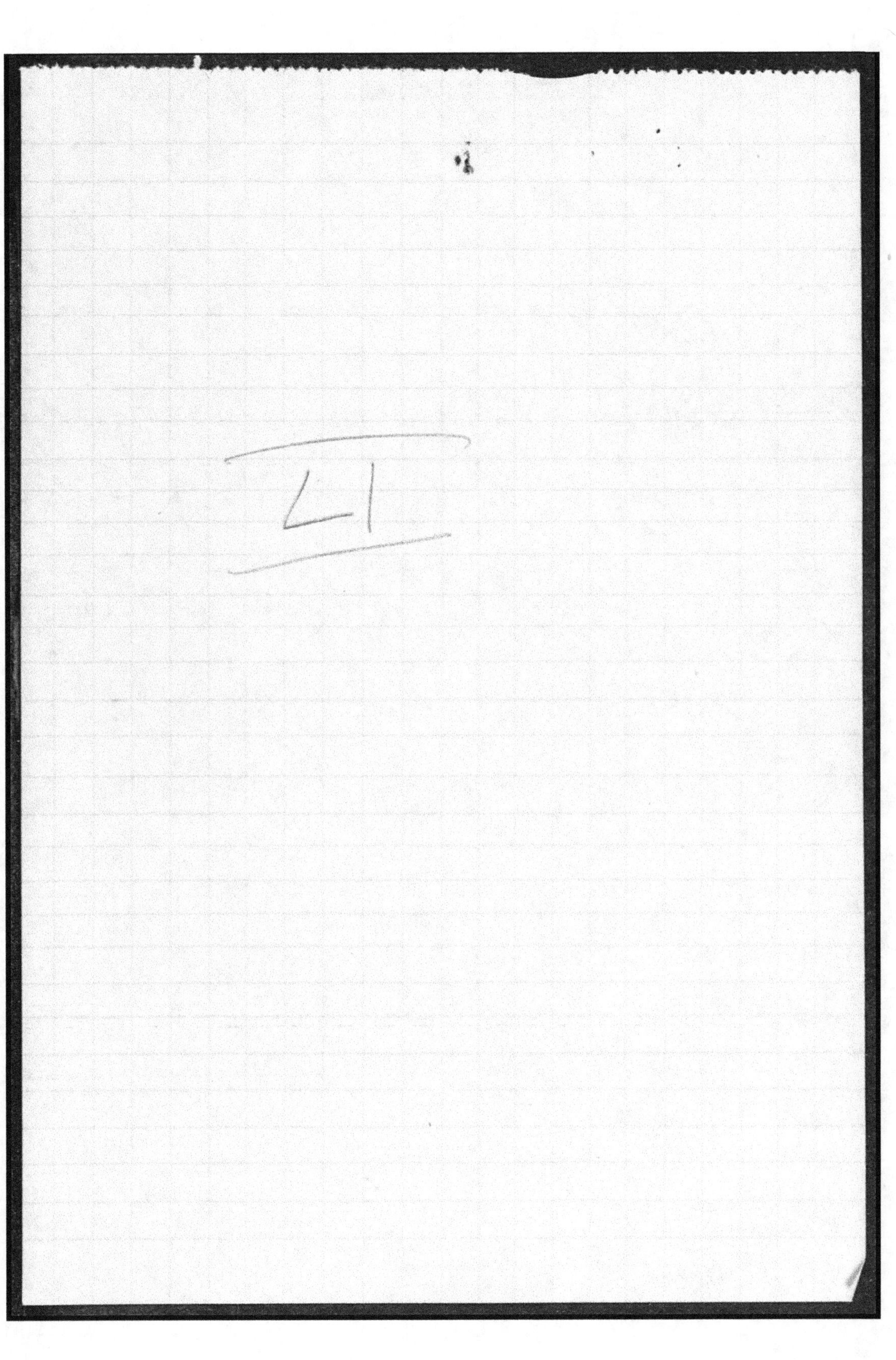

ADC

49th (W.R.) Divisional Artillery.

TACTICAL PROGRESS REPORT.

6 p.m. June 24th to 6 p.m. June 25th 1918.

1. OPERATIONS.

Nil.

2. INFORMATION GAINED.

Nil.

3. WORK DONE BY BATTERIES.

Nil.

25/6/18.

Major R.A., Brigade Major R.A.49th (W.R.) Division.

"A" Form. Army Form C. 2121.

MESSAGES AND SIGNALS. No. of Message

Prefix Code m. Office of Origin and Service Instructions.	Words. Charge.	This message is on a/c of:	Recd. at m.
	Sent At m. To By	O.H.M. Service. (Signature of "Franking Officer.")	Date From By

TO 49th W R DIVN.

Sender's Number	Day of Month	In reply to Number	AAA
* B.M./64/G	26th		

Intelligence	Summary	AAA	3	hostile
Shells	fell	near	Ldf	D
Communication	Trench	No 2	at	12.5 am
Hostile	Aeroplane	observing	during	firing.
AAA	Five	hostile	Captive	balloons
seen	one	at	180°	three
at	186°	and	one	at
186°	all	bearings	magnetic	from
A 36 b 6.2	AAA	Hostile	howitzer	battery
in	27th	DIVN	area	shelled
FLEURBAIX	ARMENTIERS	road	5.10 pm	6
Shells	AAA	Small	black	and
white	pennant	seen	in	German
front	trench	at	pt	969

From 49th W R ARTY

Place

Time 6.23 pm

The above may be forwarded as now corrected. (Z)

Censor. Signature of Addressor or person authorised to telegraph in his name

* This line should be erased if not required.

(24473). M.R.Co.,Ltd. Wt.W4848/541. 50,000. 9/14. Forms C2121/10.

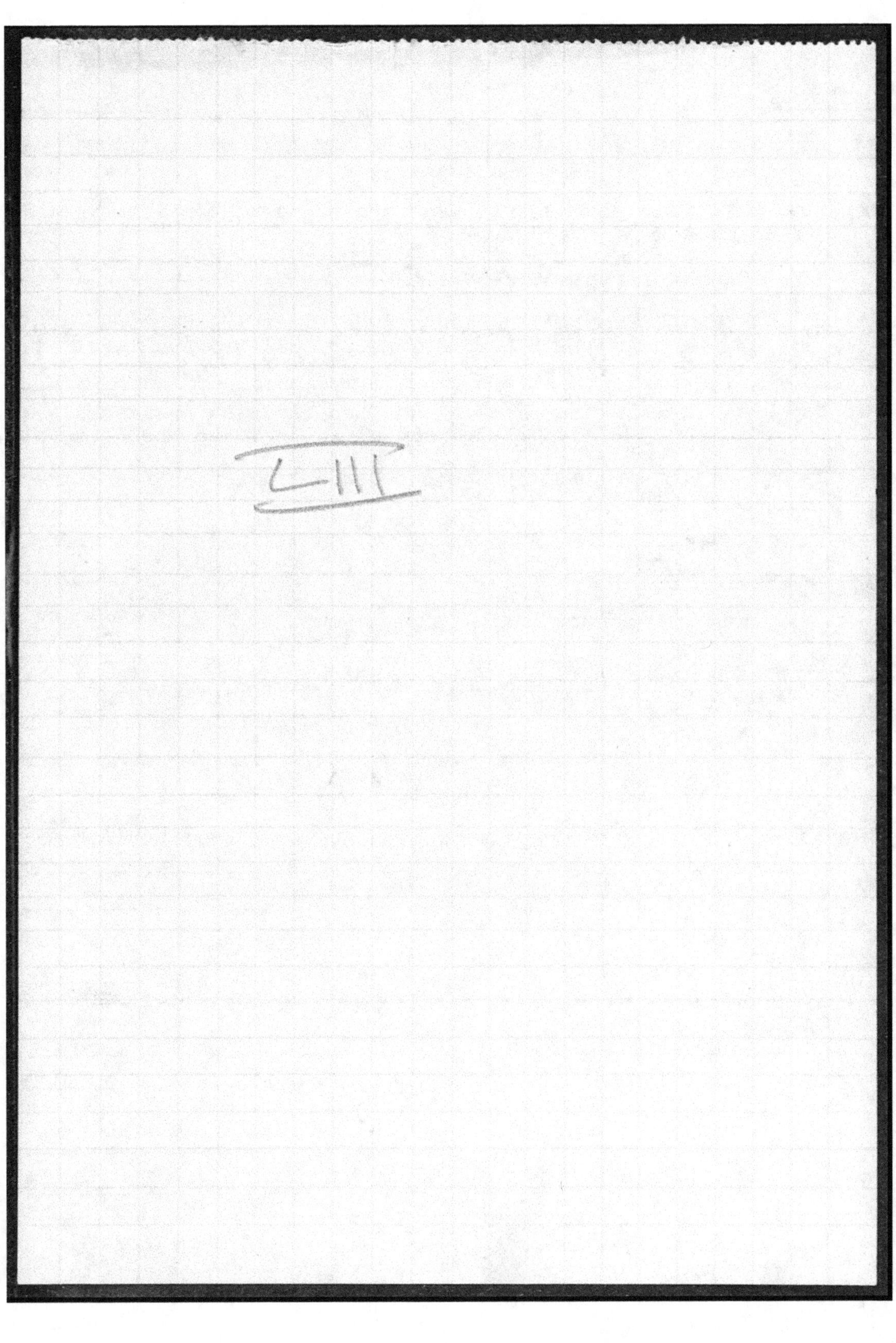
LIII

N.D.C.

49th (W.R.) Divisional Artillery.

TACTICAL PROGRESS REPORT.

1. OPERATIONS:

(a) (1) O.C. 8th W.R. Battery reports having fired 11 rounds at hostile battery, at O.8.d.7.2.

(b) (1) 3 hostile shells fell near top of communication trench number 2 at 10.45 a.m.

(2) Hostile aeroplane observing during firing.

(3) 5 hostile captive balloons seen, 1 at 180 degrees, 3 at 181 degrees and 1 at 186 degrees, all bearing magnetic from H.36.b.6.2.

(4) Hostile Howitzer battery in 27th Division area shelled FLEURBAIX - ARMENTIERS Road at 5.10 p.m. 6 shells in all.

(5) Small black and white pennant seen in German front trench at Pt.969.

2. INFORMATION GAINED.

Nil.

3. WORK DONE BY BATTERIES.

Nil.

L.W. Lewer

Major R.A.,

27/6/15. BrigadeMajor R.A.49th (W.R.) Division.

Secret.

W.R. Diary

Copy No.2.....

49th (W.R.) Divisional Artillery Order No.6.

Reference 1/20,000 Sheet 36 N.W.

26/6/15.

1. The 49th (W.R.) Division are being relieved by 8th Division.
2. Artillery reliefs for night 26th / 27th as per attached table.
3. The Brigade Headquarters will not move from their present positions till 6 a.m. 28th instant.
4. The F.O.Os 4th, 5th, 6th, 7th and 9th Batteries will stay in present forward positions until 6 a.m. on 28th inst., when the responsibility of the Artillery defence of the line PICANTIN to 6 R falls on G.O.C.R.A. 8th Division.
5. Officers Commanding Brigades 49th (W.R.) Division Artillery will take steps to ensure that they are in communication with the batteries of the 8th Division as soon as they are in line, and that F.O.Os report that they are in communication with incoming reliefs of infantry of 8th Division.
6. The G.O.C.R.A. 49th (W.R.) Division retains responsibility of the line till 6 a.m. on the 28th instant.

L W Lewer
Major R.A.,
Time of issue p.m. Brigade Major ~~R.A.~~ 49th (W.R.) Division.

Copy Nos. 1. 2 & 3 Retained.
" " 4 & 5 To H.Q.,49th (W.R.) Division.
" " 6 TO H.Q.,R.A. 8th Division.
" " 7 To 1st W.R. F.A. Bde.
" " 8 To 2nd -do-
" " 9 To 3rd -do-
" " 10 To 4th -do- (H)
11 To H.Q.,R.A. 27th Division

March Table 49th (W.R.) Division Artillery night 26th / 27th June 1915.

...

Unit.	Starting Point.	Time.	Route.	Destination.	Remarks.
2nd W.R. F.A. Bde.					
4th Battery.	Road Junction G.36.d.9.8.	9 p.m.	SAILLY SUR LA LYS - Junction roads G 9 a 3.8 - G 8 d 8.4	G 2 a 1.8	Relieved by 5th Battery R.F.A.
5th Battery.	CROIX BLANCHE.	9 p.m.	RUE DES BASSIERES - RUE BIACHE and follow 4th Battery.	A 25 d 2.5	Relieved by 2 Sections 0 Battery.
1 Section 6th Battery.	LA CROIX LESCORNEX	9.30 p.m.	Follow 5th Battery.	G 2 a 2.1	Relieved by 1 Sec: 1st Battery.
3rd W.R. F.A. Bde.					
7th Battery.	Gun position.	9.15 p.m.	FLEURBAIX - RUE DE QUESNE and follow 6th Battery. as far as G 9 a 3.8, thence via G 3 c 8.1	G 2 b 1.9 G 2 b 6.5 meadow G 2 b 3.9	Relieved by 2 Sect: 32nd Battery.
1 Section 9th Battery.	Junction Road H.28.a.8.3.	9.5 p.m.	Junction Road H.28.d.6.6 - RUE DES GRAMBIONS and follow 7th Battery. as far as G 3 c 8.1 thence via G 3 d 3.9.	G 3 a 5.6 meadow opposite for horse lines meadow behind for vehicles	Relieved by 1 Sect: 36th Battery.

N.B. 1st Line Wagons etc., will accompany Units, those of the 3rd W.R. F.A. Bde. will follow the same route as the guns.

"A" Form. Army Form C. 2121.

MESSAGES AND SIGNALS.

No. of Message ______

Prefix ____ Code ____ m.	Words.	Charge.	This message is on a/c of:	Recd. at ____ m.
Office of Origin and Service Instructions.	Sent		CRA Service.	Date ____
	At ____ m.			From ____
	To ____		[illegible]	
	By ____		(Signature of "Franking Officer.")	By ____

TO	49th	W	R	DIVN

Sender's Number	Day of Month	In reply to Number	AAA
* BM 166/Cy	27th		

Intelligence	Summary	AAA	Hostile	batteries
from	near	784	and	837
shelled	N4a3.3	LA	BOUTILLERIE	and
N26a4.2	from	11 am	to	1.30pm
AAA	1st	W	R	Battery
fired	12	rounds	at	837
battery	which	ceased	fire	at
1.30pm	AAA	1st	How	Battery
fired	at	784	battery	which
ceased	fire	with	some	effect
12	rounds	were	allotted	AAA
Battalion	HQ	at	N3c5.2	burnt
out	by	hostile	shell	1.0pm
the	shell	was	from	4.2
howitzer	battery	near	837	

From	49th	W	R	Art[illegible]
Place				
Time	[illegible] 37 pm			

The above may be forwarded as now corrected. (Z) [illegible signature]

Censor. Signature of Addressor or person authorised to telegraph in his name

* This line should be erased if not required.

(24473). M.R.Co.,Ltd. Wt.W4848/541. 50,000. 9/14. Forms C2121/10.

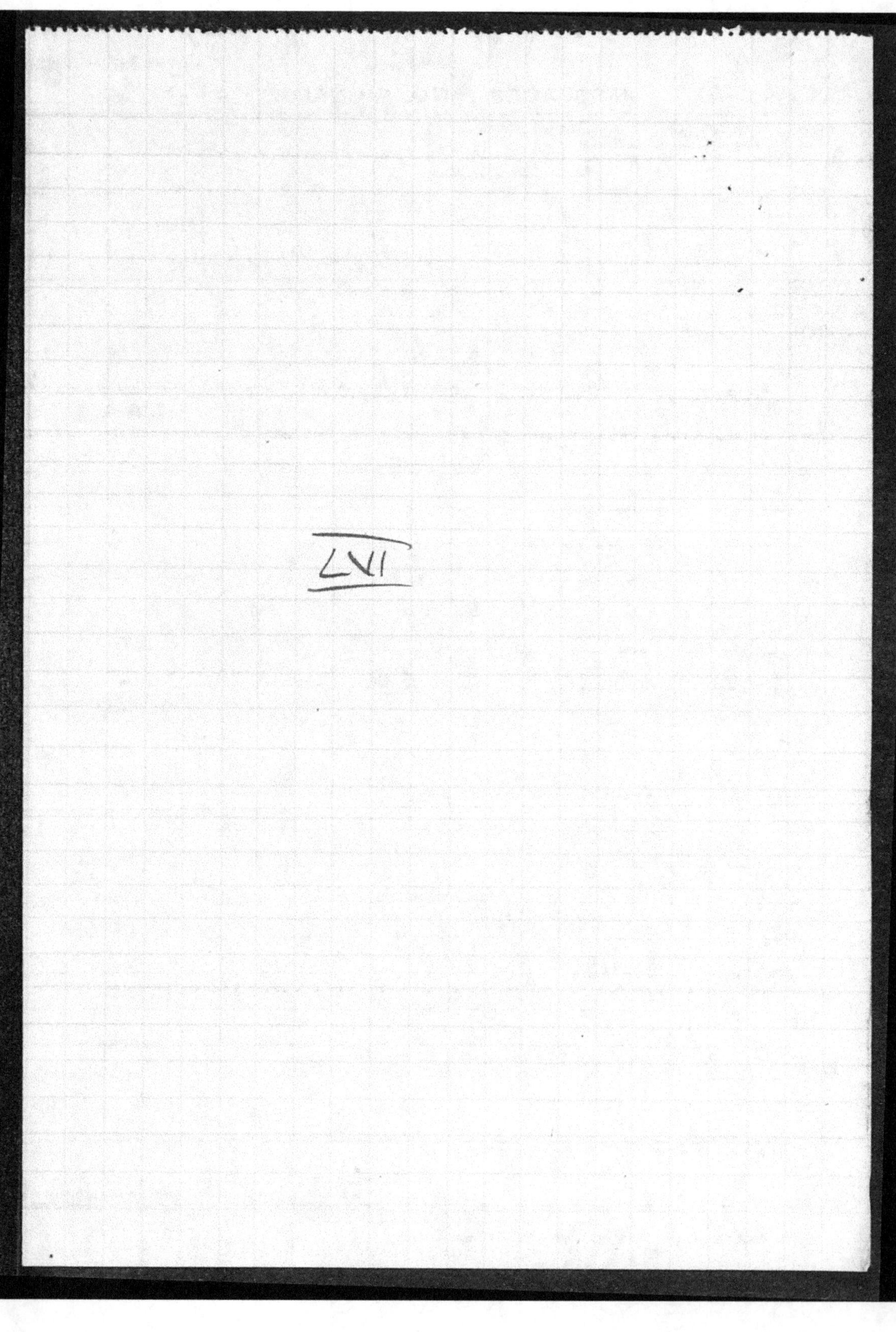
LVI

"C" Form (Duplicate). Army Form C. 2123.

MESSAGES AND SIGNALS. No. of Message

Service Instructions.	Charges to Pay. £ s. d.	Office Stamp. 29.VI.16

Handed in at F8 Office 9.10p m. Received 9.16 pm.

TO

Sender's Number	Day of Month	In reply to Number	AAA
	26		

Zeppelin travelling West to East at 8.50 p.m. time bearing 105 degrees H31 D2.4

FROM PLACE & TIME 8th Div Ark.

(24932). M.R.Co.,Ltd. Wt.W9668/1672. 50,000 Pads—1/15. Forms/C.2123.

War Diary

SECRET. Copy No. 2

49th (W.R.) Divisional Artillery Order No.8.

Reference 1/20,000 Sheet 36 N.W.

27/6/15.

1. The 1st, 2nd, and 3rd W.R. F.A. Bde. H. Qrs., will move at 8 a.m. tomorrow morning 28th instant to following positions.

   1st W.R. F.A. Bde. to G.14.c.1.3.

   2nd -do- to A.25.d.5.1.

   3rd -do- to G.2.b.7.8.

2. Brigade Headquarters will not be in telephone communication with this office from the new positions.

3. O.C. 2nd W.R. F.A. Bde., will be prepared to march with his Brigade and A.C. tomorrow evening, distance about 10 miles. Time of departure and Route will be issued later.

4. The office of the G.O.C.R.A. will not move for the present.

Issued at 8 p.m.

R W Lewer
Major R.A.,
Brigade Major R.A. 49th (W.R.) Division.

Copy Nos. 1, 2 & 3 Retained.
" " 4 & 5 To H.Q. 49th (W.R.) Division.
" " 6 " H.Q.,R.A. 8th Division.
" " 7 " 1st W.R. F.A. Bde.
" " 8 " 2nd -do-
" " 9 " 3rd -do-
" " 10 " H.Q.,R.A. 27th Division.

Copy No.2....

S E C R E T.

49th (W.R.) Divisional Artillery Order No.7.

Reference 1/20,000 Sheet 36 N.W.

27/6/15.

1. In continuation of 49th (W.R.) Divisional Artillery Order No.6 reliefs for artillery for night 27th / 28th as per attached table..

2. Bde. Headquarters 4th W.R.(How) F.A. Bde will move tonight.

3. F.O.Os 1st, 2nd, and 8th Batteries will stay in present forward positions until 6 a.m. 28th instant.
1st and 2nd Batteries for O & Z, 8th Battery for 33rd Battery.

Issued at 3.45 p.m.

Major R.A.,
Brigade Major R.A.49th (W.R.) Division.

Copy Nos	1, 2 & 3	Retained.
"	"	4 & 5	To H.Q.,49th (W.R.) Division.
"	"	6	To H.Q.,R.A. 8th Division.
"	"	7	" 1st W.R. F.A. Bde
"	"	8	" 2nd -do-
"	"	9	" 3rd -do-
"	"	10	" 4th -do- (H)
"	"	11	" H.Q.,R.A. 27th Division.

March Table 49th (W.R.) Division Artillery night 27th / 28th June 1915.

Unit.	Starting Point.	Time	Route.	Destination	Remarks.
1st W.R. F.A. Bde.					
1st Battery.	CROIX BLANCHE	9 p.m.	RUE BASSIERES - RUE BIACHE - Junction Roads G.36.d.9.8 - SAILLY SUR LA LYS - Cross roads G.16.a.2.0 - G.20.c.9.0.	G.14.c.1.3.	Covered by O Battery.
2nd Battery.	" "	9.15 p.m.	Follow 1st Battery.	G.14.c.2.4.	Covered by Z Battery.
3rd Battery.	" "	9.30 p.m.	Follow 2nd Battery as far as G.21.a.2½.2.	G.20.b.4.9.	Covered by Z Battery.
2nd W.R. F.A. Bde.					
Remaining Section 6th Battery.	LA CROIX LESCORNEX	8.55 p.m.	RUE BIACHE - G.36.d.9.8 - SAILLY SUR LA LYS - G.9.a.3.8 - G.8.d.8.4.	G.2.a.2.1.	Relieved by 1st Battery.
3rd W.R. F.A. Bde.					
8th Battery.	Gun position.	9.15 p.m.	RUE DES BOITEUX - FLEURBAIX - FORT ROMPU - SAILLY SUR LA LYS- G.9.a.3.8 - G.3.d.3.9.	G.3.a.7.4.	Covered by 33rd Batty. Guns to be taken up RUE DES BOITEUX singly.
Remaining Section 9th Battery.	H.28.a.8.3.	9.15 p.m.	To proceed 8th Battery by same route.	G.3.a.5.6.	Relieved by 36th Battery.
4th W.R.(H) F.A. Bde.					
10th Battery.	CROIX MARECHAL.	9.30 p.m.	GRANDE RUE - FLEURBAIX and follow 8th Battery Route as far as G.16.a.2½.0 thence via G.21.a.6.4.	G.21.a.5.5. }	H.Q. Bde. G.21.a.4.6.
11th Battery.	" "	9.40 p.m.	Follow 10th Battery.	G.21.a.3.7. }	Relieved by 57th Battery.

49th (W.R.) Divisional Artillery.

TACTICAL PROGRESS REPORT.

6 p.m. June 26th to 6 a.m. June 28th 1915.

1. OPERATIONS.

(a) (1) 11th W.R. Battery fired at Pt.784 battery, hostile battery ceased firing, our fire appeared effective.
12 rounds were allotted.
Enemy retaliated about 2.20 p.m.

(2) 1st W.R. Battery fired 12 rounds at Pt.837 battery, which ceased firing at 1.30 p.m.

(b) (1) Headquarters of Battalion at H.3.c.5.2 were shelled about 12.30 a.m. to 1.15 p.m. yesterday. H.Qrs. were burnt out at 1 p.m. The above shell was from 4-2 Howitzer battery near Pt.837.

(2) Hostile Batteries from near Pt.784 and 837 shelled N.4.a.3.3, LA BOUTILLERIE and N.3.b.4.2. from 11 a.m. to 1.30 p.m.

2. INFORMATION GAINED.

(1) Zeppelin travelling West to East passed over at 8.59 p.m. (26th) true bearing 145 degrees H.31.d.2.4.

3. WORK DONE BY BATTERIES.

Nil.

L. W. Lewer

28/6/15.

Major R.A.,
Brigade Major R.A.49th (W.R.) Division.

LXII

49th (W.R.) Divisional Artillery.

TACTICAL PROGRESS REPORT.

6 p.m. June 26th to 6 a.m. June 28th 1915.

1. OPERATIONS.

(a) (1) 11th W.R. Battery fired at Pt.784 battery, hostile battery ceased firing, our fire appeared effective. 12 rounds were allotted. Enemy retaliated about 2.20 p.m.

(2) 1st W.R. Battery fired 12 rounds at Pt.837 battery, which ceased firing at 1.30 p.m.

(b) (1) Headquarters of Battalion at H.3.c.5.2 were shelled about 12.30 a.m. to 1.15 p.m. yesterday. H.Qrs. were burnt out at 1 p.m. The above shell was from 4-2 Howitzer battery near Pt.837.

(2) Hostile Batteries from near Pt.784 and 837 shelled N.4.a.3.3, LA BOUTILLERIE and N.3.b.4.2. from 11 a.m. to 1.30 p.m.

2. INFORMATION GAINED&

(1) Zeppelin travelling West to East passed over at 8.59 p.m. (26th) true bearing 145 degrees H.31.d.2.4.

3. WORK DONE BY BATTERIES.

Nil.

L W Lewer

28/6/15.

Major R.A.,
Brigade Major R.A.49th (W.R.) Division.

W.a. Diary

Copy No....2

S E C R E T.

49th (W.R.) Divisional Artillery Operation Order No.8.

Reference 1/40,000 Sheet 27.
1/100,000 Hazebrouck 5a.

1. The Division will move to join 8th Corps.

2. Orders for march of Divisional Artillery less D.A.C. will be issued by Group Commanders.

3. The D.A.C. will move in accordance with attached march table.

4. Trench Mortars will leave their present billets at 9 a.m. tomorrow 29th instant, 3 Motor Lorries will be at their disposal, and will move to area NORTH of WATOU via NEUF BERQUIN - STRAZEELE - CAESTRE - STEENVOORDE - DROGLANDT - WATOU.

5. O.C. 2nd W.R. F.A. Bde. will arrange for accommodation, drawing of rations, etc., for Trench Mortars, which will be attached to his Brigade H.Qrs. for administration.

6. Divisional Artillery Headquarters will move to PROVEN on June 29th, opening at that place at 6 p.m.

R.W. Lawes

Major R.A.,
Brigade Major R.A.49th (W.R.) Division.

Issued at 1.10 p.m.

Copy Nos.		1, 2 & 3	Retained.
"	"	4 & 5	TO H.Qrs. 49th (W.R.) Division.
"	"	6	" 1st W.R. F.A. Bde.
"	"	7	" 2nd W.R. F.A. Bde.
"	"	8	" 3rd -do-
"	"	9	" 4th -do- (H)
"	"	10	" 49th (W.R.) D.A.C.
"	"	11	" Trench Mortars.

49th (W.R.) Divisional Artillery Units allotted to Groups vide 49th (W.R.) Division O.O. No.16.

Unit.	Position of H.Qrs.	Position of Units.		Groups allotted to.
2nd W.R. F.A. Bde.	A.25.d.5.1.	4th Battery. 5th Battery. 6th Battery Bde. A.C.	G.2.a.1.8. A.25.d.2.5. G.2.a.2.1. G.3.d.2.6.	Group I 146th Infantry Brigade.
3rd W.R. F.A. Bde.	G.2.b.7.8.	7th Battery. 8th Battery. 9th Battery. Bde. A.C..	G.2.b.1.9. G.3.a.7.4. G.3.a.5.6. G.10.b.1.1.	Group II 147th Infantry Brigade.
1st W.R. F.A. Bde.	G.14.c.1.3.	1st Battery. 2nd Battery. 3rd Battery. Bde. A.C.	G.14.c.1.3. G.14.c.2.4. G.20.b.4.9. G.9.d.2.2.	Group III 148th Infantry Brigade.
4th W.R. F.A. Bde.	G.21.a.4.6.	10th Battery. 11th Battery. Bde. A.C.	G.21.a.5.5. G.21.a.3.7. G.10.a.2.4.	Group III 148th Infantry Brigade.

LVII

March Table 49th (W.R.) D.A.C.

Unit.	Date.	From	To.	Route	Date.	To	Route	Remarks.
49th (W.R.) Div.Amm: Col.	July 1st.	Present Billets.	CAESTRE area.	NEUF BERQUIN- Vieux Berquin- STRAZEELE - CAESTRE.	July 2nd.	Area N. of WATOU.	EECKE - STEENVOORDE - J.12.b.9.2. - WATOU.	To start 8 p.m. each night.

On His Majesty's Service.

H.Q. R.A. 49th Dn.

Nov.

Vol VIII

121
7668

www.ingramcontent.com/pod-product-compliance
Lightning Source LLC
Chambersburg PA
CBHW080802010526
44113CB00013B/2312

9781474527057